Uncle John's Bathroom Reader® Plunges into Ohio

Uncle John's Bathroom Reader® Plunges into Ohio

Bathroom Readers' Institute
San Diego, California
Ashland, Oregon

Uncle John's Bathroom Reader
Plunges into Ohio

For information, write the Bathroom Readers' Institute at
5880 Oberlin Drive, Suite 101, San Diego, CA 92121
e-mail: unclejohn@btol.com

Library of Congress Cataloging-in-Publication Data

Uncle John's bathroom reader plunges into Ohio.
p. cm.
ISBN-13: 978-1-59223-321-2 (pbk.)
ISBN-10: 1-59223-321-X (pbk.)
1. Ohio—Miscellanea. 2. Ohio—Humor.
F491.6.U53 2007
977.1—dc22

2007003101

Printed in the United States of America
First printing: July 2007

07 08 09 10 11   10 9 8 7 6 5 4 3 2 1

Contents

Freedom Fighters

The Great Outdoors

History

Hometowns

Innovators

It's Official

Just for Fun

Let the Good Times Roll

Let Us Entertain You

Native Sons and Daughters

Oddball Ohio

Political Shenanigans

Puzzles

Sports Central

Answers

Project Team

Gordon Javna, Editor-in-Chief
JoAnn Padgett, Director, Editorial and Production
Melinda Allman, Developmental Editor
Amy Miller, Production Editor
Julia Papps, Office/Production Manager

Thank You!

The Bathroom Readers' Institute
thanks the following additional people whose advice
and assistance made this book possible.

Jennifer Payne
Michael Brunsfeld
Sydney Stanley
Monica Maestas
Michelle Sedgwick
Ralph Webb
Charlene Cheng
Angela Kern
Mana Monzavi
Laurel Graziano
Dylan Drake
Tom Mustard
Shobha Grace
Kristine, Trudy,
and Erin
Stephanie Spadaccini

Ohio Scholars

The Bathroom Readers' Institute thanks the following talented people who contributed selections to this book.

Brian Boone
Joan Brandwein
Tobias Buckell
Myles Callum
J. Carroll
Jenness I. Crawford
Jacqueline Damian
Kristal Garcia
Debbie K. Hardin
Rebecca Kaiser
Vickey Kalambakal
Kerry Kern
Megan Kern
Toney Lee
Andy Levy-Ajzenkopf
Thom Little
Dan Mansfield
Graham Meyer
Lisa Meyers
Ryan Murphy
Jay Newman
Debbie Pawlak
Jon Preimesberger
John Scalzi
Bonnie Vandewater

Preface

Welcome to Ohio—the 17th state in the Union, the birthplace of rock 'n' roll, and the leading U.S. producer of Swiss cheese. With credentials like these, it's no wonder we chose the Buckeye State as the subject of our latest Bathroom Reader. We recruited a group of Ohio aficionados to put together this collection of the most interesting stories the state has to offer. Read all about . . .

Sports: When we thought of Ohio, the first thing that came to mind was football—specifically, OSU football. But as our experts dove into their research, they discovered that there was more to Ohio sports than meets the eye. From the first professional baseball team to pro representation in the NFL, NHL, NBA, and MLB, this state is sports central.

Business: Ohio has been home to major businesses for more than a century. Whether they are developing tires, lip balms, hamburgers, or springless scales, Ohioans are masters of innovation.

Hometowns: If you want to visit the rubber capital of the world, see a medieval castle, or jam at the Rock and Roll Hall of Fame, you can do it in Ohio.

History: Whether providing a safe haven for escaped slaves, raising presidents, or offering the first interracial and coeducational college, Ohio's history is chock full of stories that affected America's social and political evolution.

Say What?

We also asked around and found answers to some of the public's most burning Ohio-related questions:

- What 1970s Soap Box Derby star was stripped of his title?
- Who introduced Script Ohio to OSU?
- How did the Underground Railroad get its name?
- How much did it cost to attend the first Ohio State Fair?
- What wicked witch grew up in Cleveland?
- How many years did Jack Nicklaus play golf for Ohio State before going pro?
- Where does the name "Ohio" come from?
- How long is the Ohio Turnpike?
- Where can you see three preserved human fingers, a calf with two heads, and a replica of John Dillinger's jail cell?
- How many Ohioans fought in the Civil War?

From settlement to statehood to abolition and beyond, Ohio has had ups and downs as dramatic as the steel hills at Cedar Point. So pull on an OSU sweatshirt, buckle your seat belt, and join us on this exciting roller-coaster ride through the Buckeye State. Please keep your hands and feet inside the car, and whatever you do, don't stand up!

As always, go with the flow . . .

—Uncle John and the BRI staff

Did You Know?

Ohio was the first state west of the Allegheny Mountains.

The Gravity Grand Prix

Here's how a neighborhood race became a spectacle for thousands.

Serendipity Strikes

In 1933, *Dayton Daily News* photographer Myron Scott came across three boys racing homemade engineless carts down a brick road in Dayton. Sensing a good story, Scott asked the boys if they'd like to participate in an organized race that awarded a trophy to its winner. The kids agreed, and they scheduled a race time for the following week. On the appointed day, 19 boys showed up, hauling their homemade cars behind them. The vehicles were strange conglomerations made from junk-heap scraps: old buggies, orange crates, and spare pieces of sheet metal. A few hundred spectators also assembled to watch the race, and the group had so much fun that Scott realized he was on to something big.

He managed to convince his boss at the newspaper to sponsor another—this time, official—event. Scott called it the Soap Box Derby (even though there's no record of anyone ever actually racing in a soap box). On August 19, 1933, about 360 kids showed up on a street in Dayton with their creations. The contestants included one girl, who took second place. Forty thousand people came to watch. Scott's Soap Box Derby was a hit.

Kid-Built, Kid-Raced

Word got out about the kid's cart race in Dayton, and Chevrolet signed on as a sponsor. Chevy dealerships around the country held local races, and the next year, 34 of these local champs joined the race in Dayton.

In those early days, the derby's rules were pretty simple. Cars had to be built by the children themselves (no help from parents or other adults). After the first two years, when girls were allowed to race, participation was restricted to boys ages nine to fifteen years old. (Later, the rules were expanded to include boys and girls of a wider range of ages.)

The 1934 race also included a handicap system that Scott implemented in the hopes of giving everyone a fair shot. The racers who proved to be the fastest in the early heats had to begin with delays of a few seconds in later heats. The result: one of the slower carts took advantage of its head start and won. Scott scrapped the handicap system after that.

Finding Fame

In 1935, the Soap Box Derby moved to Akron because it had more hills than Dayton. That year, the derby also garnered attention from national media. Reporters descended on Akron to cover the event.

During one heat, NBC sportscaster Graham McNamee crossed the safety barriers to get closer to the action at the finish line. Officials warned him back, but he said, "I've broadcast from a plane high in the sky, from a submarine on the ocean bottom, from the fastest cars at Indianapolis. I'm not afraid of a little thing like a kiddiecar!" Just then, as if taunted by his words, one of the contestants lost control of his car and crashed right into McNamee. The sportscaster escaped serious injury, but the accident was caught on newsreels and shown in theaters across the country. And the derby just got more popular.

Derby Downs

In 1936, some Soap Box enthusiasts decided that the derby needed its own racetrack. B. E. "Shorty" Fulton, a member of the

Akron city administration, was one of the main lobbyers for the track. He managed the Akron Municipal Airport (adjacent to the proposed track) and would become the track's manager. Even President Franklin D. Roosevelt agreed; he sent Works Progress Administration employees to Ohio to construct the track.

Named Derby Downs, the new cement raceway was 1,600 feet long. It had 200 feet of runoff space below the finish line and room for thousands of spectators. More than 70 years later, the derby still takes place at Derby Downs.

Today, the All-American Soap Box Derby is sponsored by Goodyear, and the rules have changed a bit. There are tournaments in three racing divisions, and parents are encouraged to help their children. The race attracts about 200 to 300 contestants each year. Racers range in age from eight to seventeen and have had many famous fans over the years: Ronald Reagan, Richard Nixon, heavyweight boxer Jack Dempsey, *Star Trek* cast member George Takei, and Jimmy Stewart (who postponed his own honeymoon to catch the 1949 race).

To read about some of the kids who've competed in the derby, turn to page 137.

Did You Know?

A tornado touched down in Highland County, Ohio, in May 2006. What's so strange about a tornado in the Midwest? It struck the city of Hillsboro, right along Wizard of Oz Drive.

A Grand Ol' Burgee

Ohio's state flag is unique and packed with symbolism.

The Design

- Ohio's flag is a burgee, a tapered pennant with a swallowtail.
- It's the only U.S. state flag that is nonrectangular and one of only two such flags in the world: Nepal has the other.

The Images

- The blue triangle represents Ohio's valleys and hills. The red and white circle inside stands for both the first "O" in Ohio and the state's best-known symbol, the buckeye. Thirteen stars surround the circle, representing the original 13 American colonies. The four stars in the triangle's point bring the number up to 17 because Ohio was the 17th state to enter the Union.
- The red and white stripes on the flag's swallowtail symbolize the state's roads and waterways.

The Fold

- In 2005, the Ohio State Legislature passed and Ohio's governor signed House Bill 552, a law that laid out exactly how to fold the state's uniquely shaped flag. Eagle Scout Alex Weinstock of Junction City came up with the process for his Eagle Scout Service Project (one of the requirements to become an Eagle Scout).
- Weinstock's method requires two people and 17 folds (Ohio was the 17th state, after all) to turn the burgee into a neat rectangle.

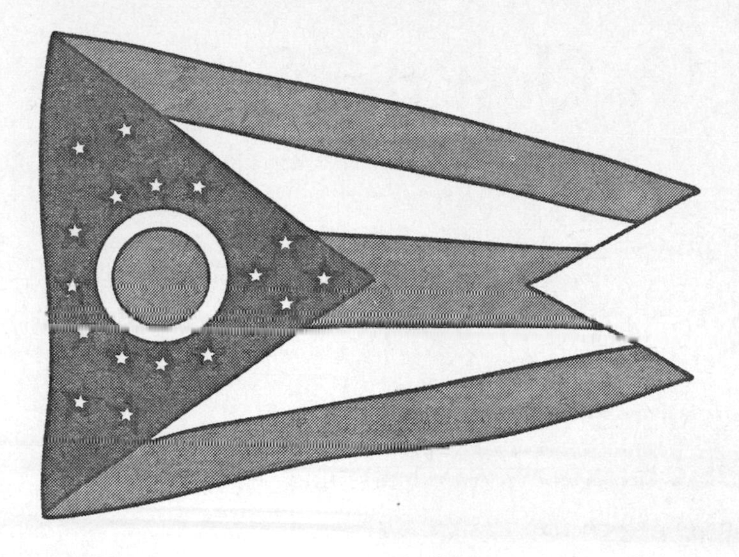

The Creator

- Cleveland architect John Eisenmann designed the flag at the turn of the 20th century. He based it on Civil War and Spanish American War–era cavalry flags carried by Ohio soldiers.

Did You Know?

The Adams County town of West Union . . .

- Actually lies about 100 miles east of Union, Ohio.
- Is the only county seat in Ohio that was never connected to a railroad line during the 1800s railroad boom.
- Was first settled by the Amish.
- Is a dry town; no alcohol can be sold in the city limits.

Just the Facts

Take a quick look at Ohio.

Gained statehood: March 1, 1803 (17th state)

Population: 11,464,042

Capital: Columbus

Nickname: The Buckeye State

State motto: "With God, all things are possible."

Land area: 40,948 square miles

Highest point: Campbell Hill (1,550 feet)

Lowest point: Ohio River (455 feet)

Congressional Representatives: 18

Counties: 88

State parks: 74

National parks: 1 (Cuyahoga Valley National Park)

Borders: Pennsylvania, West Virginia, Kentucky, Indiana, and Michigan

Average high temperature: 85.8°F

Average low temperature: 15.5°F

Record high temperature: 113°F at Gallipolis (1934)

Record low temperature: -39°F at Milligan (1899)

On the Map

Your guide to some of the cities, towns, and communities discussed on the following pages.

A Capital City

Got Buckeye fever? You're in good company in Columbus.

Town: Columbus

Location: Franklin County

Founding: 1812

Current population: 728,432

Size: 212.6 square miles

County seat: Yes

What's in a Name?

In 1812, Ohio's legislature decided that the area just across the Scioto River from the small settlement of Franklinton would make a good, permanent state capital. (Ohio's capital had already moved twice since statehood in 1803.) The legislators named the new capital Columbus—for explorer Christopher Columbus—and the state's government officially moved there in 1816. Soon after, the capital crossed the river and absorbed little Franklinton, incorporating it as one of the city's neighborhoods.

Claims to Fame:

- In 1838, German immigrants in Columbus began the first kindergarten in the United States. Seventy-one years later, in 1909, Indianola Junior High opened in the city; it was the first middle school in the United States.
- Ohio State University opened its doors in Columbus in 1876, originally under the name Ohio Agricultural and

Mechanical College (it became Ohio State University in 1870). Today, OSU is one of the largest universities in the United States and is home (of course!) to the world-famous Buckeyes.

- In the late 1800s, Columbus became the self-proclaimed "buggy capital of the world." The city housed several buggy manufacturers, but the biggest was the Columbus Buggy Company founded by local businessman C. D. Firestone (uncle of Harvey Firestone, who went on to make Firestone tires). In its heyday, the company could turn out a buggy every eight minutes.
- In 1886, British-born Samuel Gompers established the American Federation of Labor (AFL) in Columbus and became its first president. During his tenure, the AFL became the largest, most influential labor union in the United States.
- Columbus is the birthplace of the National Football League (NFL). The organization began in Canton under the name the American Professional Football Association, but in 1922, it moved to Columbus and officially adopted the moniker of the National Football League.
- The Columbus Zoo and Aquarium opened in 1927 and has been a destination for animal lovers ever since. Among the zoo's most famous inhabitants is Colo, born in December 1956 and the first western lowland gorilla born in captivity. Colo still lives at the Columbus Zoo and Aquarium and celebrated her 50th birthday there in 2006.
- Columbus is Ohio's largest city.

Getting to Know Cy Young

They don't make pitchers like Cy Young anymore. Born in Gilmore and raised in Newcomerstown, Young rewrote the record books by winning 511 games during his 22 seasons in the major leagues. Learn more about the man who inspired the pitcher's coveted Cy Young Award.

1. "Cy" was his nickname.

Young earned the nickname in his teens when he tried out for a Canton, Ohio, minor league baseball team. According to legend, the catcher assigned to warm up with him was so impressed by the velocity of Young's fastball that he immediately renamed the young man "Cyclone." Local reporters eventually shortened the moniker to "Cy." (His real name was Denton True Young.)

2. He pitched the first perfect game in American League history.

On May 5, 1904, Young retired all 27 batters he faced in a 3-0 victory over the Philadelphia Athletics. Athletics manager Connie Mack was so impressed by Young's performance that he later called the game the most impressive one ever pitched.

3. He had some power at the plate.

Pitchers don't usually have great reputations as hitters, but Young helped ensure a number of victories for his team by getting on base himself. In his 22 seasons in the major leagues, he clubbed 18 home runs and 290 RBIs. (By comparison, Tom

Glavine, one of the best-hitting pitchers of the modern era, tallied only one home run and 85 RBIs during his first 20 major league seasons.)

4. He has more losses than any pitcher in baseball history.

As dominant a pitcher as Young was, he also weathered his fair share of tough outings. In 906 regular season starts, he lost 316 games, the most in major league history.

5. He had a unique approach to spring training.

Young believed that he generated the blazing speed on his pitches from his legs, not his arm. So when spring training began every February, he held off on throwing a baseball for the first three weeks to concentrate on conditioning his legs instead. "I figured the old arm had just so many throws in it, and there wasn't any use wasting them," he explained. The unorthodox approach allowed him to pitch 7,356 innings, the most in major league history and 1,353 more than Pud Galvin, his next closest competitor.

6. His final outing was a bust.

Appearing for the Boston Braves at the ripe old age of 44, Young surrendered one triple, three doubles, and three singles to the last seven batters he faced. It was one of the worst outings of his career.

7. Fans still make pilgrimages to his grave.

Although Cy Young passed away on November 4, 1955, hundreds of people visit his grave in Peoli, Ohio, every year. According to one superstition, placing a baseball on his gravestone will improve a pitcher's game dramatically.

8. He won only one championship.

Despite racking up 511 career victories, Young won just one championship—in 1903 as a member of the Boston Americans. He finished that season with a record of 28–9 and a 2.08 ERA.

Career Stats:

- Young played for 22 seasons.
- He has career totals of 511 wins, 2,803 strikeouts, and an ERA of 2.63.
- He played for five major league teams: the Cleveland Spiders (1890–1898), the St. Louis Perfectos/Cardinals (1899–1900), the Boston Americans/Somersets/Pilgrims/Red Sox (1901–1908), the Cleveland Naps/Indians (1909–1911), and the Boston Braves (1911).
- Young holds the all-time major league record for wins (511), innings pitched (7,356), games started (815), and complete games (749).
- He was inducted into the Baseball Hall of Fame in 1937.
- Young's remarkable career has been honored every year since 1956 with the Cy Young Award, given annually to the best pitcher in the American and National leagues. It's the only major award in baseball named after a pitcher. Roger Clemens currently holds the record for having won the most Cy Young Awards—he has seven.

A Good Scare

When it comes to urban legends, Ohio offers up some spooky tales.

Creatures: The frog people

Haunts: Southwestern Ohio, specifically the town of Loveland

The legend: The first frog sighting took place in 1955 when a man said he saw a person—three or four feet tall, with wrinkles instead of hair and a mouth with no lips—crouching near a bridge in the town of Loveland. He said the "person" was "frog-faced," and even though authorities investigated, they found no sign of the frog person. Over the next 40 years, other locals came forward with their own tales: the frog people were actually four to five feet tall, could hop onto and over railings like amphibians, and had wet, leathery skin. One woman even reported being dragged under the water while swimming in the Ohio River; from the depths came a clawlike hand, she said, and it left scratches and a green print on her skin.

The truth (such as it is): To this day, scientists, locals, and paranormal investigators debate the authenticity of the claims. They also offer logical explanations for the sightings: Maybe the frog people were pet alligators let loose in the Ohio wilderness. Or maybe they're an as-yet-unidentified type of amphibian. Or maybe it was all a hoax exaggerated by the media.

Creature: Bigfoot

Haunts: Various parts of Ohio, but mainly the central part of the state

The legend: The term "bigfoot" was first used in the late 1950s to describe a creature spotted in California. But in Ohio, Bigfoot had been around for decades by then. In 1897, the *Cleveland Plain Dealer* published a story about two men who claimed to have seen a "wild man about six feet tall" in the woods near Rome, Ohio. Other sightings popped up over the next hundred years—from Cincinnati to Tiffin—leading many people to speculate that Bigfoot wasn't a single creature but an actual species.

The truth (such as it is): Over the years, Bigfoot became so ingrained in Ohio lore that a group was created to research the creature's authenticity and investigate reported sightings. Mike Hartman, a native Ohioan and Bigfoot enthusiast since childhood, established Central Ohio Bigfoot Research and Investigations (called C.O.B.R. for short) in 2003. Hartman and his team split into small groups that dragged cameras, tape recorders, and notebooks to the woods, and went hunting for Bigfoot. Number of Bigfeet caught: zero.

Creatures: Crybabies

Haunts: 24 bridges throughout Ohio

The legend: Rural bridges throughout Ohio are haunted by the spirits of dead children and sometimes also by their parents. The children make themselves known by crying or screaming whenever the living park their cars on or beneath the haunted bridges. Each bridge has its own (albeit similar) story: On Abbeyville Road near Medina, a young unmarried girl hid her pregnancy by throwing her baby over the bridge. In Rogue's Hollow (in Medina and Wayne counties), the ghost of a baby who died with his parents in a car crash haunts a bridge. And in Clinton, the bridge on Cleveland-Massillon Road is said to be haunted by the children of escaped slaves; mothers threw their babies into the water while fleeing slave hunters. Many didn't survive. Legend also has it that the children who haunt the crybaby bridges leave behind ghostly handprints on car windows and footprints in the dirt.

The truth (such as it is): Although some of the tales might actually be true (there are stories of slaves tossing their children into bodies of water to save them from bounty hunters), there's no evidence that the bridges are actually haunted.

Did You Know?

Two Ohio natives, Mark Mothersbaugh (Akron) and Gerald Casale (Ravenna), met when they were students at Kent State University in the late 1960s. They read some interesting books and came up with a theory about how the human race was in a state of de-evolution. (They also made art and wrote songs about it.) When the infamous shootings occurred on campus on May 4, 1970 (and Casale saw two of his friends die in front of him), and especially when the town of Kent went into lockdown in the weeks that followed the shootings, the two became more convinced that humans were devolving. Mark and Jerry formed the band Devo from this theory and went on to become one of the most influential and well loved post-punk bands to usher in the age of New Wave music. Their first performance was at the Kent State Creative Arts Festival in 1973, and they're still making music today; their MySpace page lists "Akron, Ohio" as one of their musical influences.

Literary Lions

Western author Zane Grey, humorist Erma Bombeck, and poet Hart Crane are just three of Ohio's famous writers. Fill in the blanks here for three more of the state's great authors. (Answers are on page 301.)

Across

1 Leaf through
5 Peeples and Vardalos
9 Leno's network
14 Keep fingers crossed
15 Leave one's mark?
16 "Is this your idea of ___?"
17 A thou
18 Bruins' sch.
19 New Orleans sandwich
20 Ohio-born author of *The Secret Life of Walter Mitty*
23 Indignant words that follow "Well"
24 Breadwinners
28 Stop along the line: Abbr.
29 Turns down
32 Toyota Prius, e.g.
33 Paris deserted her for Helen
35 Rembrandt works, e.g.
36 Ohio-born author of *The Devil's Dictionary*
40 Actor Cobb
41 Popeye's female foe in early comics
42 Highway, e.g.
45 Bar or bakery buys
46 HBO rival
49 Took game illegally
51 Put bubbles in
53 Lorain-born, Nobel Prize–winning author of *Beloved*
56 Egg-shaped
59 SpongeBob's pet snail
60 Ed Norton's wear
61 Screen
62 Lowdown
63 Language of Ireland
64 Hot spot
65 Bean curd
66 Title for Ivan the Terrible

Down

1 Japanese screens
2 Longtime Harvard president James Bryant ___
3 Missing links
4 Israeli desert
5 Elementary particle
6 Every seven-year event
7 Human rights org.
8 Mom's insistence
9 Table linen

17

10 Five-time Wimbledon champ
11 Corn holder
12 Match ender
13 "Oy ___!"
21 Passover meal
22 Scrooge's word
25 Noted Viking
26 Tick off
27 Radical 1960s campus org.
30 Peat ___
31 Scornful look
33 Goal
34 'Net auction site
36 Saab model
37 Intro to physics?
38 Simpatico response
39 Loom bar
40 Once around the track
43 Colossus locale
44 Kyoto cash
46 Officers' zappers
47 Greek peak
48 Football middleman?
50 Finger or toe
52 Metal fastener
54 "Look ___ hands!"
55 Antigone composer Carl
56 ___ Kosh B'Gosh
57 By way of
58 Twenty-vol. dictionary

Ohio on the Tube

Think Ohio isn't worthy of the Hollywood treatment? Think again. These TV shows recognized that Ohio was a great place to find some laughs.

WKRP in Cincinnati (1978–1982)

In the 1970s, television director and writer Hugh Wilson came up with a TV show that revolved around a woebegone collection of personalities running a radio station. He decided to set the show in Cincinnati, and *WKRP* was born.

The show premiered in 1978 on CBS and quickly became a hit. Rather than focus the storylines on character arcs or serial plotlines, the show's writers used comedic gags and character quirks, an approach that produced a collection of iconic personas. There were the irascible morning deejay, Johnny "Dr. Johnny Fever" Caravella (Howard Hesseman); the buffoonish but kind general manager, Arthur "Big Guy" Carlson (Gordon Jump); the super-cool overnight deejay, Venus Flytrap (Tim Reid); the perpetually annoying station salesman Herb Tarlek (Frank Bonner); the tightly wound newsman Les Nessman (Richard Sanders); the station's bombshell-with-a-brain secretary, Jennifer Marlowe (Loni Anderson); and several others.

WKRP ran for four seasons and 90 episodes and was nominated for 10 Emmy Awards. Finally, in 1982, it was canceled. The sitcom tried to make a comeback in 1991 as *The New WKRP in Cincinnati*, but poor writing and a cast of new characters doomed the show to cancellation two years later.

Fun fact:

Two of the show's stars—Gordon Jump, who played Big Guy Carlson, and Gary Sandy, who played program manager Andy

Travis—hailed from Ohio. Jump was born in Dayton, and Sandy is a native of Dayton and Kettering.

Family Ties (1982–1989)

Before he became a time-traveling movie star and a stem-cell research advocate, Michael J. Fox starred in a show called *Family Ties*. The program followed the exploits of the Keaton family: parents Elyse and Steven and kids Alex, Mallory, Jennifer, and Andy. The show's original premise called for the parents to be the story's focus, but Michael J. Fox, as archconservative oldest son Alex P. Keaton, proved so popular with viewers that he became the show's star. Most of the show's jokes revolved around clashes between Alex's staunch conservative values (he was an ardent supporter of Ronald Reagan) and his parents' hippie roots (Elyse and Steven had been 1960s flower children).

Family Ties was unarguably set in Ohio, though the city remains up for debate. Sometimes, the Keatons appeared to live in Columbus—as in an episode in which guests come to town for an Ohio State football game. Other times, they seemed to live in Dayton—in one episode, Alex answers the phone by saying "Keaton Manor in beautiful Dayton." But city confusion aside, the show was a hit. It aired on NBC for seven years and, for two of those, was ranked #2 in the Nielsen ratings.

Fun fact:

Many future Hollywood stars made appearances on *Family Ties*, including Tom Hanks, Courteney Cox, Daphne Zuniga, Geena Davis, and Tracy Pollan (who eventually married Michael J. Fox).

3rd Rock from the Sun (1996–2001)

The characters in this show came from a galaxy far away but

chose fictional Rutherford, Ohio, as a base of operations. Calling themselves the Solomon family, the extraterrestrials assumed human form and came to Earth to study its inhabitants. But they got more than they expected when their new physiques forced them to experience the pitfalls of human emotion, hitherto foreign to them. Plus, they quickly discover that being human had practical difficulties: in the first episode, the aliens discover that they can't rotate their heads 180 degrees anymore, thus making it impossible for them to lick their backs.

The group was led by veteran theatrical actor John Lithgow, who played the role of family patron Dr. Dick Solomon, alien leader. Joseph Gordon-Levitt, French Stewart, and Kristen Johnson rounded out the Solomon clan, and *Saturday Night Live* alum Jane Curtin portrayed Lithgow's non-alien love interest. The cast relied on sharp writing and wacky antics to prove once again that Ohio was a darn funny place to live . . . even for folks from outer space.

Fun fact:
William Shatner, of *Star Trek* fame, played the aliens' boss (called the Big Giant Head) in the show's first episode.

The Drew Carey Show (1995–2004)

Cleveland rocks! Or so says the opening theme song for *The Drew Carey Show*. Comedian Drew Carey, himself a proud Clevelander, created the show around his own character—a pudgy, geeky everyman stuck in a boring nine-to-five job but always trying to get ahead (and get a date). The show premiered in 1995 and starred a cast of unique characters that included Drew's friends—Oswald Lee Harvey (Diedrich Bader) and Lewis Kiniski (Ryan Stiles)—and the very made-up Mimi (Kathy Kinney).

The Drew Carey Show was on the air for nine years, and for the first three, it was one of the most highly rated programs on ABC. The show used slapstick and self-deprecating humor to appeal to the average Joe, and Carey often experimented with unique television techniques. Toward the end of the show's run, Carey tried out some live broadcasts and unrehearsed and minimally scripted episodes.

Fun fact:

The Warsaw Tavern, the bar that Carey and his friends often visited, was inspired by Murphy's Law, a Cleveland bar where the real Drew Carey liked to hang out.

Ed (2000–2004)

Another fictional Ohio town—Stuckeyville—was the setting for this NBC sitcom about a New York lawyer named Ed Stevens (Tom Cavanagh) who gets fired from his high-profile job, finds out his wife has had an affair, and then returns to the "simpler" life in his hometown. He buys the local bowling alley, the Stuckybowl, and forges bonds with his new (and old) neighbors. Stuckeyville was populated mostly with characters from Ed's past, including an unrequited high school love interest (played by Julie Bowen) and a childhood friend (played by Josh Randall).

Although the show was on the air for only four years, it attracted a loyal fan base. *Ed* enthusiasts petitioned ABC (unsuccessfully) to keep the show on the air and still participate in a fan Web site called Stuckeyville.com, which hosts more than 14,000 registered members from around the United States.

Fun fact:

Ed was set in Ohio, but most of the show was filmed in northern New Jersey.

Cleveland Browns By the Numbers

If you're a pro football fan in Ohio, you love either the Cleveland Browns or that "other" team. Here we go, Brownies!

0

Super Bowls in which the Browns have participated. The team did, however, win four NFL championships before the first Super Bowl was played in 1967.

1

Unofficial chant of the Browns' famous Dawg Pound. The Pound, located in the east end zone bleachers of Cleveland Browns Stadium, is home to the team's (and perhaps the league's) most rabid fans. Members of the Dawg Pound are well known for singing their team's unofficial chant—"Here we go Brownies! Here we go! Woof Woof!"—dressing up in dog suits, and taunting opposing players.

2

Number of contests held to choose the Cleveland franchise's team name before the 1946 inaugural season. In the first contest, fans chose the Panthers. The head coach didn't like it, though, so he held a second contest; that time, the Browns won.

3

Number of football teams that started in Cleveland. First was the Cleveland Rams in 1937; they later became the Los Angeles Rams and then the present-day St. Louis Rams. Second was the first Browns team in 1946; that team lasted until 1995, when team owner Art Modell decided to relocate the Browns to Baltimore and rename them the Ravens. Finally, in 1999, the modern-day Browns took to the field.

5

Players whose numbers have been retired: Otto Graham (14), Jim Brown (32), Ernie Davis (45), Don Fleming (46), and Lou Groza (76)

8

Yards gained by the Browns' all-time rusher, Jim Brown, in one of the team's worst games, a 1958 playoff match against the New York Giants. The Giants beat the Browns 10–0 in that game. Jim Brown ultimately racked up 12,312 yards over his career, retiring in 1965 after nine years of play. He led the league in rushing for eight of those years.

12

Number of wins for the franchise in its inaugural season. The team finished with a record of 12–2–0 in 1946. (There used to be only 14 games in the regular season.) The Browns' all-time best record came in 1948 when they went 14–0 before beating the Buffalo Bills 49–7 in the league's championship game.

14

Number of head coaches the Browns have had since their inception. The team's first coach was the appropriately named Paul Brown.

16

Browns enshrined in Canton's Pro Football Hall of Fame: Jim Brown, Lou Groza, Ozzie Newsome, Paul Brown, Len Ford, Mike McCormack, Frank Gatski, Leroy Kelly, Bobby Mitchell,

Paul Warfield, Joe DeLamielleure, Otto Graham, Dante Lavelli, Marion Motley, Bill Willis, and Gene Kicherson.

31

Points the Browns scored during the first *Monday Night Football* game in 1970. They won that game, beating the New York Jets 31–21.

110

Number of regular-season games played against the Pittsburgh Steelers between 1950 and 2006. The Browns' record in those games stands at 55–55.

73,200

Seating capacity of Cleveland Browns Stadium. Browns fans are among the NFL's most loyal; they've filled the stadium to 99 percent capacity throughout the last seven seasons despite the team's 36–76 record since 1999.

$1.4 million

Money raised by the Browns charitable foundation's annual golf outing between 1999 and 2006. All the money raised by the foundation goes to help Cleveland's needy.

Did You Know?

Cincinnati native Steven Spielberg knows a thing or two about money. He says, "Why pay a dollar for a bookmark? Why not use the dollar for a bookmark?"

Let's Get Down to Business!

We all know the buckeye is Ohio's state tree. But how well do you know the state's other symbols?

1. Ohio's state insect is the . . .

A. Ladybug beetle
B. Western honeybee
C. Grasshopper

2. Thirsty? Ohio's state drink is . . .

A. Milk
B. Buckeye tea
C. Tomato juice

3. If you wanted to make your sweetheart a ring with the state's gemstone, which one would you choose?

A. Diamond
B. Flint
C. Pipestone

4. The state bird is the . . .

A. Sparrow
B. Cardinal
C. Oriole

5. Ohio's state flower (the carnation) was inspired by the death of which president?

A. William McKinley
B. Abraham Lincoln
C. John F. Kennedy

6. Ohio's state fossil is a marine invertebrate called *Isotelus*. Marine?! Yes, Ohio is landlocked today, but it was once under an ocean. How long has it been since Ohio was underwater?

A. 23 million years

B. 430 million years

C. 1 billion years

7. Ohio adopted which state motto in 1959?

A. Live long and prosper.

B. Give us your poor, your tired, and your weary.

C. With God, all things are possible.

8. The state that houses the Rock and Roll Hall of Fame definitely needs a state rock song. Which one is it?

A. "Hang on Sloopy" by the McCoys

B. "Blue Suede Shoes" by Elvis Presley

C. "Back on the Chain Gang" by the Pretenders

9. Ohio's state wildflower (different from the state flower) is the white trillium. It sometimes goes by what nickname?

A. Robin's nest

B. Robin's egg

C. Wake robin

For answers, turn to page 301.

Did You Know?

Cross Creek in Eastern Ohio calls itself the smallest town in the state. Its population: 14. The town also has a general store where you can still get a 5-cent cup of coffee.

Why So Blue?

A possibly bottomless pool with blue water and no life? Sounds like a tourist attraction!

In 1761, while colonial farmer and military man Robert Rogers was exploring the area south of Lake Erie, he found a natural spring that shot water three feet out of the ground. Rogers made a note about the spring in his diary and left it to the Wyandot, a local Native American tribe who believed the spring had medicinal powers.

Fifty years later, an entrepreneur named Dorcastus P. Snow moved in and built a dam on the spring to power his gristmill. The dam slowed the water flow and caused pressure to build up underground. When the pressure became too great, a sink-hole about 75 feet across opened up in the limestone, and the Blue Hole of Castalia was born.

Setting Up Shop

The sinkhole was named for the nearby town of Castalia, which got its name from a natural aquifer in Greece called the Fons Castalius, another place where water rushes out of the ground. The Blue Hole, though, had some unique properties. For one thing, it was blue. For another, the water temperature remained pretty steady year-round, varying from about 48 to 51°F. Also nothing was living in the water and, most curiously, depth-sounding weights never seemed to hit bottom.

Recognizing a roadside attraction when they saw it, the Castalia Trout Club, which owned the land the spring was on, set up gates and started charging admission. People flocked to the odd natural creation. The Blue Hole's popularity grew during the 1930s and 1940s and topped out at 160,000 visitors in 1952.

A Hole 'Nother Story

Scientists were interested in the Blue Hole as well, and after they studied it for a time, they were able to explain its mysteries:

- It turned out that the sinkhole itself wasn't actually blue. The water was just exceptionally clear because it had no life in it. The blue sky reflecting off the water made the Blue Hole look blue.
- Water came into the Blue Hole from a rushing underground stream that discharged 4,500 gallons every minute. That was also why the temperature didn't vary much. The temperature of the underground water is fairly constant, and because the Blue Hole's water supply was continuously refreshed, it didn't have time to warm or cool according to the air temperature.
- The water was lifeless because it had no oxygen molecules floating around loose in it. (The Castalia Trout Club remedied this by constructing water wheels and creating waterfalls to churn up the water and add atmospheric oxygen to it. Then, they stocked it with fish for the tourists to look at.)
- Finally, the sinkhole wasn't bottomless. The depth-sounding weights just got caught up in the swift current of the underground stream and were pulled farther and farther along. The Blue Hole is actually about 45 feet deep.

Gone Fishin'

By 1990, the number of tourists visiting the Blue Hole had dwindled, so the owners decided to shut the place down.

Today, it's on private property and is off-limits to tourists. The State of Ohio, however, started a fish hatchery in a nearby sinkhole that is open to the public—a new Blue Hole. And it turns out that there are actually several other similar sinkholes in the area. So even if you can't see *the* Blue Hole anymore, you can still see a blue hole.

Did You Know?

Settlement for Ohio pioneers often meant displacement for the Native Americans who'd lived on the Midwestern plains for generations. So when the War of 1812 broke out between the United States and Great Britain, it isn't surprising that many Native Americans supported the British. They attacked throughout the Ohio territory, but because Johnny Appleseed had long been a friend to the tribes, they left him alone. Johnny managed to capitalize on this favored position and ran from homestead to homestead, warning the settlers of the impending attacks.

At one point during the war, a tribe surrounded a settlement in Mansfield and the outnumbered pioneers had to fight for their lives. When Johnny heard of the attack, he ran nearly 30 miles barefoot to Mount Vernon to get help. And as he ran, he blew a horn to warn anyone within earshot of the impending danger. Thanks to Johnny, help arrived in Mansfield within the day, and the Mansfield pioneers were saved.

Tomato, To-mah-toe

Thanks to an Ohioan, the star of the American vegetable garden has its roots firmly planted in the Buckeye State.

Seeds of a Career

The son of a farmer, Alexander W. Livingston was born in 1822 in Reynoldsburg, Ohio, about 12 miles east of Columbus. He showed an early aptitude for horticulture, conducting experiments with seeds and plants from a young age.

Alexander's mother warned him off the fruit, however. When he was about 10 years old, she told him that tomatoes "must be poison, for even the hogs will not eat them." Her tomato prejudice was common at the time and remained so until the mid-19th century. Tomato plants had been brought to Europe from South America during the 1500s, but many people believed the hard, sour fruit wasn't fit to eat. Alexander Livingston, despite his mother's advice, would grow up to change that.

Perfection by Selection

Livingston spent his early adulthood in Reynoldsburg, experimenting with tomato seeds, and married a local woman, Matilda Graham. (They eventually had 10 children.) Then, in 1852, he bought part of the Buckeye Garden Seed Company. Livingston was so fond of tomatoes that he believed there could be a market for them if he could just produce a sweet, meaty fruit that would grow reliably from year to year. The seeds also needed to produce plants exactly like those they came from, which wasn't always the case with the tomatoes available at the time. First, Livingston tried careful husbandry.

He planted the best varieties he could find and dried and saved the seeds to replant the following year. But the results were disappointing: the plants got weaker from one year to the next, delivering tomatoes that were not as good as the ones from which they had sprung.

Livingston kept trying, though, and the process was long. Finally, in 1865, he made a breakthrough. He noticed a particularly robust tomato plant in his garden: the vine was laden with smooth, glossy, deep-red fruits and heavy foliage. It was unique, a beautiful mutation that stood out among its less attractive relatives. Livingston saved some seeds from the unusual vine and planted them the following year. That crop bore another batch of luscious tomatoes, so he chose the best plants and again saved seeds. Livingston repeated this process for five years, and in 1870, he felt he'd finally grown a perfect tomato; he named the variety "Paragon."

The Start of Something Big

Livingston sold Paragon's seeds, and they were an instant hit with gardeners. Buoyed by the Paragon's popularity, Livingston applied the technique of single-plant selection to other varieties, seeking out succulent singletons from his rows of tomato vines. His second variety, Acme, was introduced in 1875.

Over the next 28 years, Livingston developed at least a dozen types of tomatoes, often creating varieties to meet the specific needs of his customers: for canners, he produced Livingston's Favorite; for ketchup makers, the Royal Red. He was always on the lookout for promising specimens and sometimes even asked for seeds from impressive tomatoes he spotted at county fairs or in private gardens.

Livingston's sons followed him into the business and continued the process after their father's death in 1898. They also moved the company—renamed Livingston Seed and still in business today—to Columbus. Livingston's tomatoes were eventually eclipsed by other commercial varieties, but his efforts helped form the basis of today's tomato-growing industry.

Let's Raise a Glass

In 1965, Alexander Livingston's hometown of Reynoldsburg declared itself the "Birthplace of the Tomato" and launched the annual Reynoldsburg Tomato Festival. Held the week after Labor Day—when the tomatoes are ripe on the vine—the festival draws an estimated 35,000 tomato lovers each year. They come to see horticulture exhibits and watch the crowning of the Tomato Queen. Prizes are given for the largest tomato and the tallest plant.

In conjunction with the first Tomato Festival, the Ohio General Assembly voted to make tomato juice the state's official beverage. And every year at the festival, visitors can drink their fill of tomato juice—for free.

Did You Know?

Of all the states that participated in the Civil War on the Union side, none had a higher percentage of its population enlist in the military than Ohio: 60% of all men between the ages of 18 and 45—320,000—from Ohio served. More than 5,000 of them were free blacks.

How Alan Freed the Music, Part 1

The rise and fall of the Ohioan who brought rock 'n' roll to the general public mirrors the story of rock's formative years: youthful, rebellious, confident, scorned, controversial, and misunderstood.

Right Time, Right Place

Alan Freed was born in Pennsylvania in 1921 but moved to Salem, Ohio, with his family when he was 12. He loved music and played the trombone in a swing band while in high school and then took a job as a deejay in Pennsylvania after he graduated. Over the next few years, he bounced from station to station—WKBN in Youngstown, WAXR in Akron—before landing in Cleveland in the early 1950s.

Freed made his first broadcast on Cleveland's WJW radio on July 11, 1951, and he quickly started shaking things up. Always looking for new music to play on his station, Freed paid attention when a local record-store owner named Leo Muntz told him that the new music rage among white teenagers was black rhythm and blues music. At first Freed was skeptical of playing R&B, or "race music" as it was called—not because he didn't like it, but because playing black artists on a white station was taboo at the time. Instead, white deejays played covers of black R&B tunes by white artists. But Freed felt that the covers lacked the rawness and musical prowess of the originals. So he decided to mix in a few R&B tunes with his lineup.

Freed was in a unique position in the early 1950s. He had more autonomy than one might expect because of his affiliation with a small, independent radio station and because most of radio's biggest dramatic stars had shifted to television, taking their shows with them. They left a gap on the airwaves that needed to be filled. The solution: play records. So Freed took the night shift at WJW and was let loose to spin whatever he wanted. And boy, did he ever.

King of the Moondoggers

It didn't take long for the new format to catch on in Cleveland. Freed was tapping into a market that, until that time, had mostly been ignored: white teenagers. And he connected with his audience by making himself one of them. Calling himself "Moondog," Freed began every show with his trademark intro: "Hello everybody, how y'all doin' tonight? This is Alan Freed, king of the Moondoggers!"

Still, Freed knew he was treading a thin line with the rampant racial prejudices of the time. So he was careful never to utter the words "rhythm and blues" on his show. Instead, he played what he called "rock 'n' roll," a term he took credit for coining—although some music historians argue that it was Leo Muntz who came up with it as a way to describe the beat of the "race music." But one thing is certain: Freed popularized the term on his radio show, now dubbed "Moondog's Rock 'n' Roll Party."

Interestingly, the term "rock 'n' roll" was actually much racier than "R&B." First appearing in the 1922 song "My Baby Rocks Me with One Steady Roll" by Trixie Smith, the term was slang for sexual intercourse. Freed claimed he chose the term not because of its sexual connotation, but because "it seemed to suggest the rolling, surging beat of the music." He was also careful to wait for the wee hours of the morning to play the raciest rock songs, such as 1951's "Sixty-Minute Man" by the Dominoes.

Freed quickly became a celebrity in Cleveland, and sales of

black artists' records skyrocketed there. It was an early indication that radio play for an artist could equal commercial success. This combination would lead Freed—and the music industry—down a slippery slope within a few years. But for the time being, Freed lived the rock star lifestyle, drinking heavily and cavorting with musicians and women.

For more about Ohio's groundbreaking deejay, turn to page 126.

Did You Know?

"WESTERVILLE, Ohio—A high school lunch period was disrupted Monday by a greased, naked student who ran around screaming and flailing his arms until police twice used a stun gun on him, authorities said. Taylor Killian, 18, had rubbed his body with grapeseed oil to keep from being caught, and got up after the first time he was shocked to continue running toward a group of frightened students huddled in a corner at Westerville North High School, Lt. Jeff Gaylor said. 'That prank went a little farther than he intended, I guess,' Gaylor said. Killian is in jail and charged with inducing panic, public indecency, resisting arrest, and disorderly conduct. School officials reported that Killian was a good student."

—Associated Press, 2007

Battelle Memorial Institute

This innovative, not-for-profit business continues to put Ohio at the forefront of technology and science.

The Birth of Battelle

The Battelle family can trace its lineage to 1780s Ohio; the first Battelles arrived just after the Revolutionary War. But the family really began to make its mark in the early 1900s, when entrepreneur John Battelle invested in sheet metal and steel foundries and made a fortune. When he died in 1918, he left an estate that totaled about $5 million (approximately $75 million in today's currency). His wife Annie and only son Gordon were left to decide what to do with the money.

Gordon loved science and he believed that it could be used to benefit humanity. He never got a chance to do much in his lifetime—he never married and died in 1923 at the age of 40, following an appendectomy. But in his will, Gordon insisted that his money be used to found a technology and research organization: the Battelle Memorial Institute. He even named president-elect Warren G. Harding, a family friend, as one of the trustees.

Annie died in 1925, and she added to the institute's funding. That money was used to build a new headquarters and laboratory in Columbus.

Bigger and Better

Gordon's will not only laid out how much money should be spent on the institute; it also specified what the organization should do. He wanted the organization to make "discoveries and inventions in connection with the metallurgy of coal, iron, steel, zinc." So, at first, the Battelle Memorial Institute focused on improving products for the steel and mining industries.

As the years went by, the scientists at Battelle branched out. They worked on atomic weapons, airplanes, and tanks for the U.S. government during World War II, and in the early 1950s, the company started to expand, opening its first new branch in Frankfurt, Germany. During the 1960s and 1970s, Battelle's scientists worked on numerous projects. They created food for astronauts to take into space, investigated ways to cut air pollution and treat wastewater, and produced "sandwich" coins for the U.S. Treasury. (Before 1965, quarters and dimes were made with pure metals like silver, but those metals were becoming increasingly expensive. So in 1965, the U.S. Mint used Battelle's method of sandwiching a copper core between a nickel-copper mix to make cheaper coins.)

Today, more than 20,000 people work at Battelle facilities worldwide. There are offices in Mexico, England, Russia, Ukraine, and Japan, but the headquarters remains in Columbus.

Innovations

The Battelle Memorial Institute has led the way in science and invention since its inception in 1929. Here are just some of the everyday things Battelle scientists have worked on:

- Photocopiers
- Compact discs
- The Sensonic electric toothbrush
- Universal product codes (those machine-readable bar codes)
- The HumaPen (a reusable insulin-injector pen for diabetics)
- Postal stamp adhesive

Cleansing Fire?

When the Cuyahoga River ignited in 1969, it set the ball rolling for real progress on water pollution. But surprisingly, that blaze wasn't the first—or even the worst— in the river's polluted history.

Mysterious Blaze

On June 22, 1969, oil slicks and industrial debris floating on the surface of Cleveland's Cuyahoga River caught fire. No one knows for sure how it started, but the best guess is that a spark from a train passing over the river on a bridge started the blaze. The fire didn't last long—only about 30 minutes—but it did damage two railroad trestles. The city's fire department showed up before the press, however, so the only photos taken of the 1969 Cuyahoga fire show its aftermath.

Sparking Discussion

Quickly, the river fire caught the attention of America's growing environmental movement. It became a rallying point for the media and environmental advocates. *Time* reported on the fire and the pollution that contributed to it in the magazine's August 1969 issue: "Some river! Chocolate-brown, oily, bubbling with subsurface gases, it oozes rather than flows. 'Anyone who falls into the Cuyahoga does not drown,' Cleveland's citizens joke grimly. 'He decays.' The Federal Water Pollution Control Administration dryly notes: 'The lower Cuyahoga has no visible life, not even low forms such as leeches and sludge worms that usually thrive on wastes.'"

As a result of all the attention, the city of Cleveland and the United States government (especially after the Environmental

Protection Agency was founded in 1970) got serious about cleaning up the Cuyahoga. They cracked down on companies that had long ago received permits to dump refuse in the river, and in 1972, the federal government passed the Federal Water Pollution Control Amendments, better known as the Clean Water Act. The act authorized federal spending for sewage-treatment facilities and gave a timetable for industries to clean up their waste or face hefty fines and even jail time for company leaders.

The Myth

Yet even as the state and country tried to clean up the river, most people overlooked the fact that this was neither the first time the river had caught fire nor the worst blaze in its history. In fact, between 1868 and 1969, the river caught fire 10 times. The worst was in 1952, when an oil slick and debris ignited into a massive blaze that caused $1.5 million in damages. A photo of that fire—and not the small one in 1969—actually ran with the 1969 *Time* story, making the disaster seem more dangerous than it actually had been.

The 1969 fire also wasn't the first time community leaders recognized the need to clean up the river. Fires on rivers near industrial centers were common during the 19th century. Industries routinely dumped the trash and waste that fanned a fire into nearby rivers. By the early 20th century, though, the debris was interfering with shipping, and cities like Cleveland, whose livelihoods relied on both industry and shipping, often sent out cleanup crews to remove debris from the rivers. By the time of the 1969 fire, much improvement had been made on the Cuyahoga River, and many people now believe that fire to have been a fluke.

You're My Inspiration

But no matter the reality, the 1969 fire did inspire the federal government to get involved and pass the wide-reaching Clean Water Act, which dramatically decreased water pollution around the country.

The fire also inspired musicians and activists. Randy Newman and R.E.M. both have written and recorded songs about Cleveland's 1969 Cuyahoga River fire. Newman's "Burn On" was released in 1972 (and was named one of *Rolling Stone* magazine's 500 greatest songs of all time), and R.E.M.'s "Cuyahoga" was released in 1986.

Did You Know?

No one knows for sure how the Underground Railroad got its name, but many historians accept this explanation: In 1831, slave Tice Davids made a run for freedom, slipping into the Ohio River on the Kentucky side and swimming for the safety of Ohio with his irate master following after him. The slave owner pulled his boat to shore only minutes behind Davids, yet the man was nowhere to be found. Perhaps, thought the puzzled slave owner, Davids had escaped via "an underground road." The Ohio Historical Society, though, says it's more likely that an abolitionist—probably John Parker or John Rankin, both famous in Ohio for helping runaway slaves—met Davids and took him to a safe house.

An Unlikely Visitor

In 1929, a stranger arrived in tiny Sabina, Ohio, and passed away a few days later, so the undertaker embalmed and displayed him with the hope that someone would identify him somehow.

Enter "Eugene"

In early June 1929, a man passed away just outside Sabina, near the Three-C Highway. No one knew anything about him, so the police examined the body for clues. The man was 50 or 60 years old, African American, and appeared to have died of natural causes. The only thing he carried with him was a piece of paper that had a Cincinnati address written on it.

The police in Sabina called their colleagues in Cincinnati and asked them to check on the address. It was just a vacant lot, but a man named Eugene Johnson lived next door. The cops interviewed him but got little help. Johnson didn't recognize the dead man's description and didn't know of anyone missing from his neighborhood.

Flummoxed, the Sabina police decided to embalm the man. That way, he could be identified if someone came looking for him. Olin R. Moon of Littleton's Funeral Home did the job.

Waiting and Waiting and . . . Waiting

No one came, though . . . even after weeks and months passed. Littleton's put him on display in a brick building next to the funeral home. The locals started calling him "Eugene," the only name they'd ever heard associated with him. Over the years, Eugene became a fixture in Sabina, and people got used to having him around. (Eugene spent his days sitting on a sofa.)

Word soon got out about the town's unusual resident. Sabinites took their out-of-town relatives to see Eugene, and people drove from all over to catch a glimpse of him. Over the next 35 years, 1.5 million people came to see Eugene.

Gone Missing

As Eugene's fame grew, though, tricksters began using him for pranks. One time, Ohio State University students stole him and put him on a park bench in Columbus. Fortunately, the cop who found the body recognized Eugene from a trip to Sabina. The officer called Littleton's to retrieve him. Another time, students stole Eugene and took him on a joyride through a drive-in restaurant's parking lot.

All this vandalism eventually convinced the people at Littleton's to bury Eugene. They interred him in October 1964 in the town cemetery. He's still there, and you can visit if you want—his gravestone is marked with his death date, burial date, and the name "Eugene."

Did You Know?

President William McKinley's first home in Canton celebrates some of America's most important women. The house was originally the family home of his wife, Ida Saxton McKinley. Today, it's the National First Ladies Historic Site and displays images and belongings of United States First Ladies.

The Scarlet and Gray By the Numbers

Although probably best known for its football team, Ohio State University actually has 36 varsity sports teams, the largest fully funded sports program in the country. With championships in everything from basketball to fencing to synchronized swimming, the Buckeyes—in their scarlet-and-gray uniforms—are a major force in college sports.

2

The number of years Jack Nicklaus played golf for OSU before turning professional. While he was a Buckeye, the Golden Bear won two U.S. Amateur championships and an NCAA championship and, while still an amateur, came in second at the 1960 U.S. Open, two strokes behind winner Arnold Palmer.

4

Gold medals won in the 1936 Berlin Olympics by OSU student and track star Jesse Owens. He took the 100-meter dash, the 200-meter dash, the long jump, and ran one leg of the 4x100-meter relay. Even more impressive than his gold-medal collection, though, was his performance at the Big Ten Championships on May 25, 1935. He set world records in the 200-yard dash, 200-yard low hurdles, and the long jump (where he posted a jump almost three inches longer than his gold-medal winning leap the following year) all at the same meet. He also tied the world record for the 100-yard dash that day.

6

Number of Ohio State football players who have won the Heisman Trophy since it was first awarded in 1935: Les Horvath (1944), Vic Janowicz (1950), Howard "Hopalong" Cassady (1955), Archie Griffin (1974 and 1975; he was the award's only two-time winner), Eddie George (1995), and Troy Smith (2006).

7

National championships the OSU football team has won: 1942, 1954, 1957, 1961, 1968, 1970, and 2002.

28

Number of years that Buckeye football was coached by the fiery Woody Hayes. Hayes' career with the school began in 1951 and ended in 1979 when he punched an opposing player who intercepted a pass and was tackled in front of him near the sideline. Hayes got two unsportsmanlike conduct penalties for the assault—one for punching, one for arguing about the first penalty with the referee—and he got the boot from the university soon afterward.

55

Team titles (men's, women's, and co-ed) that OSU sports teams have won. These include fencing, golf, synchronized swimming, gymnastics, basketball, and football.

103

Number of football games played between Ohio State and their biggest rival (not just in football), Michigan. The annual football matchup, which ends the regular season, is the biggest event on both schools' athletic calendars. Michigan has won 57 times, OSU 40, and there have been six ties. The fierceness of the rivalry has stoked some intense games, notably the 1950 Snow Bowl (*see page 143*), when adverse weather conditions made punting on first down seem like a good idea.

112

Buckeye trees planted in the Buckeye Grove, an orchard near Ohio Stadium. The trees honor football players who were all named first-team All-Americans.

$194 million

Cost to renovate Ohio Stadium in 2001. The horseshoe-shaped stadium has been the home of Buckeye football since 1922. The largest crowd to pack into the stadium for a single game was made up of 105,708 people who came to see OSU defeat Michigan 42-39 on November 18, 2006, earning the Buckeyes a spot in the national championship game.

Did You Know?

James Spangler, a Canton, Ohio, department store janitor, invented the electric vacuum cleaner in 1907. He did so to make his job easier. Originally, the dustbag was a pillowcase, and the rest of the machine was made of wood and tin. Because Spangler lacked resources to mass-produce his invention, he asked his childhood friend William Hoover to help him out.

Born in Ohio

Ohio has been the birthplace of some of the world's most famous folks. Here are some of the state's most celebrated native sons and daughters and the towns from which they came.

Sports Stars

Paul Brown (football coach and NFL founder, Norwalk)
Roger Clemens (baseball player, Dayton)
Sylvia Crawley (basketball player and coach, Steubenville)
Buster Douglas (boxer, Columbus)
Rob Dyrdek (skateboarder, Kettering)
Sarah Fisher (race car driver, Commercial Point)
Scott Hamilton (figure skater, Toledo)
Jim Harbaugh (football player, Toledo)
Woody Hayes (football coach, Clifton)
LeBron James (basketball player, Akron)
Bobby Knight (basketball coach, Massillon)
Jack Nicklaus (golfer, Columbus)
Ben Roethlisberger (football player, Findlay)
Pete Rose (baseball player and manager, Cincinnati)
Don Shula (football coach, Grand River)
Roger Staubach (football player, Cincinnati)
George Steinbrenner (New York Yankees' owner, Rocky River)
Cy Young (baseball player, Gilmore)

Performers

Jim Backus (actor, Cleveland)
Theda Bara (actress, Cincinnati)

Halle Berry (actress, Cleveland)
Drew Carey (actor and comedian, Cleveland)
George Chakiris (actor, Norwood)
Tracy Chapman (musician, Cleveland)
Tim Conway (actor, Willoughby)
Dorothy Dandridge (actress, Cleveland)
Doris Day (actress, Cincinnati)
Kim Deal (singer, Dayton)
Phyllis Diller (actress and comedian, Lima)
Phil Donahue (talk show host, Cleveland)
Hugh Downs (news broadcaster, Akron)
Carmen Electra (model, Sharonville)
Clark Gable (actor, Cadiz)
Teri Garr (actress, Lakewood)
Lillian Gish (actress, Springfield)
Maggie Grace (actress, Worthington)
Macy Gray (singer, Canton)
Joel Grey (singer and actor, Cleveland)
Dave Grohl (musician, Warren)
Margaret Hamilton (actress, Cleveland)
Hal Holbrook (actor, Cleveland)
Katie Holmes (actress, Toledo)
Chrissie Hynde (musician, Akron)
Marilyn Manson (musician, Canton)
Dean Martin (singer, Steubenville)
Paul Newman (actor, Shaker Heights)
Annie Oakley (sharpshooter, Darke County)
Luke Perry (actor, Mansfield)
Tyrone Power (actor, Cincinnati)
Molly Shannon (comedian, Shaker Heights)

Soldiers and Statesmen

Prescott Bush (U.S. senator and businessman, Columbus)
George Custer (general, New Rumley)
James A. Garfield (U.S. president, Moreland Hills)
Ulysses S. Grant (U.S. president, Point Pleasant)
Warren G. Harding (U.S. president, Blooming Grove [formerly Corsica])
Benjamin Harrison (U.S. president, North Bend)
Rutherford B. Hayes (U.S. president, Delaware)
Dennis Kucinich (U.S. representative, Cleveland)
William McKinley (U.S. president, Niles)
William Tecumseh Sherman (Civil War general, Lancaster)
William Howard Taft (U.S. president, Cincinnati)
Tecumseh (Shawnee chief, Scioto River)

Professionals

Neil Armstrong (astronaut, Wapakoneta)
Charles Brush (inventor, Euclid Township)
James M. Cox (governor and businessman, Jacksonburg)
Clarence Darrow (lawyer, Kinsman)
Thomas Edison (inventor, Milan)
Harvey Firestone (businessman, Columbiana)
John Glenn (astronaut, Cambridge)
Charles Kettering (inventor, Loudonville)
John H. Patterson (businessman, Dayton)
Charles Richter (seismologist, Hamilton)
Eddie Rickenbacker (World War I pilot, Columbus)
Ted Turner (media mogul, Cincinnati)
Orville Wright (inventor, Dayton)
Wilbur Wright (inventor, Dayton)

Writers and Artists

Sherwood Anderson (author, Camden)
Natalie Barney (poet, Dayton)
Ambrose Bierce (author, Meigs County)
Erma Bombeck (newspaper columnist and author, Dayton)
Vincent J. Cardinal (playwright, Ashtabula)
Hart Crane (poet, Garrettsville)
Wes Craven (film director, Cleveland)
Michael Cunningham (author, Cincinnati)
Paul Laurence Dunbar (poet, Dayton)
Harlan Ellison (author, Cleveland)
Zane Grey (author, Zanesville)
Cathy Guisewite (cartoonist, Dayton)
Virginia Hamilton (children's author, Yellow Springs)
Robert Edwin Lee (writer, Elyria)
Maya Lin (sculptor, Athens)
Toni Morrison (author, Lorain)
Dav Pilkey (author, Cleveland)
Steven Spielberg (film director and producer, Cincinnati)
Gloria Steinem (author, Toledo)
R. L. Stine (author, Columbus)
James Thurber (author and cartoonist, Columbus)

Did You Know?

The first item ever scanned by a supermarket scanner was a pack of Wrigley's chewing gum, scanned in 1974 at the Marsh Supermarket in Troy, Ohio. Today, that pack of gum is on display at the Smithsonian.

A State of Wine

Most people think of California when they think of American wines, but until the Civil War, Ohio led the nation in wine production.

The Rise and Fall . . .

Ohio's wine industry began with Nicholas Longworth, a New Jersey lawyer who moved to Cincinnati in 1803 and bought hundreds of acres of Ohio farmland. By 1850, he was one of the largest landowners in the United States, and he dedicated much of his property to growing grapes and making wine. Longworth specialized in the Catawba grape, a fruit that was hardy enough to survive southern Ohio's harsh winters. His white Catawba was a hit with Ohio's German immigrants and was one of America's first locally produced wines. Other vintners followed, and by the mid-1800s, Cincinnati and neighboring towns along the Ohio River were producing hundreds of thousands of gallons of wine every year.

During the Civil War, however, Ohio's southern vineyards suffered a double blow. The first was a series of diseases that spread through the wine crop and reduced its yield. The second was the lack of manpower to harvest the grapes because Ohio's young men were off fighting the Confederates. The vineyards never quite recovered, and by the time they could, California wine production had overtaken the lead.

. . . And Rise Again

But winemaking wasn't dead in Ohio. Winemakers had discovered that the northern part of the state—along Lake Erie—also was a good grape-growing environment. Along the shores of the lake, vineyards sprang up, though none produced quite as much as the southern Ohio River area had.

Yet more trouble was on the horizon. Prohibition—passed in 1920—all but killed Ohio's wine industry. With their product suddenly illegal, some vineyards switched to growing juice grapes; many others just went out of business. Even though other wine-growing areas rebounded in 1933 when Prohibition was repealed, Ohio vintners continued to struggle with California's dominance and the lack of local interest in Ohio wine growing.

It took almost 50 years to rebound, but by the 1980s, Ohio wineries had regained a legitimate place in the industry. Over the last several years, Ohio wines have won medals at the American Wine Society Commercial Wine Competition, the San Francisco International Wine Competition, and the Indy International Wine Competition. The rebound comes thanks to increased assistance from the state—governors James Rhodes and Richard Celeste set up the Ohio Grape Industries Program in the early 1980s, and Governor George Voinovich instituted grants and tax credits aimed at creating vineyards. Both initiatives grew from the spark provided by Ohio State University's agricultural center, which worked to provide disease-resistant grape varieties for the vineyards. More than 40 new vineyards opened during this period of growth.

Ice, Ice, Baby

Although Ohio produces everything from Pinot Noir to Chardonnay, the state has made its mark with ice wine, a dessert wine made from grapes that have frozen on the vine. Ohio vintners leave grapes on the stem late into the season: the grapes freeze, but the hardy vines don't die. The frozen grapes are then harvested, crushed, and drained, making a concentrated and sweet wine. Ohio ice wines are usually made from

Vidal Blanc grapes, and the first vineyard to offer an Ohio ice wine was Valley Vineyards near Cincinnati.

Take a Tour

Today, there are several clusters of vineyards in Ohio: the edges of Lake Erie, the Ohio River Valley near Cincinnati, central Ohio, the Akron/Youngstown area, and the southeast. Natives and visitors alike can tour many of the wineries in each region. Here are some of the most popular wineries from each of Ohio's wine areas:

- Kelleys Island Wine Company on Kelleys Island, Chalet Debonne Winery in Madison, or Ferrante Winery in Geneva.
- The Slate Run Vineyard in Winchester is just 15 minutes from Columbus, and at the Buckeye Winery in Newark, you can make your own wine at their store.
- Henke Winery in Cincinnati and Valley Vineyards Winery in Morrow.
- Breitenbach Wine Cellar in Dover—one of the most visited wineries in the country—and the Winery at Wolf Creek within quick driving distance of Akron.
- Shawnee Springs Winery in Coshocton or Flint Ridge Vineyards in Hopewell.

Did You Know?

Cincinnati Bengals quarterback Carson Palmer and Pittsburgh Steelers safety Troy Polamalu are friends and were roommates at the University of Southern California.

The Zanesville Bridge

"Drive to the middle of the bridge and turn right."

Turn Right . . . *on* the Bridge?

It's the only bridge in the United States that warrants directions of that kind. The Zanesville Bridge—shaped like the letter Y—spans the intersection of the Licking and Muskingum rivers on US highway 40. Pilot Amelia Earhart called Zanesville the "most recognizable city in the country," because pilots could identify the Y bridge from the air.

Zany!

There have actually been five Y bridges in Zanesville. The first was built in 1813, but it fell into the river a few years later. The bridge was rebuilt on the same site in 1819, and it stood for 13 years before being condemned as unsafe. A third bridge was built and stood from 1832 to 1900. The fourth bridge opened in 1902 and lasted until 1979. The latest bridge opened in 1984.

In the old days, you had to pay a toll to cross Zanesville's Y bridge. Some early fees:

- Foot passengers: 3 cents
- Horses, mules, or asses one year old or older: 4 cents
- Horses and riders: 12½ cents
- A sleigh or sled drawn by two oxen or two horses: 25 cents
- A coach with four wheels, a driver, and four horses: 75 cents

An Industrious Town

When it comes to innovation, this city's "high place" on the Ohio and Erie Canal takes the cake.

Town: Akron
Location: Summit County
Founding: 1825
Current population: 212,215
Size: 62 square miles
County seat: Yes

What's in a Name?

The name "Akron" is a Greek word that, roughly translated, means "a high place," an appropriate moniker since the city sits at about 1,000 feet above sea level, the highest point along the Ohio and Erie Canal (which connects the Ohio River to Lake Erie).

Claims to Fame

- German immigrant and Akron grocer Ferdinand Schumacher started selling oatmeal in his store in late 1854. Two years later, he bought an old wooden factory along the canal and started grinding oats. His company, called the German Mills American Oatmeal Company, could turn out 20 barrels of oats a day. Schumacher's company thrived over the next half century and earned him the nickname "the Oatmeal King"—business was especially good during the Civil War when the U.S. government started buying

Schumacher's oats to feed its soldiers. In 1901, Schumacher's company merged with two other oat producers, Ravenna's Quaker Mill Company and a cereal mill in Iowa, to form the Quaker Oats Company . . . you know the one—it's got that white-haired man on its logo.

- The first mass-marketed toy was produced in Akron in 1884 when Samuel C. Dyke and the Akron Toy Company (later known as the American Marble and Toy Manufacturing Company) started making clay marbles and selling them directly to children—one penny bought one, two, three, or a handful of marbles, depending on the style and workmanship. Dyke's company became the 19th century's most profitable and largest toymaker. Today, Akron's American Marble and Toy Museum celebrates the city's toy history with marble exhibits and tournaments.
- Akron is the "Rubber Capital of the World." Two of the largest American rubber and tire companies—B.F. Goodrich and Goodyear—got their starts in the city. (*To read more about them, turn to pages 74 and 257.*)
- The self-help group Alcoholics Anonymous started in Akron in 1935 when two struggling alcoholics—physician Bob Smith and stockbroker Bill Wilson—started holding informal meetings. The group became immensely popular and, since its inception, has helped millions of alcoholics combat their addictions.

Did You Know?

An Ohioan's word to the wise: "Man cannot live by bread alone; he must have peanut butter." **—James Garfield**

Down on the Farm

Ohio is one of the largest producers of agricultural goods in the United States. Take a look at the stats.

- The state's top industries are food and agriculture.
- Ohio is one of only five U.S. states with almost half of its land considered prime farmland; 44 percent is designated prime farmland by the Department of Agriculture.
- Ohio grows more than 200 crops, with corn and soybeans being the most popular.
- One in every seven Ohioans is employed in some aspect of agriculture, including farm production, wholesaling and retailing, marketing and processing, and agribusiness.
- In 2003, Ohio had 77,600 farms; 91 percent of those are family farms.
- Ohio is the leading U.S. producer of Swiss cheese and is second in egg production, producing 7.6 billion eggs in 2003.
- Ohio's number-one floriculture crop is the poinsettia.

Did You Know?

In his junior year of high school, Cleveland Cavaliers basketball star (and Akron native) LeBron James was the #2 ranked *football* prospect in the state of Ohio. #1: Ohio State star Maurice Clarett.

The Apple Tree Man

The myth of Johnny Appleseed depicts a man wearing an upturned pot for a hat and carrying bags of apple seeds to scatter across the land. But the real Johnny did a lot more than toss seeds to the wind: He helped save a fledgling nation from starvation.

A Legend with Great Appeal

Johnny Appleseed was born John Chapman on September 26, 1774, in Leominster, Massachusetts. Little is known about his childhood, but we do know he was apprenticed to a nurseryman at an early age. It was there that he learned to cultivate plants and trees, developing quite a green thumb by the time he was a teenager.

In the late 1700s, Johnny headed west loaded with apple seeds he had picked up from the waste of East Coast cider mills. He was a man with a mission: to bring apples to the new settlers. He predicted what areas would most appeal to settlers and then, a year or so ahead of them, claimed tracts of those lands throughout the Midwest, particularly in Ohio and Pennsylvania. When he arrived, he cleared fields for orchards and carefully cultivated his seeds into saplings. When the settlers arrived, he traded or sold them his seeds, saplings, and apples. By then, he was already called Johnny Appleseed and the Apple Tree Man. No one knows how the nicknames got started; they may have come from customers, neighbors, or even Johnny himself.

He did all the work in the orchards himself and lived alone for weeks and months at a time. Johnny was also a pacifist and vegetarian who befriended the Native Americans. He never carried a gun or a weapon of any kind and loved animals so much that he refused to ride horses because he thought it was cruel. He often used the profits from his orchards to care for lame horses that would otherwise have been put to death. And according to legend, Johnny even spared the lives of such pests as yellow jackets and mosquitoes.

An Apple a Day . . .

Naysayers discounted Johnny's work. They claimed that his plan to fill Ohio with apple orchards was folly. But growing the saplings proved to be smart for the state. Apples are both a sweet treat and a stable commodity. Fresh apples can be stored in a cellar for several months, and dried and preserved apples can be stored for as long as a year. They can also be pressed and made into hard cider, an alcoholic drink that many pioneers relied on during the long winters. Without Johnny's apples, seeds, and saplings, many early pioneers would have starved or suffered from malnutrition.

Generous to the Core

In all, Johnny Appleseed personally planted several million apple seeds and established hundreds of apple orchards south of the Great Lakes, between the Ohio and Mississippi rivers. That totals more than 100,000 square miles of orchards, many of which are still around today. The settlers he inspired planted many more.

They succeeded primarily because Johnny was generous and helpful. The settlers had little money, so he sold his saplings for just a few pennies each, usually on credit. If a settler couldn't come up with the money, Johnny would accept bartered items like cornmeal or used clothing in exchange. Johnny was said to be so generous that he would give his shoes to a friend and walk the countryside in his bare feet—even in the winter.

Johnny saw it as his mission to help others not only by supplying them with apples but by bringing them faith as well. So in addition to planting trees, he spread the gospel. He was a self-appointed minister of a Christian sect called the Church of New Jerusalem.

A Good Seed

Johnny Appleseed died in 1845 in Fort Wayne, Indiana, after spending more than 50 years planting apple trees. The Johnny Appleseed Heritage Center in Ashland, Ohio—where Johnny lived for several years—tells his story and celebrates his birthday every September. The Johnny Appleseed Triathlon held its inaugural event in 2006. The triathlon's course meanders through Knox County's Apple Valley Lake area, and organizers hope it will become an annual homage to the beloved nurseryman.

Did You Know?

The television show *Normal, Ohio* (2000) was created by the same people who made *3rd Rock from the Sun.* It centered on a 40-ish gay man named William "Butch" Gamble (John Goodman) who left Los Angeles and returned to his middle-American hometown to make amends with his son. Other cast members included Joely Fisher, Orson Bean, Anita Gillette, and Charles Rocket. Although Goodman won the People's Choice Award for Best Actor in a New Comedy Series, the show was not a ratings success and was canceled after only a few months on the air.

You Know You're an Ohioan When . . .

- . . . you think all pro football teams wear orange.

- . . . you live less than 30 miles from a college or university.

- . . . you can spell words like Cuyahoga, Olentangy, Bellefontaine, Tuscarawas, and Wapakoneta.

- . . . "Vacation" means spending the day at Cedar Point.

- . . . you end your sentences with an unnecessary preposition. Example: "Where's my pop at?"

- . . . you can identify a buckeye, and you've eaten candy ones.

- . . . your four major food groups are beef, beer, green bean casserole, and Jell-O salad with marshmallows.

- . . . you know that Serpent Mounds were not made by snakes.

- . . . "Down South" means Kentucky.

- . . . no hamburger compares to a White Castle.

- . . . you don't think of Florida when someone mentions Miami.

- . . . you find 20°F to be a bit chilly.

A Week of Water

The great flood of 1913 was Ohio's worst natural disaster. Almost no part of the state escaped unscathed. Yet heroes emerged in the form of ordinary citizens and a business tycoon.

Blame It on the Rain

It didn't begin as a deluge—just a steady shower that began on March 23, 1913. But the rain kept coming, overrunning an already saturated landscape and rivers swollen with melting winter snow. The ensuing flood came to be known as "Ohio's greatest weather disaster."

Between the 23rd and the 27th, it rained continuously. Rainfall—in some places mixed with sleet—totaled between 6 and 11 inches, and rivers such as the Muskingum, the Ohio, and the Great Miami overflowed. Bridges washed out, railroad tracks flooded, and drinking water and gas lines were lost. Food supplies, usually housed on the first floors in homes and in stores, were gone. Statewide, deaths from the flood were estimated close to 500, and more than 40,000 homes were destroyed.

The Kruckers' Great Escape

Abbie Krucker lived in Hamilton, nine blocks from the Miami River. Despite the rising water, she was not concerned about the possibility of a flood, but early in the morning on March 25, the river overflowed its banks and swept through the Miami Valley. As the water filled the street and flooded the Kruckers' basement, Abbie's husband Adam instituted a plan: carry as much food and furniture upstairs as possible and wait out the floodwaters from the second story with their infant son.

Others in the neighborhood did the same. But second stories were not safe havens. In the Krucker house, the water was rapidly climbing the stairs. Abbie saw boats being rowed down the streets. Two neighbors paddled a canoe up to the bedroom window, and Adam, Abbie, and the baby took their only chance at escape. They and the rescuers paddled safely to higher city ground and out of the flood and spent the next two nights with 100 others at a friend's farm, waiting for the floodwaters to ebb.

The Kruckers returned home to find a house full of mud and watermarks 18 inches deep on the second floor. The aftermath of the flood was devastating. No food or drinking water was available in the city. One hundred and six people were dead, and 10,000 were homeless.

Dayton Drama

The devastation in Hamilton was bad, but Dayton was the city that suffered the most—its earthen dam failed and the levees gave way. The Miami River was four miles wide and 20 feet deep downtown. An area of 15 square miles was underwater. Several fires erupted from ruptured gas lines and were unreachable by the city's firefighters. The story of Dayton during flood week was a combination of tragedy, narrow escapes, and daring rescues.

The Schneider family, trapped in the second floor of their home, rescued a next-door neighbor from the roof by throwing her a clothesline. The woman tied the line around her waist, leapt into the water, and the Schneiders hauled her to the safety. (They also fed her whiskey to help her recover from the ordeal.) Another man, E. C. Bennett, waded through neck-high water to get to a friend's house, where the two broke through the roof and then used a door as a plank to walk to the higher roof of the house next door.

The Plane! The Plane!

Dayton resident Orville Wright was out of the area that morning, but his 84-year-old father, Milton, with whom he shared a home, was alone when the floods encroached. Luckily, a neighbor used a canoe to rescue him.

The 1903 airplane that Orville and his brother Wilbur had flown at Kitty Hawk also narrowly escaped destruction. All around the bicycle shop where it was stored, buildings burned and exploded, but the shop survived, as did the plane, which was crated in sections and found under layers of mud. Old glass plate negatives of the Wright brothers' historic flight were also damaged but not destroyed. (*To read more about the Wrights, turn to page 189.*)

A Hero in Businessman's Clothing

Many of the Wrights' neighbors were not so lucky. The city's government collapsed. Half of Dayton's families were homeless, and communication with the outside world was impossible. To the rescue came John H. Patterson, owner of the National Cash Register Company. (*For Patterson's story, see page 148.*)

Patterson's plant was on high ground and still had water, heat, and electricity. So he turned over his entire factory to relief efforts, allowing refugees to live there, providing food and water, arranging medical care for the wounded, and turning the factory over to search-and-rescue boat construction. Patterson's plan allowed his employees to finish one boat every 15 minutes. During the five days until the flood receded, those boats sought and saved family after family from rooftops and trees. More than 3,000 people were sheltered in the factory and fed three meals a day. In the end, Patterson's company spent about $2 million on relief efforts.

Never Again

The floodwaters finally receded on March 30, and recovery began throughout Ohio. The National Guard brought order, rescue, and food to many areas. The trains that were still running brought donated food and clothing from across the country. As the recovery began, Ohio's governor, James M. Cox, and Patterson determined that such a disaster would never happen again.

They lobbied for change, and as a result of their efforts, the Ohio Conservancy Law was passed in 1914. This established watershed districts and provided for a system of dams and levees that would prevent such severe flooding in the future. It was the first such law in the United States. Today, Ohio officials estimate that the Conservancy Law system has prevented flooding at least 1,500 times in the Miami River area alone.

To read about more wild Ohio weather, turn to page 132.

Did You Know?

For the last 13 years of her life, Ohio sharpshooter Annie Oakley emerged from retirement only to perform in charity exhibitions. In 1926, when her health was failing, she moved back to Darke County. Oakley died there on November 3. Her husband, Frank Butler, passed away just 18 days later. The two were buried next to each other at Brock Cemetery in Greenville.

Topsy-Turvy

The lineup at Sandusky's Cedar Point includes 17 of the world's largest roller coasters. But the history of this amusement park is almost as exciting as the roller coasters themselves. (We said almost!) Here are five things you might not know about the "Roller Coaster Capital of the World."

1. Cedar Point is North America's second-oldest amusement park.

Cedar Point Amusement Park, on a peninsula that juts into Lake Erie, opened in 1870. (The oldest amusement park, Lake Compounce in Connecticut, opened in 1846.) That year, a local businessman named Louis Zistel opened a beer garden, bathhouse, and dance floor on the peninsula and, for 25 cents each, ferried vacationers to the point in his boat, the *Young Reindeer*. Over the years, other businesspeople added more attractions: a pony track, a diving platform, and bicycle boats, among others. And travelers from around Ohio and the Midwest started spending their holidays at the point.

In 1892, the first roller coaster arrived: Switchback Railway was a wooden coaster that boasted a 25-foot drop and a top speed of slightly more than 10 mph. Ten years later, the Figure-Eight Roller Toboggan opened, and in 1929, it was followed by the Cedar Point Cyclone, which was advertised as being "scientifically built for speed, thrills, and safety." The Blue Streak opened in 1964 and is the oldest coaster still operating at Cedar Point.

2. Cedar Point has employed several celebrities.

Sam Warner (one of the studio-founding Warner brothers), talk show host Arsenio Hall, and famed Notre Dame football coach Knute Rockne all worked at Cedar Point.In addition, in 1925, Helen Keller visited the park and gave a speech at its convention center.

3. The coasters at Cedar Point vary in size, intensity, and construction.

The Cedar Point craze exploded during the 1970s, when the Corkscrew, Gemini dual racer, Jr. Gemini, and Wave Swinger all opened. A new ride has been added every few years, and today, the inventory boasts 17 coasters in every design and of every type: wooden and steel, inverted, floorless, suspended, stand-up, and some made especially for children. The most recent addition—the $21 million, steel Maverick—opened in mid-2007.

In addition, Cedar Point boasts 68 other rides, including classic carousels; spinning rides with names like the Scrambler, Super Himalaya, and Monster; and the Cedar Point and Lake Erie Railroad, a ride on coal-powered locomotives through recreated Old West towns.

4. From the top of the park's three largest coasters, riders can see all the way to Canada.

On a clear day (and if you have good eyesight), from the highest hills on the Magnum XL 200, Top Thrill Dragster, or Millennium Force, riders can see the southern tip of Point Pelee on Canada's mainland, about 30 miles away. On cloudy days, Canada's Pelee Island—about 20 miles off the coast of Lake Erie—is visible.

5. The park's Hotel Breakers has the most expensive hotel room in Sandusky.

That's not to say that regular people can't stay at the Breakers, but the hotel does contain the most expensive room in the city: the Presidential Suite, which goes for $1,000 a night during the high season. Built in 1905, the hotel is also decorated with Tiffany stained-glass windows in the lobby. Over the years, presidents William H. Taft, Calvin Coolidge, Woodrow Wilson, Warren Harding, and Dwight D. Eisenhower all stayed there.

The Best Amusement Park in the World

The trade newspaper *Amusement Today* has ranked Cedar Point as the top amusement park in the world and ranks the Millennium Force and Magnum XL 200 as two of the top ten coasters in the world. Here are Cedar Point's 17 coasters, their heights, and speeds:

- Blue Streak—height: 78 feet, top speed: 40 mph
- Cedar Creek Mine Ride—height: 55 feet, top speed: 42 mph
- Corkscrew—height: 85 feet, top speed: 48 mph
- Disaster Transport—height: 63 feet, top speed: 40 mph
- Gemini—height: 124½ feet, top speed: 60 mph
- Iron Dragon—height: 76 feet, top speed: 40 mph
- Jr. Gemini—height: 19 feet, top speed: 6 mph
- Magnum XL 200—height: 205 feet, top speed: 72 mph
- Mantis—height: 145 feet, top speed: 60 mph
- Maverick—height: 105 feet, top speed: 70 mph
- Mean Streak—height: 161 feet, top speed: 65 mph
- Millennium Force—height: 310 feet, top speed: 93 mph
- Raptor—height: 137 feet, top speed: 57 mph
- Top Thrill Dragster—height: 420 feet, top speed: 120 mph
- Wicked Twister—height: 215 feet, top speed: 72 mph
- WildCat—height: 50 feet, top speed: 40 mph
- Woodstock Express—height: 38 feet, top speed: 25 mph

Bombeck's Thoughts On . . .

Dayton-born Erma Bombeck was a premier domestic wit. Here are just a few of the things she had to say over the years about home, hearth, and husbands.

Children

"My kids always perceived the bathroom as a place where you wait it out until all the groceries are unloaded from the car."

"All of us have moments in our lives that test our courage. Taking children into a house with white carpet is one of them."

"In general my children refuse to eat anything that hasn't danced on television."

"When a child is locked in the bathroom with water running and he says he's doing nothing, but the dog is barking, call 911."

Football

"Anybody who watches three games of football in a row should be declared brain dead."

"Thanksgiving dinners take eighteen hours to prepare. They are consumed in twelve minutes. Halftimes take twelve minutes. This is not a coincidence."

Marriage and Friendship

"A friend will tell you she saw your old boyfriend—and he's a priest."

"Marriage has no guarantees. If that's what you're looking for, go live with a car battery."

"A friend never defends a husband who gets his wife an electric skillet for her birthday."

And Some Sage Advice . . .

"Before you try to keep up with the Joneses, be sure they're not trying to keep up with you."

"Onion rings in the car cushions do not improve with time."

"I have a theory about the human mind. A brain is a lot like a computer. It will only take so many facts, and then it will go on overload and blow up."

"It takes a lot of courage to show your dreams to someone else."

"Never go to a doctor whose office plants have died."

Did You Know?

- Number of entries returned for "I hate Cleveland" on Google (May 2007): 2,240.
- Number for "I Love Cleveland": 18,500.

Sports City

From football to baton twirling, the folks in this hometown love their sports.

Town: Canton

Location: Stark County

Founding: 1805

Current population: 79,255

Size: 21 square miles

County seat: Yes

What's in a Name?

At the turn of the 19th century, surveyor Bezaleel Wells founded the town that became Canton. He named the new village in honor of Captain John O'Donnell, who was one of the first Americans to import goods from Canton, China. After hearing that O'Donnell had died, Wells named his new town Canton in tribute.

Claims to Fame:

- Canton is Ohio's golf capital—there are 39 golf courses within the city's limits.
- The American Professional Football Association (which became the National Football League in 1922) formed in Canton in 1920 when a group of team managers met at a local car dealership to create an organization that would oversee pro football. The association elected athletic star Jim Thorpe as its first president, selected 11 teams to comprise the league,

and instituted comprehensive rules for the sport (rival teams couldn't steal each other's players, for example).

- Canton boasts the oldest high school football rivalry in the United States—Canton McKinley High School versus Massillon High School. The annual game held between the schools is so well known and its reach is so broad that it's the only high school athletic event whose odds are posted in Las Vegas.
- Every year, Twirling Unlimited, a nonprofit group made up of baton twirlers and coaches, holds its Baton Twirling International Championship at Canton's Memorial Civic Center.
- In 1963, recognizing and celebrating its football heritage, Canton opened the Pro Football Hall of Fame. That first year, 17 people were inducted; today, there are more than 200 enshrined in the hall.

Did You Know?

Ohio native Nancy Cartwright, the voice of Bart Simpson, was visiting Buckingham Palace in London. Like most American tourists, she thought she'd try to make one of the guards—who are famous for standing perfectly still—at least smile a little. She walked up to the guard and said, "I'm Bart Simpson. Who the hell are you?" The guard couldn't take it and let out a smile.

Of Gangsters and Presidents, Part 1

Ohio is home to some of the country's most impressive museums, filled with works by legendary artists. But some museums in the Buckeye state offer more unique exhibits.

Dillinger's Cell

Where: Allen County Museum, Lima

Why: One of the 1930s' most notorious gangsters, John Dillinger (and two cohorts) robbed Bluffton's Citizens National Bank on August 14, 1933. They made off with $2,100 and a revolver. With the local authorities tracking closer by the day, Dillinger hid at his girlfriend's house in Dayton. (His cohorts were arrested in Indiana but soon escaped.) He was eventually found, arrested, and sent back to Allen County for trial. He managed to escape, however, when his friends returned to break him out. They shot and killed the local sheriff, Jess Sarber, and walked out of the jail. Eventually, Dillinger's friends were caught and convicted of the crime. Dillinger himself became the FBI's Public Enemy Number One and was killed during a raid in Chicago in 1934.

The Allen County Museum tells the story of the infamous gangster and his crimes with a re-creation of Dillinger's jail cell. The exhibit also includes wax figures of Dillinger and Sarber.

Also on display:

The Allen County Museum has an exhibit of accidentally swallowed items—collected by a local physician who worked at a local mental hospital. The exhibit includes everything from small buttons to a large wooden screw.

Mary Bach's Fingers

Where: Wood County Historical Center and Museum, Bowling Green

Why: Carl and Mary Bach emigrated from Germany in the mid-1800s and settled in northwest Ohio. They had a volatile relationship and fought a lot, so Carl ended up sleeping in the barn. In late 1881, as winter approached, Carl wanted to move back into the house, but Mary refused him. So he armed himself with a corn knife, broke into the house, and killed her. When she'd reached up to shield herself from his attack, he cut off three of her fingers. Carl turned himself in the next day, and prosecutors used the fingers as evidence in the trial. Carl was convicted and hanged shortly thereafter.

The fingers used to convict him were preserved and remained on display at the Wood County courthouse until the early 1980s, when they were transferred to the Wood County Historical Center and Museum. Today, they're featured in an exhibit that also includes the corn knife used in the murder, Carl's pipe, a German-language Bible, the noose used in the hanging, and a ticket to the public execution. Morbid? Maybe, but also extremely popular. According to one museum official, "Those fingers built this museum."

Also on display:

The museum boasts exhibits on everything from Ohio history to a timeline of laundry advertisements. Among its most interesting areas, though, are the Lunatic House—a former psychiatric hospital on the grounds that has been turned into an exhibit that looks at the history of mental health in America—and an authentic replica of a turn-of-the-century general store.

To read about more unique exhibits, turn to page 152.

B.F. Goodrich By the Numbers

In the late 1800s, a New York businessman moved to Akron and helped the city earn its nickname, "The Rubber Capital of the World." Here are the numbers behind Benjamin Franklin Goodrich's innovative empire.

2

Number of times the B.F. Goodrich Company almost went bankrupt during the 1870s. The company made tires, and sales were sluggish during the first decade. Sales only really took off after the invention of the automobile.

4

Number of names the company has had over the years: Goodrich, Tew & Co.; B.F. Goodrich Company; BFGoodrich; and Goodrich Corporation.

20

Workers employed at the Akron Rubber Works (later Goodrich) when it opened in 1870.

118

Years the company spent in the tire business. In 1988, Goodrich sold its tire manufacturing business to Michelin, but not before taking part in some historic events: In 1909, American Glenn Curtis set a high-speed flying record of 47 mph; his plane was outfitted with Goodrich tires. Goodrich tires were also on Charles Lindbergh's plane during his famous 1927 transatlantic flight.

1910

Year scientists at Goodrich added carbon to rubber, which made tires last longer. Goodrich scientist Waldo Semon invented vinyl in 1926. In 1937, company scientists invented synthetic rubber. The latter invention proved invaluable during World War II, when America's access to the world's rubber plantations was cut off.

$13,600

Amount of money that Akron's residents raised and paid Goodrich in the late 1800s to encourage him to move his rubber company from New York to Ohio. At that time, there weren't any rubber manufacturers west of the Appalachian Mountains, and Akron (and Goodrich) saw the move as a way for the fledgling town to boost its economy.

These Days

Today, Goodrich has its headquarters in North Carolina and is a leader in the aerospace industry, having participated in everything from building space suits for the *Mercury* astronauts to perfecting de-icing technology and aircraft brakes. The division of Goodrich devoted to making wheels and brakes for airplanes remains in Ohio, though it moved to Troy in the 1940s.

One Taft After Another

New York had the Roosevelts; Massachusetts claims the Kennedys—and Ohio has bragging rights to its own political dynasty: the Tafts.

The Taft family has been rooted in the Buckeye state since the early 19th century when Alphonso Taft, who was born in Vermont, moved to Cincinnati after getting his law degree at Yale. In the more than 150 years since, the Tafts have become an integral part of Ohio and U.S. history. Here are some of the principal players.

The Progenitor: Alphonso Taft

Accomplishments: Alphonso served as a Cincinnati Superior Court judge from 1866 to 1872 and as President Ulysses S. Grant's secretary of war (a position now called secretary of defense) in 1876. Three months into the job Alphonso became the 35th U.S. attorney general. After two unsuccessful bids to win the Ohio governor's seat (in 1875 and 1879), Alphonso became a U.S. ambassador—first to Hungary (1882) and then Russia (1884).

The President: William Howard Taft

Accomplishments: Alphonso's most famous son, William Howard, attended Yale and became a lawyer like his father. He worked first as a judge for the Ohio Superior Court and then, in 1890, became U.S. solicitor general under President Benjamin Harrison. After Spain ceded the Philippines to America in 1898 following a defeat in the Spanish-American

War, President William McKinley sent Taft to the islands to serve as the new territory's first civilian governor-general.

In 1904, President Theodore Roosevelt appointed Taft to be secretary of war—the same position his father had held 28 years earlier. During his tenure, Taft oversaw the start of construction on the Panama Canal, negotiated a peaceful end to General Enrique Loynaz del Castillo's 1906 rebellion in Cuba, and even became the "acting president" when Roosevelt was away.

Taft really wanted to be a Supreme Court justice (a dream since his law school days), but Roosevelt had other ideas. When Roosevelt decided not to run for a third term in 1908, he decided to back Taft as his successor. With Roosevelt's support, Taft easily won the election to become the 27th president of the United States. He spent one term in office, and during that time, he expanded the civil service, fought for a federal income tax on businesses, and lobbied for the election of senators by voters, rather than appointment by state legislatures. He also oversaw the admission of New Mexico and Arizona to the United States.

When Taft lost his reelection campaign to Woodrow Wilson in 1912, he took a job as a Yale law professor and as president of the American Bar Association. Then, finally, in 1921, President Warren G. Harding nominated Taft for the job he'd always wanted: he became the 10th U.S. Supreme Court justice and the only person in American history to head both the executive and judicial branches of the government. This position gave William Howard Taft the unique opportunity of swearing in two more presidents, Calvin Coolidge and Herbert Hoover.

Mr. Republican: Robert Alphonso Taft

Accomplishments: William Howard Taft's son, Robert Alphonso, was a well-respected Republican senator whose career also began in Cincinnati. A graduate of Yale University and Harvard Law School, his first federal job was with the Food and Drug Administration during World War I, where he acted as assistant counsel. In 1921, he became a congressional representative and, within five years, Speaker of the House. From there, he ran for and won a seat in the Ohio State Senate in 1939.

Robert Alphonso Taft was known as "Mr. Republican" for his staunch GOP views: he was against the U.S. entering World War II until the attack on Pearl Harbor and disagreed with President Franklin D. Roosevelt's plans to give more power to the federal government. But that wasn't enough to help him gain his party's presidential nomination; he mounted three unsuccessful bids, in 1940, 1948, and 1952.

Taft is best known, however, for his part in the creation of the Taft-Hartley Act—a law passed in 1947 that restricted the power of labor unions. Taft-Hartley is still around today and is responsible for banning closed shops (companies that required employees to be union members), banning unfair union practices, and requiring that unions give 60 days notice of a strike.

The Governor: Bob Taft

Accomplishments: Robert Alphonso "Bob" Taft II (his father was Robert Taft Jr.) was born in Massachusetts but grew up in Cincinnati—he even attended and graduated from the city's Taft High School before heading off to Yale University. He was a U.S. representative and held a variety of state political positions between 1976 and 1998 before finally serving two terms as Ohio's governor—the first Taft to do so—from 1999 to 2007.

Ohio Underground

Without Ohio, there probably would not have been an Underground Railroad. Here's a look at Ohio's role in that famous escape route and the story of some of the Ohioans who made their marks helping Southern slaves find freedom.

To Ohio and Beyond

Before the Civil War, Ohio was the major hub of the Underground Railroad. The shortest and most direct route from the slaveholding South to Canada was through Ohio. Thirteen station stops, or safe houses, have been identified in Ohio so far—more than in any other state. The organization's unofficial president was even part of Ohio's Underground Railroad network: Levi Coffin, an abolitionist who moved to Cincinnati in 1847, saw 13,000 slaves pass through his home (called "Grand Central Station") and make it safely to freedom in Canada, where slavery had been abolished in 1833. At least 40,000 African Americans had made their way through Ohio's Underground Railroad network by the time of the Emancipation Proclamation in 1863.

Against All Odds

The Underground Railroad birthed many heroes—religious communities (especially the Quakers), white people of conscience, Ottawa Indians, and free blacks, who risked their lives and their own freedom to fight slavery. Harboring escaped slaves was dangerous. Even in free states like Ohio, many citizens supported slavery, and after the Fugitive Slave Law of 1850 banned assisting runaways, slave catchers and bounty hunters roamed Ohio's countryside with impunity, often capturing free African Americans and selling them into slavery. And federal marshals threatened to fine and imprison anyone who assisted escapees. Yet the Underground Railroad flourished, as thousands of Ohioans worked as conductors (guides) and stationmasters (who ran safe houses) and led their passengers to freedom.

The African American Guide

One of the conductors was John P. Parker of Ripley, who was born a slave in Norfolk, Virginia. He was sold at the age of eight by his own white father/owner and was marched barefoot and in chains to Alabama. Eventually, Parker was sent to a factory in New Orleans, where he was able to work extra hours, save some money, and buy his freedom.

In 1848, he moved to Ohio, where he became a successful manufacturer of engines and reapers. By day, Parker was a respectable businessman, but by night, he was a conductor on the Underground Railroad. In the wee hours, he sneaked across the Ohio River into the slave state of Kentucky, gathered fugitives from a prearranged meeting place, led them back across the river, and delivered them to a safe house in Ripley. His efforts earned him a $1,000 bounty in Kentucky, but the Kentuckians never caught him. In Ohio, he was safe as long as he wasn't caught in the act. (He never was.) Parker later described leading more than 400 escaping slaves into freedom.

A Songwriting Abolitionist

Near Columbus, in Westerville, there's another stop on the Underground Railroad: the family home of Benjamin Russell Hanby, best remembered as a composer—he wrote the famous Christmas song "Up on the Housetop (Ho! Ho! Ho!)." But, like his minister father, Hanby was also an ardent abolitionist.

While Hanby was a student at Otterbein College, a fugitive slave named Joseph Selby took shelter at the Hanby home. Selby died soon after of pneumonia and never realized his dream of finding freedom for himself and his fiancée, Nelly. But he told Hanby his story, how Nelly had been sold away from their Kentucky home. In the early 1850s, Hanby immortalized Selby's story in his song "Darling Nelly Gray," which describes Nelly being led away in chains, taken to Georgia, and condemned to a life in the cotton and sugarcane fields, never to be seen again by the man who had lost her.

Over the years, Hanby and his father aided many slaves to freedom, but some historians believe that Benjamin Hanby's antislavery song was his most important contribution, as effective as Harriet Beecher Stowe's revolutionary *Uncle Tom's Cabin* at galvanizing American sentiment against slavery. "Darling Nelly Gray" became a wildly popular campaign song for the Union Army during the Civil War, and Hanby came to represent the many heroes of Ohio's Underground Railroad. Today, the Hanby home in Westerville is on the National Register of Historic Places and is open to the public.

To read about Harriet Beecher Stowe and how Ohio affected her writing of Uncle Tom's Cabin, *turn to page 237.*

Did You Know?

In 1993, John Gorski of Avon, Ohio, threw a boomerang that caught a thermal updraft and flew to a height of 600 feet. It stayed aloft for 17 minutes before it descended.

Ohio Firsts

Ohio is home to many innovations. Here are just a few.

First Automobile Accident: Ohio City

Ohio was an important place in the early history of the automobile. One of the state's automotive firsts occurred in 1891 when James William Lambert, driving the first single-cylinder gasoline automobile (which he had converted from a three-cylinder engine), struck a tree root in Ohio City. The car flew into the air and smashed into a hitching post.

First Speeding Ticket: Dayton

Thirteen years later, another Ohioan, Harry Myers, received the first speeding ticket: police ticketed Myers for driving 12 miles per hour on West Third Street in Dayton.

First Emergency Parachute Jump: Dayton

On October 20, 1922, Lieutenant Harold R. Harris, Chief of the Flying Section of Dayton's McCook Field, made an emergency jump from his plane, which had malfunctioned and started to nosedive. Harris left the plane at approximately 2,500 feet, and his parachute opened at 500 feet. The pilot landed safely in a grape arbor, but the plane wasn't so lucky—it landed a block away and was completely destroyed.

First African American Politician: Brownhelm

John Mercer Langston, a lawyer living in Brownhelm, was elected to the post of town clerk in 1855, making him the first African American in the United States to be elected to a public office.

First Rubber-Wound Golf Ball: Cleveland

Coburn Haskell, a Cleveland golfer, and Bertram G. Work of the B.F. Goodrich Company patented the three-piece rubber golf ball at the turn of the 20th century. Previously, balls had been made of wood, leather stuffed with feathers, or a type of latex called gutta-percha. The new ball used rubber threads tension-wound around a solid rubber core, an invention that made it possible for the ball to fly and roll farther than its predecessors. Although there were concerns about how well golfers could control the new ball, both the 1901 U.S. Amateur and the 1902 U.S. Open champions proved that they could win major competitions using it.

First Interracial and Coeducational College in the United States: Oberlin

In 1835, Oberlin College was the first institution of higher education to admit students of color. Six years later, it became the first college to give bachelor's degrees to women in a coed program.

First Pressurized Flight Suit: Akron

Russ Colley, an engineer at B.F. Goodrich, invented the first pressurized flight suit in 1934. The suit enabled pilots to fly higher than 30,000 feet for the first time. In 1961, Colley also helped develop the space suits worn by the *Mercury* astronauts. Alan Shepard (the first American in space) and John Glenn (the first to orbit the earth) both wore the Goodrich suits.

First Junior High School: Columbus

In 1909, responding to high drop-out rates for high schoolers (only 48 percent made it to the 10th grade, and only 7 percent actually graduated), the Columbus Board of Education created the first junior high in the United States: Indianola Junior High School at 140 East 16th Avenue. Previously, students went to elementary school through the eighth grade and then continued on to high school. Splitting up the early years into elementary and junior high, though, helped to prepare kids for the rigors of high school and made it more likely that they would stick with it until graduation.

Did You Know?

William Henry Harrison set a number of records as the ninth U.S. president. At 68, he was the oldest man ever elected, until Ronald Reagan took office in 1980 at age 69. And with a term that lasted just one month, he's the commander-in-chief who spent the least time in office. Harrison's inaugural address, however, remains the longest ever given: It lasted one hour and 40 minutes and included 8,445 words. Indeed, some historians believe that speaking so long in the cold Washington weather contributed to the pneumonia that killed Harrison a month later. Perhaps recalling this lesson, Ohio native Benjamin Harrison—William Henry's grandson and the 23rd president—asked his predecessor Grover Cleveland to hold an umbrella over his head when he gave his own inaugural address on a rain-soaked day in March 1889.

Open-Minded Oberlin

This little town gives new meaning to the term "liberal" arts.

Town: Oberlin

Location: Lorain County

Founding: 1833

Current population: 8,195

Size: 4.4 square miles

County seat: No

What's in a Name?

Founders and ministers John Jay Shipherd and Philo P. Stewart named this town after a German pastor, Jean Frédéric Oberlin, who stressed the importance of religious education and community service. Shipherd and Stewart arrived in Ohio wanting to create a community of church-centered folks who supported a local school for preachers and Christian teachers.

Claims to Fame:

- Oberlin's biggest claim to fame is Shipherd and Stewart's school: Oberlin College. Founded simultaneously with the town, the college had a unique early recruitment tool: it allowed students (who otherwise could probably not have afforded a college education) to pay for classes by working in the community. This "Learning and Labor" idea became the school's motto. The idea is currently reflected in the college's AmeriCorps Learning and Labor Program, in which students can receive an AmeriCorps Education Award by performing community service.

- In 1835, the Oberlin Anti-Slavery Society formed; its objective was "the immediate emancipation of the whole colored race within the United States." With this goal in place, Oberlin became a key stop on the Underground Railroad—thousands of escaped slaves passed through and were sheltered by the town on their way to freedom in Canada. (*For the story of the 1858 Oberlin-Wellington rescue case, in which 37 people were indicted for helping a slave escape to freedom,* *see page 160.*)
- The first meeting of the Ohio Anti-Saloon League took place in Oberlin on May 24, 1893. The league eventually joined with its counterpart in Washington, D.C., to create the Anti-Saloon League of America, the organization mainly responsible for the 18th Amendment to the U.S. Constitution, which prohibited alcohol.
- Oberlin is home to the Weltzheimer/Johnson House, Frank Lloyd Wright's first Usonian home built in Ohio. ("Usonian" was Wright's term for the utilitarian, inexpensive, and small American houses he created for the post–World War I nuclear family.) Designed in 1948 and completed in 1950, the house is now run by the Allen Memorial Art Museum, which is part of Oberlin College.

The Eagle Has Landed

Neil Armstrong, an Ohio-born astronaut and the first man on the Moon, shares his thoughts on . . .

Flying and Space Travel

"Gliders, sail planes, they're wonderful flying machines. It's the closest you can come to being a bird."

"Pilots take no special joy in walking. Pilots like flying."

"I was born and raised about 60 miles north of Dayton, so the legends of the Wright brothers have been in my memories as long as I can remember."

"The important achievement of Apollo was demonstrating that humanity is not forever chained to this planet and our visions go rather further than that and our opportunities are unlimited."

Life

"I believe that every human has a finite number of heartbeats. I don't intend to waste any of mine running around doing exercises."

The View of Earth from Space

"It suddenly struck me that that tiny pea, pretty and blue, was the Earth. I put up my thumb and shut one eye, and my thumb blotted out the planet Earth. I didn't feel like a giant. I felt very, very small."

Eight Things You Don't Know About Annie Oakley

Annie Oakley, the famous female sharpshooter, was one of the most recognizable citizens of the Wild West—but she was born in Ohio and lived nearly all of her nontouring life east of the Mississippi River. What else don't you know about this famous Wild West icon?

1. Annie Oakley wasn't her given name.

Oakley was born Phoebe Ann Mosely in 1860, in Darke County, Ohio. The still-tiny village of North Star (population 209, according to the 2000 census) claims to be her hometown, but the annual Annie Oakley Days festival takes place in the county seat of Greenville. "Annie" clearly comes from young Phoebe's middle name, but "Oakley" comes from the Cincinnati suburb of Oakley, near where Oakley and her husband (fellow sharpshooter Frank Butler) lived during the early years of their marriage.

2. Annie Oakley and Frank Butler were smitten with each other from the start.

It's well known that Butler became enamored with Oakley after she outshot him in a competition—he hit 24 targets, she hit 25. What's less known is the day of the competition (Thanksgiving Day, 1875) and the amount of money the competition was for ($100, which would be worth about $2,000 today). Butler originally hired Oakley as his assistant but then switched their roles when she proved to be the bigger star. They married on August 23, 1876.

3. Annie Oakley and Sioux chief Sitting Bull were old friends.

The pair was a big draw in Buffalo Bill Cody's Wild West Show, but the two knew each other before either joined the show. They met in 1884, after Sitting Bull saw Oakley shoot in a show in Minneapolis. He was so impressed with her skills that he gave her the name Watanya Cicilla, meaning Little Sure Shot. Oakley joined Buffalo Bill's show in 1885, and Sitting Bull joined shortly thereafter.

4. Annie Oakley wasn't the only female sharp-shooter in Buffalo Bill's show.

Another, younger sharpshooter named Lillian Smith toured with the show for a time, and Oakley was fiercely competitive with the younger woman—enough to lop six years off of her age so the two would be the "same" age. Relations got so bad between the two that Oakley left Buffalo Bill's show in late 1887 rather than appear with Smith. When Smith was dropped from the show two years later, Oakley came back.

5. In 1889, the king of Senegal tried to buy Annie Oakley for 100,000 francs.

He wanted her to kill the tigers that roamed the country. Oakley turned down the offer, as well as another offer that same year from the president of France, who didn't want her to kill tigers, merely to accept a commission in the French army.

6. She tried a new career at the age of 41.

Oakley and Frank Butler stayed with the Wild West show until 1901, when a train crash injured and frightened them enough that they decided to do other things. One of those things was performing in the theater: Oakley starred in the 1902 play *The*

Western Girl. Annie Oakley's life, of course, would be later immortalized in another stage play, the 1946 Rogers and Hammerstein musical *Annie Get Your Gun*.

7. Oakley had a unique request for Thomas Edison.

Annie Oakley also met Thomas Edison in 1889 and had an unusual request for him—she wanted him to build her an electric rifle. No one knows if he complied, but Oakley did perform in some of Edison's early films, showing off her shooting skills.

8. Oakley sued William Randolph Hearst.

In 1903, Hearst's newspapers falsely reported that Oakley was in prison because she stole a man's trousers to buy cocaine. Oakley was enraged and sued, eventually filing 55 separate libel suits against Hearst and his newspapers. She won 54 of the suits but spent most of the settlement money on legal fees.

Did You Know?

Toledo resident Mildred Wirt Benson, who authored many Nancy Drew mysteries, wrote for several young-adult series during her lifetime, and she published under a variety of names and pseudonyms: Frank Bell, Mildred Benson, Joan Clark, Julia K. Duncan, Alice B. Emerson, Frances K. Judd, Carolyn Keene, Don Palmer, Helen Louise Thorndyke, Dorothy West, Ann Wirt, and Mildred A. Wirt.

Offbeat Ohio

From the world's largest rubber stamp to a moving ball of granite, Ohio is home to some incredible attractions.

Oldest Concrete Street: Bellefontaine

Ohio really paved the way for U.S. roads! In 1891, George Bartholomew persuaded his hometown of Bellefontaine to test his new invention: concrete pavement. (Concrete had been around since the late 1700s, but it was Bartholomew who figured out how to turn it into pavement.) After a successful test on Main Street outside the Logan County Courthouse, the city council agreed to pave Court Avenue. Today, this street in Bellefontaine still exists, making it the first and oldest concrete street in America. Bartholomew was honored for his invention at the 1893 World Columbian Exposition in Chicago, and the technique was adopted throughout the country, and around the world, soon after.

Hartman Rock Garden: Springfield

Breaking rocks is labor usually reserved for chain gangs, but for Ben Hartman of Springfield, it was part of his art. The Great Depression left Hartman out of a job, and in order to keep busy, he built a cement-and-stone fishpond in his backyard . . . then he decided to keep building. Some of his many yard creations include a four-foot-high teacup and saucer, Philadelphia's Independence Hall, Custer's Last Stand, and Noah's Ark. Hartman got most of his rocks from a nearby lot that was being cleared for housing, and his yard soon became a local attraction as neighbors stopped by to chat. Sometimes, they also donated small change, which Hartman saved for supplies like cement and hammers. In just seven years, he wore out three of those hammers and broke nearly 250,000 stones. Although Ben Hartman died in 1944, his youngest son still owns and maintains the property and garden, which is open to visitors.

The World's Largest Basket: Newark

The world's largest basket is actually a building for the Longaberger Basket Company. In 1976, David Longaberger started what would become America's premier handcrafted basket company. As its success grew, so did Longaberger's architectural ambitions. His first project was a house-sized basket that served as the company's first headquarters in Dresden. Next was the Longaberger Homestead in Frazeysburg, where visitors can still tour the basket factory, make their own baskets, and see a 29-foot-tall apple basket, complete with giant fake apples (vendors offer regular-sized food as well).

Longaberger's business kept expanding, and when it came time to build a new, larger home office, he proposed his grandest idea yet: a seven-story building in the shape of a basket. No one took the idea seriously at first, but in 1995, construction began on the 180,000-square-foot building. Stucco and steel give the building's exterior its wicker texture and shape, and 150-ton basket handles adorn the top—the handles are even heated in winter to discourage ice buildup. Longaberger and his employees moved into the new basket in 1997.

The Moving Granite Ball: Marion

The laws of physics seem to be openly defied in Marion. In 1886, members of the Merchant family erected a memorial to their ancestors in the town's cemetery. The memorial was a block of white granite topped with a smooth and polished five-ton ball of black granite. It seemed a stoic, fitting memorial for a stable local clan. After about two years, though, cemetery personnel realized the ball had rotated. How could they tell? There was one spot on the ball that was unpolished: the place where it sat on the base. That rough spot was showing. Cemetery officials used a crane to return the ball to its original position, with the unpolished spot sitting directly on the white granite. As an extra precaution, they put a seal around the base to keep it immobile. Soon after, the ball was shifting again. Rather than continue the game, they left the ball alone.

Over the last century, many people have offered theories to explain this mystery. These include changes in temperature or shifts in the earth's surface, although no one can explain how the ball moves on the base without scratching itself. If you want to take a look for yourself, drop by the Marion Cemetery on Vernon Heights Boulevard. (Let us know if you figure it out.)

For more attractions, turn to page 164.

Did You Know?

In Wooster, Ohio, just days after the disastrous flood of 1913, rescuers caught a large salmon in the cellar of the First National Bank. (No word on whether they ate it or let it go.)

Wacky Ohio

Strange stuff happens all over the world, but Ohio seems to have more than its share.

Vidiots

In 2006, alarmed residents of Ravenna contacted the Portage County Hazardous Materials Unit when 17 suspicious objects were discovered downtown. The mysterious items: large boxes wrapped in gold paper with question marks spray-painted on them. Five teenage girls later turned themselves in. The boxes were intended to be part of a "real-life" version of the 1980s video game *Super Mario Brothers*. In the video game, the boxes contain flowers and mushrooms that give Mario special powers. These boxes, however, were empty.

For the Love(land) of Money

Deborah Combs of Loveland was arrested for tax evasion in 2005. She hadn't filed her city income tax forms in five years and, as a result, owed Loveland . . . one dollar and sixteen cents. Police arrested Combs at a routine traffic stop. "What they've spent in stamps is more than what I owe," Combs told reporters. Loveland city manager Fred Enderle said the miniscule amount Combs owed was irrelevant: "Whether a taxpayer owes us $1 or $1,000, it's not fair to the rest of the public not to pursue that person."

Back to the Future

Athens chiropractor James C. Burda had his license revoked in 2006 after an investigation by the state chiropractic board found that he had promised to cure patients of back pain via telepathy and time travel. Burda called his telepathic body healing technique "bahlaqueem" and told patients he could go back in time to realign bones and joints before they were damaged.

Old-Fashioned Irony

Ohio has a large Amish community. In January 2005, a 17-year-old Amish boy got the wheels of his buggy entangled in some power lines near the town of Chardon. However, the boy—whose religious beliefs require him to abstain from using electricity—was electrocuted when he tried to remove the power lines by hand. (He survived.)

Breaking the Rules

In 2005, the embarrassed Ohio High School Athletic Association apologized to Bobby Martin, a football player at Colonel White High School in Dayton. Referees had kicked Martin out of a game because he wasn't wearing shoes or knee pads, which the rule book explicitly require. But Martin had a reason: he was born without legs and moves around the field on his arms.

A Fat Head, Maybe

Brian Monfort of Springfield was arrested in 2005 for approaching children and offering them $40 to make fun of him for being fat. Monfort said he was trying to inspire himself to lose weight.

For more wacky stories, turn to page 121.

Ohio in Song

If it wasn't for Ohio, would we have any music?

Jewel: "Cleveland"

From the Alaskan folk-pop star's 2001 album, *This Way,* the song became popular among young men and boys in the city for one scintillating line, sung to a young man from Cleveland: "I want to make your toes curl."

The Pretenders: "My City Was Gone"

Written by band leader Chrissie Hynde, this song is a lament for the state of her home state. Since 1984, conservative talk-radio host Rush Limbaugh has used the tune as his radio show's theme song—without the band's permission. In 1997, Hynde's lawyers contacted Limbaugh, and he now makes royalty payments for use of the song. Hynde stipulated that the payments go directly to the animal rights group PETA—People for the Ethical Treatment of Animals—a frequent target of ridicule by Limbaugh.

John Hiatt: "All the Lilacs in Ohio"

On his 2001 CD *The Tiki Bar Is Open*, the folk-rocker sings about a drunk lamenting his lost youth and lost girl who smelled like "all the lilacs in Ohio." That line is from the 1945 Billy Wilder film *The Lost Weekend* (based on the 1944 novel by Charles R. Jackson) about a writer named Don Birnam, who struggles with writer's block and goes on a five-day drinking binge. "Love is the hardest thing in the world to write about," Birnam (played by Ray Milland) says in the film. "It's so simple. You've gotta catch it through details . . .

the ringing of a telephone that sounds like Beethoven's *Pastorale*, a letter scribbled on her office stationary that you carry around in your pocket because it smells like all the lilacs in Ohio."

The novel was Johnson's first and was a huge success; the film won four Academy Awards, including Best Picture. Hiatt's album (released on September 11, 2001) didn't do as well.

Randy Newman: "Dayton, Ohio, 1903"

Newman wrote this nostalgic ballad in 1972 to reminisce about the good old days, pictured in the sleepy town of Dayton in the year 1903. Newman later admitted that when he wrote the song, he'd never been to Dayton.

Ian Hunter: "Cleveland Rocks"

No, it's not about Cleveland geology . . . it's about how Cleveland rocks! And it's by Ian Hunter—who's from England. Hunter was the singer for Mott the Hoople ("All the Young Dudes"), and, so the story goes, Cleveland held the group's biggest fan base. So Hunter penned a tune in honor of the city. It was later used as the theme song of *The Drew Carey Show*.

These days, Cincinnati radio station WLW plays a parody of the song in its Cincinnati Reds promotions. In that version: "Cleveland sucks!"

To quiz yourself about more Ohio-themed songs, turn to page 177.

Ohio in Primes

When the BRI writers read that Ohio was the 17th state in the Union, they didn't think of American history. They noted that 17 is a prime number—it can be divided only by itself and one. That's why they wrote this page. Really.

Ohio has 2 . . . main climate regions: the southern part of the state is "humid subtropical," with average summer temperatures above 80°F and winter averages of about 45°F; the north is "humid continental," with summer temperatures averaging around 70°F and winter's average temperature below 32°F.

Ohio has 3 . . . distinct topographical regions: the foothills of the Allegheny Mountains in the east, the Erie lakeshore region, and the central plains in the west of the state.

Ohio has 7 . . . cities with more than 100,000 people. Only California, Florida, and Texas have more.

Ohio has 11 . . . Historic lighthouses, as designated by the National Park Service's Inventory of Historic Light Stations. The oldest is Marblehead Light, on Sandusky Bay on Lake Erie, built in 1821.

Ohio has 19 . . . species of native crayfish.

Ohio has 29 . . . counties (out of 88 total) in what is officially designated the United States' Appalachian Region. (There are 410 counties in the region scattered over 13 states.) Ohio's area is nearly one third of the state.

Ohio has 31 . . . drive-in movie theaters as of 2007. That's the most of any state. (Thanks, Ohio!)

Ohio Stars: the Classics

Ohio has produced some of Hollywood's most beloved movie and TV stars. See if you can match the celebrities to their descriptions.

1. Jim Backus
2. Dorothy Dandridge
3. Tim Conway
4. Doris Day
5. Clark Gable
6. Margaret Hamilton
7. Bob Hope
8. Jack Paar
9. Roy Rogers
10. Lillian Gish

A. She was one of the first actresses to star in Hollywood romantic comedies. Her first film was a 1959 hit that costarred Rock Hudson.

B. Better watch out, or this Cleveland native will get you . . . and your little dog too!

C. Born in Cleveland, this Ohioan was the first African American to be nominated for an Academy Award.

D. As a child, this megastar of the 1930s and 1940s lived in many Ohio towns: Cadiz, Hopedale, Ravenna, and Akron.

E. Born in Willoughby and raised in Chagrin Falls, this TV funnyman also went to college at Bowling Green State University.

F. In 1912, family friend and silent film star Mary Pickford introduced this Springfield native to director D. W. Griffith, who helped her get a contract with the then-prolific Biograph Studio.

G. From James Dean to the cast of *Gilligan's Island*, this star of radio, television, Broadway, and the silver screen worked with some of the most famous people in Hollywood.

H. This singing cowboy was born in a Second Street tenement in Cincinnati. In 1970, Riverfront Stadium was built on the site.

I. In 1960, when NBC censors edited a *Tonight Show* segment that included a joke about a toilet, this host walked off the show for one month.

J. This USO star was actually born in England but moved to Cleveland when he was five years old.

For answers, turn to page 303.
For more Ohio celebrities, turn to page 212.

Did You Know?

There are several theories to explain the origin of the term "upper crust," but one comes from 19th-century America, when many cooks saved money on food wherever they could. Apple pies—a favorite dessert in Ohio and elsewhere—were often made with just a bottom crust to save on flour and lard. Families that were rich enough to bake their apple pies with both a top and bottom crust became known as the "upper crust."

Major Reward

In the beloved film A Christmas Story, *little Ralphie Parker wants nothing more for Christmas than an official Red Ryder carbine action 200-shot range model air rifle. But his requests are always thwarted by the same response: "You'll shoot your eye out!" Now, one Ohio city is home to a museum celebrating Ralphie's myriad attempts to outwit the adults who stand between him and his perfect Christmas present.*

An Icon on eBay

A Christmas Story, staring Peter Billingsley, Darren McGavin, and Melinda Dillon, was released in 1983. It wasn't an instant hit in theaters (though it did earn a respectable $19 million at the box office). However, when cable television stations got ahold of the film in the late 1980s, it became one of the most popular (and most rerun) Christmas movies on TV. The film tells the story of nine-year-old Ralphie Parker, who wants a BB gun for Christmas. It's set in Indiana during the early 1940s, but many of the movie's exterior shots were filmed in Cleveland's Tremont neighborhood.

The two-story house where the Parker family lived has long sat at 3159 West 11th Street in Cleveland (Cleveland Street in the movie). And for years, fans of the film made pilgrimages to the site, which was a private residence. In 2005, one fan decided to buy the place.

San Diego, California, resident Brian Jones had loved the film for years, so when his wife told him that the Parkers' house was being sold on eBay, he didn't need a triple-dog dare to act on the news. He bought the place, sight unseen, for $150,000. Jones spent the next year remodeling and furnishing the house to match the movie sets. Then, in November 2006, just in time for Christmas, the house opened to visitors. Jones says that more than 22,000 people showed up to see the place in the first month.

Leg Lamps, Ovaltine, Secret Decoder Pins . . . It's All Here!

Jones also bought the house across the street and transformed it into a gift shop and museum filled with original movie artifacts. Here guests can buy Leg Lamps (Ralphie's dad's Major Award), Little Orphan Annie secret decoder pins, Ovaltine, and Life Buoy soap. The museum features little brother Randy's snowsuit and the zeppelin he receives for Christmas, toys from the Higbee's Department Store window display, and a uniform from the marching band that leads the Christmas parade.

Jones plans to expand the collection over the next few years so that returning guests will always have something new to see. Would it be too much to hope for the pink bunny suit Ralphie receives from Aunt Clara? Or maybe the frozen flagpole that Flick sticks his tongue to? Of course, the real crowning glory would be a coveted Red Ryder carbine action 200-shot range model air rifle—but then Jones would have to caution guests against touching it, lest they shoot their eye out.

Did You Know?

The power outage that occurred on August 14, 2003, in the Northeastern United States and Canada—the largest in North American history, with more than 10 million people affected—began at a generating plant in Eastlake, Ohio.

Ain't No Mistake By the Lake

From boom to bust and back again, Cleveland is a city on the rise.

Town: Cleveland
Location: Cuyahoga County
Founding: 1796
Current population: 461,324
Size: 82.4 square miles
County seat: Yes

What's in a Name?

The city was named for 18th-century general Moses Cleveland, who led a group of surveyors on an exploration of the area. Cleveland and his group founded the town in 1796 and helped design a plan for its downtown area, including the Square (Public Square to out-of-towners). The city was officially incorporated in 1814 and changed its name to Cleveland in 1831 so it could easily fit its newspaper's masthead.

Claims to Fame:

- On April 28, 1865, the funeral train carrying the body of President Abraham Lincoln stopped in Cleveland on its way to Illinois, where Lincoln was to be buried. A horse-drawn hearse picked up Lincoln's casket at the train station and carried it to Public Square, where more than 90,000 people viewed the casket throughout the day.
- Many well-known businesses got their start in Cleveland,

including the Ajax Manufacturing Company, the American Greetings Corporation, and the Sherwin Williams Company.

- Love great tunes? Then check out the Rock and Roll Hall of Fame in downtown Cleveland. Designed by renowned architect I. M. Pei, the museum opened in 1995 and is housed in Cleveland because the city was the site of the first rock-and-roll concert (1952's Moondog Coronation Ball). Today, the museum features all kinds of rock-related memorabilia—everything from the bass guitar used by Paul Simonon of the Clash to handbills promoting the Dave Clark Five to Jim Morrison's Cub Scout uniform.
- Playhouse Square Center in downtown Cleveland is the second-largest theater complex in the United States, after Lincoln Center in New York. The center wasn't always profitable, though. It began in 1921 as five theaters that were built to show silent movies. As talkies became popular in the 1930s and cheaper theaters sprung up around town, the Playhouse Square theaters fell into disrepair. They languished until 1970, when a nonprofit group stepped in and decided to revitalize them. Today, all five historic theaters have been restored, and Playhouse Square is Cleveland's premier performing arts center.
- Cleveland is home to the 57-story Key Tower (the largest building in Ohio), Case Western Reserve University (the highest-rated university in Ohio), and three big league professional sports teams—the Cleveland Browns, the Cleveland Indians, and the Cleveland Cavaliers.
- In October 2005, the Economist Intelligence Unit (an analysis firm linked to the *Economist* magazine) called Cleveland "America's most liveable city" based on factors such as health care, culture, education, and environment.

Cincinnati Reds By the Numbers

Baseball is a game of numbers, and nowhere is that more apparent than in the Queen City, where the hometown Cincinnati Reds have been racking up wins since 1869.

2

Number of times the Reds changed their nickname to the "Redlegs" between 1953 and 1959. The change was an effort to disassociate the team from the so-called red menace of communism. However, players and fans continued to refer to the team as the Reds, and the new moniker eventually disappeared altogether.

4

Number of times the Reds have hosted Major League Baseball's annual All-Star Game (1938, 1953, 1970, 1988) and the number of 100-win seasons in the Reds' history (1940, 1970, 1975, 1976).

5

Number of times the Reds have won the World Series (1919, 1940, 1975, 1976, and 1990).

9

Number of National League pennants won by the Reds (1919, 1939, 1940, 1961, 1970, 1972, 1975, 1976, and 1990).

12

Number of inside-the-park home runs hit by Sam Crawford during the 1901 season. The total represents a major league record.

14

Jersey number of former Reds player and manager Pete Rose, nicknamed "Charlie Hustle." Rose played for the club for 16 seasons and owns the major league records for most career hits (4,256), most career games played (3,562), and most career at-bats (14,053). He also led the National League in hitting in 1965, 1972, 1973, and 1977. Rose is not eligible for the Reds Hall of Fame or for the National Baseball Hall of Fame, though, after he admitted to betting on major league games in the 1980s.

15 years

Age of pitcher Joe Nuxhall when he made his major league debut with the Reds on June 10, 1944. Nuxhall appeared in only one game that season, posting an ERA of 67.50.

59

Number of years the Reds played their home games at Crosley Field. The stadium, which was built for $225,000, began to fall into disrepair in the mid-1950s, so in 1970, the team moved to Riverfront Stadium along with the newly formed Cincinnati Bengals. Over the years, the Reds have called nine ballparks home: Lincoln Park Grounds (1876), Avenue Grounds (1876–1879), Bank Street Grounds (1880–1883), League Park I (1884–1893), League Park II (1894–1901), Palace of the Fans (1902–1911), Crosley Field (1912–1970),

Riverfront Stadium (1970–2002), and Great American Ballpark (2003–present).

389

Number of career home runs clubbed by catcher Johnny Bench. The only catcher in major league history with more home runs is Mike Piazza, who broke Bench's record on June 18, 2004.

1869

Year the Cincinnati Red Stockings became the first all-professional team in baseball history. The infusion of professional talent propelled the team to a 45–9 victory in their first game against the Great Westerns of Cincinnati.

1931

Year the Reds went bankrupt due to the ravages of the Great Depression. Radio tycoon and Cincinnati native Powel Crosley Jr. bought the team in 1934 and brought them out of bankruptcy. During his 27 years as owner, the Reds won two National League titles and one World Series.

52,953

Seating capacity of Great American Ballpark, the Reds' home stadium. The team attracted an average of 26,351 fans per game during the 2006 season.

2,629,708

Number of fans who came out to support the Reds during the 1976 season, the most in the team's history.

Dumb Crooks: Ohio Style

Some crooks just aren't especially bright.

Super(Stupid)man

Dim-Witted Criminal: Matthew Binegar of Dayton, Ohio

Dumb Idea: Being incredibly conspicuous

The Crime: Ohio teenager Matthew Binegar decided to shoplift from a Kmart in Fairborn. Inside the store, he shoved a DVD movie and a video game into his clothing and fled the scene. He might have made off with the goods if not for his work "uniform"; as a street promoter for a local apartment complex, Binegar had to wear a Superman costume and was still dressed as the Man of Steel when he stole the merchandise. After a brief chase, the police nabbed Binegar, who was easily identified by employees who had watched Superman steal the goods.

The Punishment: Binegar was found guilty of one count of criminal theft, served 52 days in jail, and was fined $200. He also had to face ridicule from his older sister Michelle, who calls him "America's Dumbest Criminal." (We bet she's not the only one who calls him that.)

The Ignorant Delinquent

Dim-Witted Criminal: Adam Brown of Columbus, Ohio

Dumb Idea: Wasting time by asking too many questions

The Crime: Seventeen-year-old Adam Brown broke into an elderly woman's home and ordered her to hand over the keys to her car. He tried to steal her vehicle but was thwarted when he couldn't open the garage door. He reentered the house to ask his victim how to open her garage door; after a second try, he returned for a more detailed explanation. Eventually, he managed to figure it out but was further hindered by his inability to drive a car with a manual transmission. Once again, he went back into the house and asked the woman for instructions, but by then she'd had plenty of time and opportunity to call the police. They arrived as he was attempting to leave her driveway.

The Punishment: The delinquent was arrested on the spot.

When Daily Errands Foil a Heist

Dim-Witted Criminal: Darren Wallace of Columbus, Ohio

Dumb Idea: Using his unsuspecting mother as his getaway driver

The Crime: Wallace thought he had what it took to be a successful bank robber. He had targeted a local bank and secured a getaway driver. The only hang-up? His escape plan included his mother, who had no idea what her son was up to. Mrs. Wallace agreed when her son asked her for a ride to the bank. But while he was inside, she decided to run some errands. When Wallace escaped from the bank with his stash, his driver was shopping at a grocery store a few blocks away. Needless to say, the bank robber didn't get far.

The Punishment: Wallace was captured and cuffed before Mom returned from running her errands.

The Panty Thief

Dim-Witted Criminal: Larry Edmonds of Barberton, Ohio

Dumb Idea: Wearing the evidence

The Crime: Edmonds was under suspicion of burglarizing an Ohio home: the resident had caught him scrounging around in her bedroom and had given his description to police, but little tangible evidence linked him to the crime. Still, the cops brought him in for questioning, and during the interrogation, something sparkly caught an officer's eye. Edmonds' pants were hanging low, and sequins were showing around his waist. Turns out he was wearing a pair of sequined panties. Underneath those, he had on a red string bikini. Beneath those were a seven other pairs! The woman whose home had been robbed had reported all of those garments missing.

The Punishment: With such sparkling evidence against him, Edmonds was sentenced to jail time.

The Good Deed

Dim-Witted Criminals: An identified group of bozos in Fostoria, Ohio

Dumb Idea: Robbing the poor

The Crime: A group of crooks broke into the Fostoria Bureau of Concern. The agency serves the poor and needy and keeps little cash on hand. But the criminals found a safe in the organization's administrative office and took off with the stash. But—oops!—the safe was empty. The bureau's money was actually in a new safe that the criminals hadn't found. The agency had been meaning to get rid of the old safe but hadn't found anyone willing to cart the heavy thing off.

The Punishment: So far there's been none; the crooks weren't caught. But their good deed didn't go unnoticed by the bureau. Susan Simpkins, director of the Fostoria Bureau of Concern, said, "They did us a favor by taking it."

Fun Fests: The Best (and Wurst)

From sauerkraut doughnuts to frog jumps, Ohio's festival circuit offers a bigger collection of curiosities than your grandmother's attic.

Twins Days

Where: Twinsburg

When: Early August

What: Every summer for more than 30 years, identical and fraternal twins have been gathering here to celebrate twinhood. They can participate in the festival's parade, talent show, charity walk, and a variety of contests—from the best movie-themed costumes to the most similar- and dissimilar-looking twins.

The festival, which lasts three days, began in 1976 with 37 sets of twins; today, more than 2,500 pairs participate. Over the years, Twinsburg's festival has gotten plenty of good publicity. It's been profiled on television programs like *Nova* and *That's Incredible* and is mentioned in the *Guinness Book of World Records* as the largest gathering of twins. Science has also benefited from Twins Days; having so many sets of people with identical DNA in one place gives researchers an opportunity to study genetic and environmental influences on human beings.

Valley City Frog Jump Festival

Where: Valley City

When: August

What: In 1962, looking for a special way to celebrate their township's 150th anniversary, the inhabitants of Valley City started a frog-jump festival. (They were inspired by Mark Twain's story "The Celebrated Jumping Frog of Calaveras County.") There are food booths, carnival games, and the Great Rocky River Frog Race (in which festivalgoers try to pick the frog that will reach the finish line first), but the highlight of the festival is the frog jump. The frogs jump one at a time. Contestants place their amphibians in the middle of a parachute and measure the distance they travel after three jumps. The frog that jumps the farthest from the starting place wins—and gets a trophy. The all-time record—set in 1988 by a North American bullfrog named Space Jumper—is 19 feet 1 inch (about 2 feet shy of the real Calaveras County world-record holder, Rosie the Ribeter, who jumped 21 feet 5¾ inches in 1986). And have no fear: If you come to the festival frogless, you can still participate. The festival organizers catch some frogs beforehand for attendees who don't bring their own.

New Year's Eve Sausage Drop

Where: Elmore

When: December 31

What: Instead of the giant lighted ball that descends in New York's Times Square during the countdown to the New Year, the town of Elmore drops a giant lighted sausage. The first celebratory wurst was dropped for the 2001 New Year's celebration. It was made from a drainpipe decorated to look like a local meat company's award-winning wurst. The current sausage—a 10-foot-long hotdog—is covered in 1,500 tiny lights, evoking the Tiffany ball in New York. The party also features contests, including a sausage toss and a sausage-eating competition.

DUCKtona

Where: Gallipolis

When: Early August

What: This half-mile race takes place on the Ohio River. Participants set their rubber duckies loose in the river and cheer them on to the finish line; the ducks that cross the finish line first win their owners prizes—including a camper, a boat, a hot tub, and furniture. The race began in 2006 (more than 10,000 ducks participated that year) and raises money for the Ariel-Ann Carson Dater Performing Arts Centre, a local theater.

For more festivals, turn to page 222.

Did You Know?

Dayton's Schuster Center for the Performing Arts, built in 1991, was designed by Argentinean architect Cesar Pelli, who is also well known for his designs of the Petronas Towers in Kuala Lumpur—the world's tallest buildings until 2004—the Washington Reagan National Airport Passenger Terminal, and the Canary Wharf Tower in London.

Pelli's goal in designing the Schuster Center was to show that Dayton is a city moving into the future. In an interview with the *Dayton Daily News*, Pelli called the Schuster Center's design "an exclamation point for Dayton!"

Ladies First

At a time when few women even went to college, Florence Ellinwood Allen graduated from law school, was admitted to the Ohio bar, and fought for women's rights.

A Melodic Beginning

Florence Ellinwood Allen was born in Utah in 1884. Her family was headed by activists: both of her parents championed women's and labor rights, and her father was elected to Congress in 1895. When she was eleven, Allen met Susan B. Anthony, and a suffragette was born.

In 1900, Allen moved to Ashtabula, Ohio, to live with her grandfather, a schoolteacher. She attended Western Reserve University's College for Women (now Case Western Reserve University), where she studied music. Allen originally wanted to be a pianist. After graduation, she studied music for two years in Berlin, and when she returned home, she put her musical expertise to work writing for a newspaper, the *Cleveland Plain Dealer*. But in the end, her sense of civic duty won out. She thought she could do more good in politics than she could as a musician.

Break on Through

Initially, Allen dabbled in political journalism, but that didn't satisfy her. She soon turned to the law. She applied to Western Reserve University's law school but was rejected because of her gender. So she moved on to the University of Chicago, where she was second in her class, and then to New York University, where she graduated with her law degree in 1913. She was admitted to the Ohio bar in 1914 (and ranked seventh among all the takers of the bar that year), established a private law practice in Cleveland, and worked for the Legal Aid Society, where she campaigned for women's suffrage.

Making History

Being one of the only female attorneys in the country didn't satisfy her, though. During her lifetime, Allen was the first woman in Ohio (and sometimes in the country) to do the following:

- Be appointed assistant prosecutor (1919). She worked in Cuyahoga County.
- Be an elected judge (1920). Her position was on Ohio's Court of Common Pleas.
- Be elected to the Ohio State Supreme Court (1922). In fact, she was the first woman to be elected to *any* state supreme court.
- Be appointed to the U.S. Court of Appeals, Sixth Circuit (1934). She was the first woman to be appointed to a federal-level court.
- Be chief judge of a U.S. Court of Appeals (1958).

Allen retired in 1959. She died in 1966 and is buried in Waite Hill, Ohio.

Did You Know?

Gloria Steinem says, "Without leaps of imagination, or dreaming, we lose the excitement of possibilities. Dreaming, after all, is a form of planning."

Legalese

Travelers and Ohioans alike could easily find themselves on the wrong side of the law in the Buckeye State. Here are some little-known wacky laws that everyone in Ohio should keep in mind.

Animal Control

- Across the state of Ohio, it is illegal to get a fish drunk.
- State law mandates that anyone who wishes to kill a fly within 160 feet of a church must obtain a license.
- In McDonald, a goose may not be paraded down Main Street.
- It is against the law to display colored chickens for sale in Akron.
- In Cleveland, people must procure a hunting license before they catch mice.
- Policemen in Paulding can bite a dog to silence it.
- In Marysville, it is illegal for a dog to urinate on a parking meter.
- In Toledo, throwing a snake at anyone is prohibited. In the rest of Ohio, throwing a snake at another person is allowed (presumably), but shaking a snake at someone is illegal.

Getting Around Town

- Be careful when running your horse in Lowell. The speed limit for horse riders is five miles per hour.
- In North Canton, you must notify the police before you roller-skate.

- Just a bit south, in Canton, it is illegal for anyone to drive a Power Wheels car on the street.
- In Ohio, it's illegal to run out of gas.
- In Fairview Park, drivers must take special care not to honk their car horns excessively. One grandmother was fined for beeping her horn twice at her neighbor.
- No one may steer a car around Oxford's town square more than 100 times in a single driving session.
- Car drivers are breaking the law if their vehicle spooks a horse in Centerville.
- Any walker or jogger who needs to take a rest in Clinton County should know that it's against the law to lean up against a public building.

Blue Laws

- In Ohio, no one may be arrested on a Sunday.
- State legislation also bans fishing for whales on Sunday.
- In Columbus, the law prohibits stores from selling cornflakes on Sunday.

That's Indecent!

- Mothers in Ohio are prohibited from breast-feeding in public.
- Women in Cleveland may not wear patent leather shoes in public. The reason: men might catch a reflection of their underwear.
- In Oxford, it is unlawful for a female to take off her clothing in front of a picture of a man.
- In Bexley, a 1919 ordinance bans slot machines in outhouses.
- In Ironton, cross-dressing is against the law.

A Long and Winding Road

From the Baby Seals to the Blue Jackets . . . here's a look at the tumultuous history of professional hockey in Columbus.

Check!

The first professional hockey franchise in Columbus was the Checkers, a short-lived team that lasted from 1966 to 1970. They were part of the International Hockey League (IHL)—which included major and minor league teams and tried to compete with the National Hockey League (NHL)—but the Checkers were never able to best their more talented rivals. The Checkers missed the playoffs three times in four years—they made it in their second season but were ousted in the first round—and by 1970 were the IHL's worst team. That spring, the team folded.

Hey, Baby

For one year, there was no hockey in Columbus. Then, in 1971, a minor league team arrived: the Seals (nicknamed the "Baby Seals" by the media because they were a farm team). Owner Charlie Finley (who also owned the Oakland A's baseball team) blew into Ohio determined to make hockey successful in the Buckeye State. The Seals' logo: "It's time for hockey to return!"

Triumphant, however, they were not. In the Seals' first year, the team posted a record of 15–55–2. The next year, they got worse: 10–62–2. By 1973, the Seals were on the auction block.

Whoo . . . Whoo

Enter Al Savill, a Columbus investment broker who wanted to make hockey in Columbus a success. He bought the Seals, brought in new management, and changed the team's name again . . . to the Columbus Owls.

Unfortunately, nothing seemed to be able to change the woeful fate of Columbus hockey. In their first few seasons, the Owls did all right. They posted winning records in 1975 and 1977 but were unable to build enough of a fan base to keep them going—they also never made it through the play-offs or captured a championship.

In 1977, Savill moved the team to Dayton, hoping to get more support from citizens and the city. (The City of Columbus was notorious for booking events at the Owls' arena that conflicted with the team's schedule.) The team later moved to Grand Rapids, Michigan, and eventually folded, lacking the money and the fan base to continue.

The Big Chill

For the next 14 years, Columbus did without professional hockey, but in 1991, a new team and owner emerged to resuscitate the sport. Chicago businessman Horn Chen bought a minor league expansion team, moved them to Columbus, and named them the Chill.

Hoping to learn from the mistakes of his successors, Chen focused his attention on developing a strong fan base. He decided to market the new team to fans outside traditional hockey circles and hoped to appeal to casual sports fans. He relied on print and radio ads and outrageous promotions to give the Chill a reputation as a team that entertained, not just played good hockey. It worked.

Between 1991 and 1999, the Chill played at Columbus' Fairground Coliseum, and for several of those years, the team drew big crowds; in fact, between January 1992 and April 1994, they sold out 83 straight home games, a minor league record that still stands. Fans came for zany activities like the "Scream 'Til Your Brain Hurts" promotion during the 1995–96 season: team representatives handed fans a roving microphone and urged them to scream into it. One fan took the promotion to the extreme, using his turn at the mic to unleash a verbal diatribe against the opposing goalie.

Putting on the Blue Jackets

Meanwhile, the Chill's owners were laying the groundwork for an NHL club. In 1996 Columbus Hockey Limited, a partnership of five determined investors applied to the NHL to bring an expansion team to Columbus. The next year, the league approved the request. The team would be called the Blue Jackets, a reference to the blue uniforms Union soldiers wore during the Civil War and an homage to Columbus' proud abolitionist past.

In 1998, work began on the Nationwide Arena, and in October 2000, the Blue Jackets played their first game there. (The beloved Chill closed down in 1999, presumably to make room for the Blue Jackets.)

Today, the Blue Jackets are an up-and-coming team. Their best season came in 2004–2005, when they posted a record of 35–43–4. They have yet to reach the playoffs but remain popular in Columbus and continue to enjoy capacity crowds in the 18,500-seat Nationwide Arena.

Wacky Ohio, Part 2

More strange tales from the Buckeye State.

Bad Prisoner, No Doughnut!

No one said prison life is easy, but it just got a lot tougher for Franklin County's inmates. Why? Doughnuts have been taken off the menu. The low nutrition and high fat content of the bakery treats are being blamed for the removal. (The fact that Franklin County taxpayers were outraged when they found out they were coughing up $55,000 per year for the glazed and jelly doughnuts, may have had something to do with it, too.)

That's Gotta Hurt!

Jason Houston, 25, of Akron, was injured and subsequently awarded $786,760 in a lawsuit. Although we usually take pause when it comes to large sums being awarded in civil suits, in this case we have to take Houston's side. (Warning: graphic description ahead.) "I can barely walk," he said. "There's a constant throbbing of pain in a very uncomfortable spot."

The incident that led to the suit occurred in 2004. Houston was working out at an Akron YWCA when a cable on the machine he was using—a leg press holding 150 pounds of weights—snapped, causing "a center steel rod with an adjusting ball to swing 180 degrees into his groin." Houston's lawyer, Robert Meeker, explained that the injury has not only hampered Houston's sex life, but he can't even walk right. "I'm bow-legged," explained Houston, who had to leave college because he was unable to get to his classes on time. Meeker added that the bizarre injury has caused emotional distress to some of Houston's male friends. "Everyone who hears his story just kind of winces."

Girls Gone Stupid

Four 17-year-old girls were driving down Interstate 75 near Toledo in October 2006. According to several witnesses, they were flirting with other drivers, yelling things, and sticking out their (pierced) tongues at them. It was all harmless fun until one of the teens decided to stick her red bra out of the window of the Mercury Sable and hang it on the antenna. James Campbell, 47, and his friend Jeff Long, 37, were driving along the same stretch of road in Campbell's Dodge Neon. They saw the girls in the car ahead of them gesturing to other cars, but chalked it up to normal teenage shenanigans. That's when Campbell saw a flash of red approach his windshield. He swerved to avoid it, but the Neon flipped over and rolled several times, landing in the median and throwing Campbell from the car. Both men were flown to the hospital with serious injuries.

To make matters worse, when Campbell awoke in his hospital bed, he was informed that he'd received a citation for failure to maintain control of his vehicle. "I got a ticket, and I'm not even the one who did anything," Campbell complained to the press. The girl who hung the bra on the antenna was cited for littering, but she had an excuse: she explained to police that earlier that morning, her dog had chewed on the bra and torn the strap, prompting her to hang it from the antenna when she realized it was broken. (We don't understand her logic, either.)

Boys Gone Stupid

In April 2007, four teenage boys from Michigan were riding in a car on Interstate 75 near Findlay, Ohio. One boy was driving, another boy was operating a video camera, and the remaining two were mooning cars while the amateur videographer captured surprised motorists' reactions. Their antics were put to a stop when their car pulled past Bob Burd, an Ohio state trooper driving an unmarked car. He told reporters that the two teenagers "were hanging almost completely out of the vehicle." Burd pulled the boys over, found the camera, and charged them all with disorderly conduct. "The video showed everything they had been doing," he said. "They were apparently making one of those homemade *Jackass*-type videos while on their way to a skate park in Dayton."

Money for Nothing

Joe Randolph, a 42-year-old father from Upper Arlington, was told by the Licking County Child Support Enforcement Agency (CSEA) that he must continue paying $1,300 per month in child support to his ex-wife until the court tells him he can stop. Yet according to Randolph, there are two problems with this order: 1) His ex-wife is dead; and 2) Randolph himself has had custody of his three children for two years. His lawyer, Jerry Swank, made a statement to reporters: "I ask the burning question, 'Who are they going to send the money to?'"

The CSEA agrees, but insists that they have no right to terminate child support payments; only a court order can do that. "It's certainly a very unfortunate situation and something we've done everything we can to rectify." So even though everyone agrees that Randolph has been paying money to no one, he must keep doing so until the bureaucratic red tape has been worked through—and then he and his lawyer can try to get the money back.

From Ada to Youngstown

We've crammed 50 cities into this Ohio-shaped word search. How many can you find?

ADA
AKRON
ALLIANCE
AMHERST
ANDOVER
ANTWERP
ARLINGTON
ASHTABULA
ATHENS
AURORA
AVON
BATH
BELLAIRE
BEREA
BETHLEHEM
BOWLING GREEN
CADIZ
CALCUTTA
CALDWELL
CANTON
CHAGRIN FALLS
CINCINNATI
CLEVELAND
COLDWATER
COLUMBUS
DAYTON
DEER PARK
DEFIANCE
DOVER
DUBLIN
ELYRIA
EUCLID
FRANKLIN
GENEVA
GENOA
GERMANTOWN
HOLLAND
INDIAN HILL
KENT
LIMA
MEDINA
MILAN
NEWARK
OBERLIN
OTTAWA
RAVENNA
SANDUSKY
SPRINGFIELD
TOLEDO
YOUNGSTOWN

N
Z P I
I A T X S O A C A Y D T G U W C
T T L M H W D Q E G T P O U C Y K J D
W N E S A R I C C E P N R E D S L R N M Y D C G
T A T T U C L A C C K I S G D B L O U E D X U J
X V T Q R T C L R R A U Z S Y I R F G E G J O P
U O P W O T U D A L B G N O K K E N T Y R O A
I N D X R J E W L M I E U L A L S Y R R Q L J
I O F K A F E E U W H N O T Y A D U B L I N I R
H T R R I N B L B T G E G R H L N F D M K N J F
I N A A K N O L A S F V I T A N N I C N I C I W
P A N P X C I Q T P Z A C B O N D H D L A X C L
R C K R V M U O H R A N W O T N A M R E G S Q
E T L E A A W Q S I O L A W A G Z E R R M D P
W N I E I N D I A N H I L L R H B E I E P V S
T O N D V N D F O G Z F L I I O B N H L C W
N N T O L E D O F F Z O N N A M H E R S T N
A D V G S V L N V I H F R G E N L K E K C
X F J M M A D A D E A V H G S H C H R
Y L D E R Q A N L R T L R T F H E R
K I C C O L D W A T E R J F R
P G S T I F K B E G D
V W V B N U C
U B E

For answers, turn to page 304.

How Alan Freed the Music, Part 2

On page 33, we introduced you to revolutionary Cleveland deejay Alan Freed. Here's the rest of his story.

Birth of the Rock Concert

On March 21, 1952, Freed organized what many consider to be the world's first rock concert. The Moondog Coronation Ball took place at the Cleveland Arena and included artists like the Dominoes, Tiny Grimes, the Rockin' Highlanders, Danny Cobb, and Varietta Dillard. Freed promoted the concert heavily and called on all his "Moondoggers" to come on down for a night of swinging and dancing. And come they did.

Tickets to the concert cost $1.50 and $1.75 (depending on where a seat was). Initially, Freed and his concert promoters printed 7,000 tickets. When those sold out, they printed another 2,000—all of which sold in one day. Then, on the day of the show, more than 20,000 people showed up at the Cleveland Arena, even though the venue could hold only about 10,000. Despite the fact that more than half of them didn't have tickets, the audience rushed the arena's gates, prompting the show to be canceled by fire marshals after just one song by R&B artist Paul "Hucklebuck" Williams.

Segregation, Riots, and *The Big Beat*

Word of Freed's concert and his radio success spread across the nation, leading other stations to drop their formats and start playing rock 'n' roll records. Meanwhile, Freed's audience (especially his white audience) continued to grow. With this success came promotions, and in 1954, Freed left WJW for WINS in New York City. He dropped the Moondog name (after a blues artist called Moon Dog sued him), but maintained his manic style and continued to push "race music" to white teenagers. Freed also defended the rock 'n' roll genre to critics who thought it was a passing fad. Freed said, "Anyone who thinks that rock 'n' roll is a flash-in-the-pan trend along the music road has rocks in their head, dad!"

Suddenly, Freed was rock's unofficial spokesman and a movie star to boot after he appeared in a string of 1950s rock movies. Unfortunately, Freed's success was soon muddied by violence, racial politics, and money. The first sign of trouble came in 1957 when ABC hired him to host a nationally televised rock 'n' roll show called *The Big Beat*. The program ran for only one episode, though; racial politics got in the way when Frankie Lymon, a black performer on the show, danced with a white girl. That was more than ABC's Southern affiliates could stand. They were livid and dropped the show, which led many sponsors to pull their ads. With no sponsors and little affiliate support, the network canceled the program.

Banned!

In 1958, Freed suffered another setback when a riot broke out at a concert he'd organized in Boston. Freed was criminally charged for inciting the violence, even though most of the fighting took place outside the arena by non-ticket holders. After paying some hefty legal fees, the charges were dropped, but both rock music and Freed were feeling the heat—Boston banned rock concerts and WINS fired its most famous deejay. Freed now had to scour local markets to find work.

Beleaguered but still enthusiastic about rock 'n' roll, Freed landed a job hosting a rock show on WABC TV in New York.

But that didn't last long, either. Rock's biggest scandal to date was just around the corner, and once again, Freed found himself at the center of it.

Payola

When the potential power of radio became apparent in the mid-1950s, record companies started paying radio stations and deejays to push their artists. Although the practice, dubbed "payola," had been around in some form since the 1920s, the new demographic of post-war baby boom teenagers promised dividends unlike any that the music industry had seen before. The kids—millions of them—liked rock, had access to money, and were willing to spend it on records. The laws surrounding payola were murky at the time. But everyone was doing it, and they defended themselves by pointing out how common the practice was. Alan Freed had done it . . . to an extent. He was mostly paid as a "consultant," listening to new records and telling record executives which ones might fly with the kids. In some cases, he even accepted cowriting credits on songs he played, such as on Chuck Berry's "Maybelline."

In November 1959, fearing a scandal, WABC ordered Freed to sign a statement saying that he'd never taken money to play a song. Freed refused and was immediately fired. Soon after, Congress held hearings on the payola scandal. Most of the nation's deejays were left alone, but the high-profile Freed was charged with 26 counts of commercial bribery. He was found guilty, fined, and received a suspended sentence. Already nearly bankrupt from the massive legal fees surrounding the incident in Boston, the payola scandal effectively ended Freed's career.

Freed tried to deejay at a few California radio stations over the next few years, but he never regained his early glory. He lived out the rest of his life on the West Coast and died of cirrhosis of the liver in January 1965. He was 43 years old.

The Beat Lives On

Freed's impact on rock 'n' roll, though, remains. Just listen to any rock deejay and you'll hear shades of the man who pioneered the form. What Freed did in the 1950s had more far-reaching ramifications than popularizing a new type of music. The civil rights movement of the 1960s can be traced, in part, to the dance halls that Freed's music had integrated a decade earlier. Through music, he preached racial harmony. And music has, at times, had a very loud voice.

In 1986, Freed was among the first group of inductees into Cleveland's Rock and Roll Hall of Fame. In 1988, he was inducted into the Radio Hall of Fame at Chicago's Museum of Broadcast Communications. "More than any other man," wrote *Billboard*'s Paul Ackerman, "he brought us rock 'n' roll."

Did You Know?

In 1948, long before he opened the first Wendy's fast-food restaurant in Columbus, Dave Thomas dropped out of high school to take a job as a busboy in Indiana. Forty-five years later, he earned a GED from Coconut Creek High School in Fort Lauderdale, Florida (where he lived during his retirement).

A Drive on the Pike

Take a look at the Ohio Turnpike by the numbers.

0

Number of major cities through which the turnpike passes. The highway skirts the major cities because it was designed as a long-distance route. Planners avoided urban centers and the short-distance traffic they bring.

1 mile

Amount of roadway that turnpike crews laid each day at the peak of the road's construction in late 1953.

$3

The price per car to drive the length of the turnpike in 1955. Today, it costs $10.25—that's about 4 cents per mile.

14

Number of service plazas on the turnpike. These are placed about 30 miles apart in seven pairs: one on the eastbound side, one westbound.

30

Number of turnpike exits (not including the service plazas).

65 mph

Speed limit for all vehicles on the turnpike.

75 percent

Turnpike motorists who are from states other than Ohio.

241 miles

Length of the turnpike. It runs across the northern part of the state and connects the Pennsylvania Turnpike to the Indiana Toll Road.

1955

Year the turnpike was completed. At the time, it was the longest freeway project ever completed.

51.8 million

Number of vehicles that traveled the turnpike in 2006. They logged more than 3 billion miles of driving.

$184 million

Toll money collected on the turnpike in 2006. Total revenue—including concessions at the service plazas and other miscellaneous moneymakers—was $220 million, none of which included federal funding. (The only state funding comes from a 5-cents-per-gallon tax on gas at turnpike service plazas.) The turnpike cost only $104 million to operate that year.

Did You Know?

The longstanding Ohio–Michigan rivalry lives on . . .

Q: What's the only sign of intelligent life in Ann Arbor?
A: Columbus: 187 Miles

Q: Why did Michigan change their field from grass to artificial turf?
A: To keep the Michigan cheerleaders from grazing at halftime.

Wild Weather

When it comes natural disasters, these two storms prove that Ohio is one wild and crazy place.

The Xenia Tornado: April 3, 1974

On April 3 and 4, 1974, the United States experienced a series of tornadoes—148 across 13 states. It was the costliest and deadliest series of tornadoes of the 20th century, and the worst one touched down in Xenia, Ohio.

The F5 tornado arrived at about 4:30 in the afternoon, just outside Xenia, and blew into town about ten minutes later. The residents had little warning as winds of up to 300 mph blasted the county. Within half an hour, more than 1,000 buildings had been destroyed, and 33 people were dead. President Richard Nixon, who visited a week later, called it "the worst disaster I've ever seen."

Yet even with all the damage, within a year the town of Xenia had rebuilt most of its structures. And residents were proud of their accomplishment; cars in the area boasted bumper stickers declaring "Xenia lives!"

The White Hurricane: January 25–27, 1978

The National Weather Service called this blizzard a "storm of unprecedented magnitude." To many Ohioans, it was the storm of the century. In fact, the 1978 "white hurricane" remains the most costly and most deadly: damages totaled more than $70 million, and 51 people died.

The blizzard was actually made up of two storms: one had formed over Louisiana and the other over North Dakota. They met in Ohio on January 25, 1978, and merged into one large tempest. The storm started as rain but turned to snow overnight. Temperatures dropped to 10°F or below, snow accumulations topped three feet, and the barometric pressure in Cleveland dropped to 28.28 inches, the lowest ever recorded in Ohio. But what made this storm especially bad was the wind. Bitter air blasted in from the north and blew across the state at more than 70 mph. The winds lifted houses off their foundations, blew cars off the roads, and created snowdrifts up to 20 feet high.

Ohio shut down. School was canceled. Offices closed. Even the Ohio Turnpike was off-limits. Then-governor James A. Rhodes called in the state's National Guard to rescue stranded families, help utility crews access downed power lines, escort doctors and nurses to work, and distribute food to Ohio's neediest residents. In all, more than 5,000 National Guardsmen heeded the call, and President Jimmy Carter even dispatched an additional 300 U.S. Army troops to help out.

To read about the flood of 1913, the greatest natural disaster in Ohio's history, turn to page 61.

Did You Know?

Ohio resident Joseph P. Crowley is one lucky guy. In 1987, he won $3 million in the Ohio lottery. Six years later, he retired to Boca Raton, Florida, played the lottery there . . . and won again. That time, he took home $20 million.

Battle of Fallen Timbers

In the late 18th century in the forests near Maumee, U.S. soldiers battled Native Americans for control of Ohio.

At War Again

At the end of the 18th century, with the Revolutionary War behind them, the British agreed to withdraw to Canada and cede the Northwest Territory—a region that included what is now Ohio and its neighboring states—to the Americans. Local commanders, though, didn't want to comply with the agreement; they weren't happy about their country having surrendered to the colonists and some refused to vacate the area.

This defiance was initially helpful to the Native Americans in the area. Local tribes—the Shawnee, Iroquois, Miami, Wabash, and others—had formed an alliance called the Western Lakes Confederacy and started battling the Americans for control of the area. The British supported the tribes, giving them provisions and arms and encouraging them to resist the Americans. As a result, the Northwest Indian War raged from 1785 to 1795.

Enter Mad Anthony

For many of those years, the Americans were losing. In 1790 and 1791 especially, U.S. soldiers took many beatings from the warriors of the Western Lakes Confederacy. President George Washington saw these defeats as a threat to the new nation, so he decided to call in one of his star Revolutionary War generals to lead an army against the tribes. "Mad" Anthony Wayne was a veteran of Valley Forge and had commanded his troops to many victories during the Revolution. He got his nickname because of his temper.

Wayne spent several months training his militia. The men were inexperienced volunteers, but their general turned them into a fierce fighting unit. Then he marched them to Ohio, where they occupied Fort Washington in Cincinnati and built Fort Recovery in Mercer County and Fort Greenville in Darke County. In skirmishes throughout the summer of 1794, Wayne's men tasted battle and suffered casualties.

An Uneasy Alliance

The Western Lakes Confederacy was by far the strongest tribal alliance in history to stand up to the Americans, but it was unstable. The different tribes didn't really get along, and they didn't stand together as a solid unit. Plus, as their homes and villages came under attack, many tribes abandoned the larger fight and returned home to defend their own land.

This left only a few warriors to battle Wayne's advancing army. The Native American warriors and American soldiers first met at Fallen Timbers, an area outside Toledo where a recent tornado had felled a grove of trees. But the natives were outnumbered. Only about 400 warriors were available to fight. Wayne commanded an army of more than 1,500.

The Battle

Fighting began on August 20, 1794. Wayne's troops advanced into Fallen Timbers and were ambushed by small groups of tribal warriors who fired muskets from behind trees and tall grass. The Americans returned fire, regrouped, and kept advancing. This surprised the tribal warriors; the Americans had never shown such discipline before. In previous fights, they'd been quick to panic and run away. At Fallen Timbers, though, the Americans charged and swept around to outflank the natives, who were eventually forced to retreat.

The tribes followed the Maumee River to a British fort, hoping their allies would protect them. But the fort's commander, afraid to start a fight with the Americans, closed the gates. The Native Americans continued downriver and eventually got away, but General Wayne and his men swept across the countryside and destroyed all the Native American camps and villages they found.

The Western Lakes resistance collapsed, and Wayne demanded surrender. Most tribes signed the Treaty of Greenville, which ended the war and opened up most of Ohio to American settlement.

The Warrior and the President

Among the Shawnee warriors who fought at Fallen Timbers were three brothers: one was killed, the second became a religious leader, and the third—Tecumseh—distinguished himself as a great warrior. Tecumseh spurned the Treaty of Greenville and continued to unite tribes to fight the Americans until he was killed in 1813.

One of Wayne's soldiers was William Henry Harrison, who led the army that eventually killed Tecumseh during the War of 1812. Harrison also won the U.S. presidency in March 1841, but he developed pneumonia and died on April 4, 1841, after just one month in office.

Stars of the Derby

On page 1, we covered the history of Akron's All-American Soap Box Derby. Here are some of the more innovative and mischievous characters to participate in the race over the years.

Cliff Hardesty

In 1939, this contestant from White Plains, New York, was the subject of 52 letters of complaint . . . and that was before he'd even hit the track. Parents of racers he'd beaten in local competitions complained that Cliff's racer was too flawless—the suspension too sophisticated—to have been built by an 11-year-old. Race officials grilled Cliff about building his car and then brought him to a garage, where they told him to build from scratch the front suspension of his racer. After only half an hour, Cliff had built one even better, though he apologized that he couldn't get it quite right because the tools were unfamiliar. The stunned officials let him race, and he went on to win.

Gilbert Klecan

California's Gilbert Klecan was the derby's 1946 champ. Spectators called him the "angel with a dirty face" because he coated himself and his cart in graphite powder—commonly used as a lubricant—to cut down on wind resistance. He zipped well ahead of his competitors and won the race. The next year, it appeared that Gilbert had started a trend. Almost every racer in 1947 showed up covered in graphite. This proved both messy and dangerous—volunteers had trouble keeping the cars from slipping out of their hands when they carried them to the track. So from 1948 on, covering oneself and one's car in graphite was not allowed.

Kenny Cline

In 1964, several racers showed up with cars that required drivers to lie flat on their backs to cut down on wind resistance and make the cars go faster. The designs were the brainchild of a few boys from Texas, but Kenny Cline, originally from Midland, Texas, improved it. His racer, the "Grasshopper," required that he lie on his stomach while steering. Seemingly cumbersome but successful, his needle-nosed car shot to victory in 1967, and the "lie down" design has been popular ever since.

Karren Stead

Although a girl raced and placed second in the first derby in 1933, girls were prohibited from competing in the Soap Box Derby for 40 years. Girls were officially allowed to race again in 1971, but it wasn't until 1975 that a girl, Karren Stead from Pennsylvania, won the crown. (Eleven-year-old Karren won the race despite dislocating her thumb in a water balloon fight just before the starting whistle blew.) That year, girls occupied five of the top ten spots.

Jim Gronen

Some of the derby's most famous contestants gained their notoriety because of scandal. In 1973, 14-year-old Jim Gronen from Colorado, cousin of 1972 winner Bobby Lange, snagged the crown. But shortly after the race, rumors started that Jim had cheated. His race times were consistently and substantially ahead of those of his competitors, and a review of video footage showed his cart leaping out of the gate at the start of the derby. Because the racers' cars are supposed to start by gravity alone, one contestant shouldn't be able to gain an advantage right out of the gate. An inspection of Jim's car revealed a button on his headrest that triggered an electromagnet concealed in the nose. The electromagnet had been pulling the racer toward the metal starting gate, so that when the gate dropped, Jim's car got an extra boost down the hill.

Jim Gronen was stripped of his title, and his uncle, Robert Lange (father to Bobby Lange), confessed to urging the boy to use the magnet. Lange's rationale? He believed everyone else was cheating, too. Lange was convicted of encouraging the delinquency of a minor and was fined $2,000. His involvement also led to speculation that his son Bobby had cheated as well. But when derby officials tried to investigate, they found that Bobby's racer, which was supposed to be kept at Derby Downs after the win, had mysteriously vanished.

Did You Know?

Self-taught German artist Heinz Gaugel worked for 14 years on his masterpiece *Behalt*, a 10-by-265-foot mural whose name means "to keep" or "remember." The painting commemorates the history of the Amish, Mennonite, and Hutterite people and today hangs in the Amish and Mennonite Heritage Center in Berlin, Ohio. It's a *cyclorama*, a cylindrical painting that surrounds viewers and makes them feel like they're standing inside the action of the artwork itself. Gaugel's is one of only three cycloramas in the United States. (The other two depict Civil War battles and hang in museums in Atlanta, Georgia, and Gettysburg, Pennsylvania.)

Some Like It Hot

With more than 180 chili parlors, Cincinnati has the highest per capita density of chili parlors in the country. And Cincinnati residents eat more than 2 million pounds of chili every year.

Chili, Cincy Style

Cincinnati chili is a unique concoction: there are no beans, onions, or chili peppers in this mix. There aren't even any large chunks of beef. Instead, Cincinnati chili is a thick sauce of finely ground beef served over spaghetti or on hot dogs. The sauce is cooked slowly and seasoned with an elusive mix of spices that can include cinnamon, cloves, allspice, cardamom, cocoa, or even licorice. The exact recipes, though, are closely held secrets at Cincinnati's chili establishments.

Melting Pot

Cincinnati chili traces its origins to 1922, when two brothers—Tom and John Kiradjieff—opened a hot dog stand in downtown Cincinnati. The stand was next door to a burlesque theater from which the Kiradjieffs took their establishment's name: the Empress. Borrowing from Mediterranean cuisine, Tom concocted an Americanized version of Greek stew that used finely ground beef instead of lamb. He added chili powder and pinches of cinnamon and cloves, the spices often used in Greek cooking, and served the result over spaghetti. Tom also ladled the chili sauce on top of hot dogs, a dish he called the "Coney dog" for Coney Island in New York. He'd passed through Coney Island when he immigrated to the United

States, and the place (and, no doubt, its carnival fare) had impressed him.

By the 1940s, another immigrant—Nicholas Lambrinides—was working as a cook at the Empress. Inspired by memories of his mother's and grandmother's cooking back in Greece, Lambrinides started experimenting with a chili recipe of his own. He tried to introduce the new recipe at work, but Tom Kiradjieff kept tinkering with its ingredients. Finally, in 1949, Lambrinides and three of his sons opened their own restaurant: Skyline Chili, named for the panoramic view of Cincinnati visible from its site on Price Hill.

The Sky's the Limit

In the beginning, customers didn't know what to make of Lambrinides' unusual dish. "People had never heard of chili on top of spaghetti," Nicholas' son William told a newspaper reporter in 1999. But Skyline offered free samples to introduce customers to its product. The strategy worked, and soon word of mouth had made Skyline Chili one of the most popular restaurants in Cincinnati.

It was so popular, in fact, that the family opened a second location in 1953. Today, there are more than 110 Skyline Chili parlors in Ohio and the surrounding states, making Skyline one of the two most popular purveyors of Cincinnati chili. (The other, Gold Star Chili, was founded in 1965 by the Daoud brothers from Jordan.)

Skyline Chili is still made from the secret recipe Nicholas Lambrinides cooked up more than 60 years ago. "Dad always said, 'Don't change a thing with the recipe—don't add anything, don't take out anything,'" William recalled. "'It's perfect the way it is.'"

Every Which Way

For out-of-towners, Cincinnati chili is eaten by the numbers:

- Two-way means chili on top of spaghetti.
- Three-way, the most popular, adds a layer of shredded cheddar cheese.
- Four-way piles on onions.
- And five-way adds red kidney beans.

Oyster crackers crumbled on top are de rigueur. Chili dogs, long ago named "Coneys" by Tom Kiradjieff, are still popular, and there's been a recent addition: baked potatoes topped with a mound of Cincinnati chili.

Did You Know?

"As a result of a 2003 traffic stop in Ohio, Catherine Donkers was convicted of a child-seat-restraint violation (specifically, holding her baby in her lap for breast-feeding while driving), but she appealed, and in April 2007, a court ruled in her favor. The story made *News of the Weird* in 2003 because Donkers' husband, Brad Barnhill, who was not in the car, demanded that he be charged instead because his First Christian Fellowship for Eternal Sovereignty religion teaches that the husband must take responsibility for all of his wife's public actions (especially when the 'public action' involves 'the Beast,' which is what the religion calls 'government')."

—*News of the Weird*, 2007

The Snow Bowl

Ten degrees, five inches of snow and counting, 28-mph winds: ahh . . . the perfect conditions for a college football game.

Putting the "Fan" in "Fanatic"

November 25, 1950, dawned as the worst blizzard the citizens of Columbus, Ohio, had seen in 37 years. Rain, sleet, and snow pelted the ground; winds topped 28 mph, whipped up snowdrifts a foot high, and downed tree branches. In the end, more than a foot of snow fell on Columbus that Thanksgiving weekend, but the Ohio State Buckeyes and the Michigan Wolverines played on.

Neither rain nor sleet nor whiteouts were going to stop the big showdown. It was, after all, the most anticipated game of the year for the rival schools, and this year was particularly important: the game would determine the Big Ten title and who would go to the Rose Bowl. If the game were canceled, Ohio would get the title by default. But Michigan didn't want that, and Ohio State's athletic director, Dick Larkins, didn't want his players to win unless they did so fair and square.

Initially, the organizers wondered how many spectators would actually show up at the stadium. But diehards couldn't let a little snow and wind keep them away from the year's biggest matchup. Despite the fact that snow was piled high in the bleachers, more than 50,000 fans piled into Ohio Stadium.

Wait . . . Where's the End Zone?

When the game started, more than five inches of snow was on the field, and the fierce wind blew it into drifts that obscured the yard markers and goal lines. Special sweepers hired by OSU tried to keep the sidelines and goal lines clear, but often, players and referees had to call time-outs so the sweepers could clear away enough snow to allow everyone to see the field markers.

The weather made traditional football plays impossible. Players were slipping and sliding in the snow, and no one seemed to be able to complete a pass. So the coaches got creative. Both sides mostly punted and tried to take advantage of turnovers. Over the course of the game, the teams punted 45 times, yet even this wasn't easy. Snappers usually couldn't see the punters, and neither team got a single first down.

May the Best Team Win

Somehow, though, they managed to score. OSU kicked a field goal (after recovering a fumbled punt) and put the first points on the board. Then the Wolverines scored when a blocked kick rolled into their end zone for a safety. Finally, Michigan's Tony Momsen sealed the win for his team when a blocked punt landed in the end zone and he fell on it for a touchdown. Michigan won the game 9–3 and went on to play in the Rose Bowl in January 1951. (They beat the University of California, Berkeley, 14–6.) The Ohio State coach, Wes Fesler, was fired.

The 1950 Michigan/Ohio State game went down in history as one of the most difficult (and comical) games in college football. Vic Janowicz, the Ohio State halfback and winner of that year's Heisman Trophy, said of the game, "It was a nightmare. My hands were numb. I had no feeling in them and I don't know how I hung onto the ball. It was terrible. You knew what you wanted to do, but you couldn't do it." It wasn't until 1955 that the Buckeyes made it back to the Rose Bowl, where they scored a decisive 20–7 victory over the University of Southern California.

That's Nutty!

Here's how a tree came to represent a state, its citizens, and their sports teams.

When the first settlers crossed the Allegheny Mountains into the region that became Ohio, they encountered a tree that most of them didn't recognize. The Native Americans called the tree *hetuck*, or "buckeye," because they thought its nut—dark brown on the outside with a lighter tan circle within—resembled the eye of a deer.

The buckeye was a hardy tree, and the settlers often carved its soft wood into bowls or into logs for a cabin. The tree was so tenacious, in fact, that Cincinnati physician Daniel Drake quipped during an 1833 speech, "Even after it is cut down and worked up into the side of a cabin, it will send out young branches, denoting to all the world that buckeyes are not easily conquered."

The Name Game

Ohioans have been calling themselves Buckeyes since at least 1788, when the Native Americans nicknamed the 6-foot 4-inch tall pioneer colonel, Ebenezer Sproat, "Hetuck" for his height and girth. The name caught on among other settlers, and by the 1830s, it was not unusual for newspaper and magazine writers to refer to Ohio locals as Buckeyes. The nickname didn't fully catch on, though, until 1840, when William Henry Harrison—a former U.S. senator from Ohio—was elected president. Harrison campaigned as a frontiersman and a man of the people, and the buckeye became his symbol, its nut serving as a campaign button. Harrison's backers distributed walking sticks carved out of buckeye wood and built buckeye log cabins as parade floats.

By the turn of the 20th century, the term "Buckeye" was being used to refer to athletic teams at Ohio State University in Columbus. The school's athletic department officially adopted the moniker in 1950, and today, OSU players have the distinction of belonging to one of the few teams named for a tree. OSU football players who make big plays on the field get decals of the buckeye's leaf to stick on their helmets.

In 1902, Ohio established its official state flag: a red, white, and blue pennant with a swallowtail design that bears a large circle. This "O" represents both the state's name and the shape and configuration of the buckeye nut. Then, in 1953, Ohio made it official: the buckeye became the state tree, and the "Buckeye State" was adopted as Ohio's nickname.

How Sweet It Is . . . and Isn't

The fruit of the buckeye nut isn't edible. In fact, it contains a poison called tannic acid, which is toxic to humans. Native Americans, though, used to extract the tannic acid from buckeye nuts—they used the acid to tan leather and could then eat the nut (without the acid, it was no longer poisonous).

In later years, Ohio cooks concocted a candy version of the buckeye nut called the "buckeye ball." Cooks shape morsels of peanut-butter fudge into buckeye-size "nuts" and then coat them with chocolate. The dish has become a popular Christmas treat throughout the United States.

Famous Buckeyes

It seems you can't turn a corner in Ohio without running into something or someone called "Buckeye." Here are some of the most famous Buckeyes:

- It may not be easy to personify a nut, but OSU students managed to do it in 1965. That's when Brutus Buckeye, now the school's official mascot, debuted. Brutus' outfit is simple: he's clad in the school colors of scarlet and gray and has a giant buckeye for a head.
- Ohio fielded three teams in baseball's Negro leagues; all bore the name Buckeye. The Columbus Buckeyes played one season (1921) in the Negro National League. In the Negro American League, the Cincinnati Buckeyes played for one year in that city (1942) and then moved to Cleveland, where they remained through 1948. On May 20, 2006, the Cleveland Indians and Pittsburgh Pirates paid tribute to the Negro leagues by wearing the uniforms of the Cleveland Buckeyes and the Homestead (Pennsylvania) Grays in an exhibition game in Cleveland.
- Before they moved to Texas, the Bush family put down roots in Ohio. Samuel Prescott Bush—grandfather of George Herbert Walker Bush and great-grandfather of George W. Bush—was the longtime president of the Buckeye Steel and Casting Company, a Columbus-based steel foundry established in 1881. Samuel, who became one of America's best-known industrialists of the 20th century, spent the rest of his adult life in Columbus. He died there in 1948 and is buried in Green Lawn Cemetery.
- Pennsylvania's Punxsutawney Phil may be the most famous groundhog in America, but Ohio has its own woodchuck—Marion's Buckeye Chuck—to predict the regional weather every February 2. The Ohio State Legislature named Chuck the state's groundhog of record in 1979.

Ka-ching!

"Every time you sell a merchant a National Cash Register, you are doing him a big favor." —*John H. Patterson*

John Henry Patterson—founder of the National Cash Register Company (NCR)—was born outside Dayton in 1844. He was well educated, attending both Miami University and Dartmouth, and spent much of his young adult life working a variety of jobs: in his father's grist and saw mills, as a soldier in the Union army during the Civil War, and as a toll collector on the Miami and Erie Canal. By 1883, he was running a company general store with his brothers. The store did good business, but it never showed a profit.

A Handy Contraption

Soon, the Patterson brothers heard about and ordered a newfangled contraption called a "mechanical money drawer," invented and produced by Dayton's own James J. Ritty. (*To read about Ritty's cash register, turn to page 230.*) Called "Ritty's Incorruptible Cashier," the device turned the Patterson brothers' profits around. The machine revealed employees with sticky fingers by keeping an accurate count of the day's receipts. Patterson was so impressed by the value of the cash register that he bought stock in Ritty's company and, in 1884, bought the company itself.

Ritty's company had been failing, though, and made no profit; it had sold only about a dozen registers in a year. Patterson was so ridiculed by Daytonians for his seemingly frivolous purchase that he tried to sell the company back the next day—at half price. His offer was refused.

The Product Nobody Wanted

So Patterson took over the operation and its 13 employees and decided to prove to the nation's businessmen that, though they didn't know it, they all needed cash registers. Patterson had little money and knew almost nothing about manufacturing. But he was an inspired and natural salesman.

He changed the company's name to National Cash Register and instituted selling techniques that flattered "P.P.s" (probable purchasers) and persuaded them to buy cash registers. He also made several improvements to the original product and patented it in his name. He added a cash drawer and changed the original "bong" sound at sale to the pleasant "ding" known today. Soon, National Cash Register was a success.

Getting Comfortable

In 1888, Patterson married his wife Katherine and made plans to build a state-of-the-art manufacturing plant on his family farm. (He and Katherine went on to have two children, Frederick and Dorothy. When Katherine died young, Patterson raised the children himself.) Although the new factory would be built with mostly borrowed money, Patterson was determined to make it an innovative place. In an era of dark, dingy sweatshops, he built a light, airy factory with tall windows and parklike grounds. He also shortened the workday for his employees from 12 hours (standard at the time) to eight for women and nine and a half for men.

Visionary

National Cash Register became more successful with each passing year, and by 1910, it had 90 percent of the U.S. cash register business. Patterson was a wealthy man who poured the money back into his factory. He landscaped the acreage around the factory with flowers and shrubs. When he noticed workers heating a bucket of coffee on a factory radiator, he put in lunchrooms where his employees could enjoy hot meals. He added swimming pools, pushed sanitary factory conditions, and provided medical care. His peers ridiculed him, but productivity at his factory increased dramatically, as did the loyalty of his many employees. When asked why he did all this "welfare" work, he said simply, "It pays." The phrase became a company slogan, which Patterson posted around the factory.

And pay it did. By 1913, Patterson employed 7,000 people at his Dayton company, and many of them were trained in sales. He was the first businessman to institute employee training in a time when people believed you either had it or you didn't when it came to selling. He developed a training manual, paid commissions, assigned territories, and gave passionate lectures that made employees believe they could make a fortune selling cash registers. But he also ruled his company with an iron fist and scared some salesmen. Patterson's training seminars became legendary for his quick-fire questions and extreme criticism. Some salesmen even fainted from the pressure.

Robber Baron or Saint?

Competitors in the cash register industry considered Patterson's business tactics unfair, and in 1913, the federal government brought Patterson to trial for violating the Sherman Antitrust Act. He was found guilty and given the maximum penalty: a $5,000 fine and a year in jail.

Meanwhile, the great flood of 1913 arrived in Dayton, and Patterson almost single-handedly saved his city and its citizens. (*For more on the story of the flood and Patterson's heroics, see page*

Dayton under Patterson's control and the Salvation Army chief declared him an "instrument of the Lord." In Dayton and across the country, Patterson was hailed as a hero. His supporters protested the guilty verdict in his antitrust trial, and finally, President Woodrow Wilson pardoned him.

The Legacy

For the rest of his life, Patterson remained a benevolent force in Dayton. He was one of the founders of the Dayton Association, a group devoted to charitable works. He supported women's suffrage, providing local activists with office space. He also organized support for a flying field, Wright Field (now Wright-Patterson Air Force Base), to encourage the new aviation industry.

In 1922, Patterson died suddenly while visiting Atlantic City; he left National Cash Register to his son. But the city he'd loved honored his memory. In Dayton, you can drive down Patterson Boulevard, visit Wright-Patterson Air Force Base, and even buy an NCR product (the company is still headquartered in Dayton).

Did You Know?

On May 24, 1935, the Cincinnati Reds became the first team to win in a major league night game. They beat the Philadelphia Phillies 2–1 at Crosley Field.

Of Gangsters and Presidents, Part 2

On page 72, we told you about two unique museum exhibits. Here are two more.

Balto (Stuffed)

Where: Cleveland Museum of Natural History, Cleveland

Why: In January 1925, Nome, Alaska, was in crisis. A diphtheria epidemic had struck the town, and there was no antitoxin serum available. The doctor in Nome radioed for help. There was plenty of serum in Anchorage, but that city was almost 1,000 miles away. Plus, it was winter; most of the route to Nome was covered with ice and snow. Fierce winds made it impossible for airplanes to fly into or out of the city, and the railroad line stopped several hundred miles short. The only way to get the antitoxin serum to Nome was to use sled dog teams and mushers.

The serum traveled by train to the town of Nenana, 674 miles from Nome. And then the musher relay began. More than 20 teams took turns pushing through the ice, wind, and snow; they crossed frozen lakes, bore temperatures as low as 40 below, and took six days. But the mushers—and the serum—made it to Nome and saved the town.

The dog who led the last team, the one that drove the final 53 miles into Nome, was named Balto. He was initially hailed as a hero, but as the 1920s wore on, Balto and several of the other dogs on his team were passed from one inattentive owner to the next until 1927 when George Kimble, a Cleveland businessman, found them hungry and sick at a zoo in Los Angeles.

It would cost $2,000 for Kimble to buy the dogs and bring them to Ohio. He didn't have the money on hand, so he established the Balto Fund. Ohioans responded in droves. Children offered coins. The Cleveland *Plain Dealer* ran stories about the dogs. Factory and retail workers scraped up whatever cash they could and donated it to the cause. Less than two weeks later, Kimble had enough money to buy the dogs. He brought them to Cleveland, where they lived out their days at the Brookside Zoo (now the Cleveland Metroparks Zoo). Balto lived at the zoo until 1933, and when he died, his body was stuffed, mounted, and put on display at the Cleveland Museum of Natural History. With the exception of a five-month visit to Alaska in 1998 and 1999, the dog has been there ever since.

Also on display:

A variety of dinosaur and other fossils, a titanium-coated planetarium that shows the position of more than 5,000 stars, and an outdoor wildlife center that's home to bald eagles, bobcats, hawks, and other animals.

Roosevelt Portrait and the Ex-Lax Thermometer

Where: Canton Classic Car Museum, Canton

Why: Marshall Belden Sr. established this homage to all things automotive in 1978, and the museum's collection contains numerous cars and pieces of car memorabilia. But what's most unique about the museum are its non-car-related items. Take the typing paper portrait of Franklin D. Roosevelt, for example. An inmate at the Ohio Penitentiary used a typewriter to create the portrait in 1941.

There's also that Ex-Lax Thermometer . . . it's just what it sounds like. Its round face is about the size of a wall clock, and it boasts the slogan "Keep regular with Ex-Lax."

Also on display:

Cars, of course! Everything from a 1901 Oldsmobile to a 1937 Packard hearse to a 1962 Amphicar (a German-made automobile that doubled as a boat).

Did You Know?

East Liverpool, Ohio, boasts a very odd attraction. In fact, it's the only one of its kind in the country: a bed-and-breakfast/mortuary museum. It all started in 1934 when murderer and bank robber Charles "Pretty Boy" Floyd was gunned down by the law in what is now Beavercreek State Park. Floyd's body was taken to the home (also a mortuary) of East Liverpool local E. G. Sturgis for embalming. Frank Dawson, who worked with Sturgis, did the procedure, but when word got out that the FBI's most wanted fugitive lay dead in their town, local residents converged on the funeral home, demanding that they be allowed to see Pretty Boy Floyd. The crowd grew so large and unruly that police feared a riot and, to placate the group, ordered Dawson to put the body on display in the viewing room. Over the next three hours, approximately 10,000 people filed through to see the body. The next morning, Charles Floyd's body was returned to his family in Oklahoma.

Frank Dawson's son, who took over the former funeral home in 1993, converted it into the Sturgis House bed-and-breakfast. There are six guest rooms, paraphernalia from Floyd's last stand in the basement, and breakfast is served in the very room where Pretty Boy Floyd was laid out.

Ohio Literati

The Buckeye State has produced some of America's most famous writers. See if you can match these Ohio authors to their descriptions.

1. Toni Morrison
2. Jack Miles Bickham
3. Erma Bombeck
4. Adrienne Miller
5. Hart Crane
6. James Thurber
7. Ambrose Bierce
8. Sherwood Anderson
9. Zane Grey
10. Rita Dove

A. This Garrettsville-born poet took great inspiration from the works of T. S. Eliot.

B. Having lived in Camden, Clyde, Springfield, Elyria, and Cleveland, this author's most famous work was a collection of short stories about small-town life entitled *Winesburg, Ohio*.

C. This Lorain native, a winner of Nobel and Pulitzer prizes, was named Chloe Anthony Wofford at birth. As a young adult, she changed her name because she thought "Chloe" was too hard to pronounce.

D. An author and literary critic, this Ohioan's biting critiques for the *San Francisco Examiner* earned him a "bitter" nickname.

E. This author was born in Columbus and grew up in Akron. Her childhood hometown plays a major role in her first novel.

F. This Akron-born writer, and only the second African American poet to win the Pulitzer Prize (Gwendolyn Brooks was the first), graduated summa cum laude from Oxford's Miami University in 1973.

G. Born and raised in Columbus, this author wrote 75 novels; two of them were made into movies.

H. A humorist and cartoonist, this Ohioan began his career at the *Columbus Dispatch* and later found success at the *New Yorker*.

I. This author graduated from the University of Dayton in 1949 and went to work as a reporter for the *Dayton Journal Herald* before finding fame in the 1960s with a syndicated column for the *Kettering-Oakwood Times*.

J. This Ohio writer occasionally worked as a dentist before he wrote his first story (about fishing) in 1902.

For answers, turn to page 304.

Did You Know?

• In April 2007, a four-year-old boy in West Alexandria was run over by a riding lawn mower. Police couldn't determine what had caused the accident; they could say only that one of his siblings may have done it, hopefully by accident. (The boy was okay.)

• In 2006, the world lawnmower land speed record was broken at the Bonneville Salt Flats in Utah. Speed: 81 mph. The champion was Bob Cleveland from Georgia. (But c'mon—his name's *Cleveland*.)

Funny Ohioans

"I hate women because they always know where things are."

—James Thurber

"Oh, you hate your job? Why didn't you say so? There's a support group for that. It's called EVERYBODY, and they meet at the bar."

—Drew Carey

"The embarrassing thing is that the salad dressing is outgrossing my films."

—Paul Newman

"Through years of experience I have found that air offers less resistance than dirt."

—Jack Nicklaus

"What I don't like about office Christmas parties is looking for a job the next day."

—Phyllis Diller

"I once shook hands with Pat Boone and my whole right side sobered up."

—Dean Martin

"Never accept a drink from a urologist."

—Erma Bombeck"

Good Ol' Youngstown

From art to ice cream to movies, Youngstown has given us some of our favorite things.

Town: Youngstown

Location: Mahoning County

Founding: 1797

Current population: 79, 271

Size: 34 square miles

County seat: Yes

What's in a name?

Youngstown was named for surveyor John Young, who settled the area in 1796.

Claims to Fame:

- In 1904, four brothers from Youngstown sold their family's delivery horse to buy a used Edison Kinetoscope projector. They showed their first movie, *The Great Train Robbery*, soon after, using the side of a tent as a screen. They soon took the movies on the road, traveling through small towns in the area and finally establishing a permanent nickelodeon in Pennsylvania in 1906. Then, in 1910, Harry, Albert, Sam, and Jack Warner set themselves up in Burbank, California, producing films through their new company: the Warner Bros. Studios.
- We can all thank Youngstown for Good Humor bars. In 1920, a local candy maker named Harry Burt created the

Jolly Boy Sucker, a piece of candy on a stick. That same year, he developed a smooth chocolate coating. Burt's son suggested combining the two treats by freezing ice cream onto wooden sticks and covering them with chocolate—and Good Humor bars were born.

- The first institution dedicated to American art opened in Youngstown in 1919. At the Butler Institute, visitors can see more than 20,000 pieces, including Winslow Homer's *Snap the Whip*, works by Mary Cassatt and Seth Eastman, and an entire gallery dedicated to American sports art.
- The city is the subject of Bruce Springsteen's song "Youngstown," which refers to the decline of Youngstown's steel mills in the late 1970s and the impact it had on the city's residents. It all began on September 19, 1977, when the president of Youngstown Sheet and Tube announced that most of the company was closing down because its aging mills were no longer efficient in the modern world. Rather than update the mills, though, the steel company shut down; others followed, and thousands of workers lost their jobs. In "Youngstown," Springsteen sings, "My sweet Jenny, I'm sinkin' down," a reference to the Jeanette furnace, a blast furnace that once stood along the Mahoning River at Youngstown Sheet and Tube's Brier Hill plant.

Did You Know?

According to MSNBC, Ohio has three of the best children's hospitals in the United States: Cincinnati Children's Hospital Medical Center, Rainbow Babies and Children's Hospital/Cleveland, and Columbus Children's Hospital.

A Daring Rescue

Here's how a raid to liberate a captured former slave contributed to the outbreak of the Civil War.

Hunting John Price

The year was 1858, and Kentuckian Anderson D. Jennings showed up in Oberlin, Ohio, looking for one of his escaped slaves. He didn't find the man, but he did spot 18-year-old John Price, who had escaped a couple of years before from the plantation of Jennings' neighbor, John G. Bacon. Jennings got permission from Bacon to recapture Price and then assembled a posse—which included a local sheriff and a U.S. marshal—to apprehend him and bring him back to Kentucky.

Bacon and Jennings were within their rights under federal law. The 1850 Fugitive Slave Law required federal authorities to help slave owners recapture escaped slaves . . . even if the slaves were living in free states. The law was controversial: Northern abolitionists called it unconstitutional and a violation of states' rights. And many local citizens did everything they could to subvert the authority of the Southern slave owners and the federal officials.

Resorting to Trickery

One of the Ohio towns most unwilling to follow the Fugitive Slave Law was Oberlin. Notoriously antislavery, white residents in Oberlin lived shoulder-to-shoulder with African Americans—freemen and fugitive slaves. Their children even went to school together.

The marshal working with Jennings was well aware of the antislavery sentiment in Oberlin, and the fact that John Price lived and worked within the town's limits posed a problem. So he hired a local boy named William Shakespeare Boynton, whose family was among the few slavery sympathizers in the area, to lure Price out of town by telling him he'd hire him to do some day labor digging potatoes. Once the two were outside of Oberlin's borders, the posse would pounce.

When Boynton approached Price and made his proposition, however, Price said he couldn't do it. He suggested another man who might be able to take the job, and when Price climbed into Boynton's buggy for the ride to and from the friend's home, Boynton steered the buggy out of town. The posse then caught up with the two and captured John Price.

Break Him Free!

The posse headed for nearby Wellington, where public sentiment was decidedly antislavery but less passionate than in Oberlin. From there, Jennings and his cohorts planned to put Price on a train and take him back to Kentucky. The posse skirted downtown Oberlin on their way to Wellington, but they ran into one of Oberlin's citizens on the road. When the man arrived home, he spread the word of John Price's capture.

The posse confined Price on the second floor above a tavern in Wellington to wait for the train. But as word got out, a crowd of about 200 abolitionists from Oberlin, Wellington, and other towns assembled outside. First, the antislavery advocates tried to talk Price's captors into letting the young man go. When that didn't work, they stormed the building and broke Price out. Then they put him on a wagon heading north. No one heard from John Price again, but he most likely escaped to freedom in Canada by taking a boat across Lake Erie.

Bushnell and Langston Take the Fall

In the wake of the rescue, a Cleveland grand jury (which included Lewis Boynton, young William Shakespeare Boynton's father) indicted 37 of the rescuers for violating the Fugitive Slave Law. Federal marshals rounded them up, and the U.S. government put them on trial.

The first defendant was Simeon Bushnell, a white store clerk and printer. He was convicted by a jury of unsympathetic antiabolitionists, sentenced to 60 days in prison, and ordered to pay a $600 fine. The second defendant, Charles Langston, was a black schoolteacher who demanded a new jury, arguing that he'd never receive a fair trial from a jury full of proslavery advocates. He got the new jury but was still found guilty. Langston was sentenced to 20 days in prison and given a $100 fine.

The Trial That Wasn't

Meanwhile, state officials arrested the posse, charging Jennings and three others with violating Ohio's kidnapping laws. The men were held in the county jail for eight days, until local slavery sympathizers posted bail for them. They spent the next two months waiting to go to trial.

While they were waiting, Jennings and his posse went to Canada to search for John Price, whom they hoped would testify at their trial. He was the only one who could verify Jennings and Mitchell's testimony that they'd "kidnapped" the right guy. (Taking a fugitive slave was legal, but rounding up random African Americans in free states was not.) Without Price, it looked like the posse would be convicted. But then the state officials holding them and the federal officials holding the remaining 35 rescuers reached a compromise: everyone would go free. The feds didn't want to proceed with so many expensive trials, and the state officials just wanted the Oberlin rescuers to be released. So it was. The remaining rescuers went home, and the posse skulked out of Oberlin.

Impact

The Oberlin-Wellington rescue case ended in a stalemate, but it drove the wedge of slavery deeper into the country's North-South rift. The tension between the national government and state governments over the Fugitive Slave Act remained unresolved, and the publicity the Oberlin-Wellington case received inflamed both pro and antislavery passions. It was only two years later that the first shots of the Civil War were fired at Fort Sumter.

To read more about the town of Oberlin, turn to page 85.
To read about Ohio and the Underground Railroad, turn to page 79.

Did You Know?

The Web site of Cleveland-born cartoonist and Captain Underpants creator Dav Pilkey reveals the answer to a question that perplexes many of his fans: How does he pronounce his first name? The answer is that you can pronounce it to rhyme with either "rave" or "have." The spelling was the result of a botched name tag for a job he had at Pizza Hut. (His real name is David.)

More Offbeat Ohio

Our discussion of Ohio attractions began on page 91. Here are a few more.

World's Largest Amish Buggy: Berlin

The world's largest Amish buggy is on display in the Holmes County town of Berlin. The county also has the largest Amish and Mennonite communities in the world. Coincidence? We think not. In 1994, local business owners decided to capitalize on tourism by building a giant Amish buggy and putting it on display in the showroom at Wendell August, a local gift shop. The vehicle is about 10 feet tall, nearly 14 feet wide, and weighs more than a ton.

Big Muskie: Reinersville

Between 1969 and 1991, Big Muskie, the world's largest dragline crane, cleared rock and soil to expose coal seams at sites in southeastern Ohio—the crane cleared more than 608 million cubic yards over its lifetime. It was retired in 1991 and dismantled in 1999, but Big Muskie's enormous bucket is still on display at Miner's Memorial Park in Reinersville. Although it once held up to 220 cubic yards of dirt (that's 325 tons), the bucket's most impressive cargo was the entire McConnelsville Marching Band; a picture of that feat is on display at the park.

The Cow with Two Brains: Brookville

In the basement of the Brookville Historical Society's Spitler House, there's a freak attraction of bovine proportions. The story begins in 1941 when Spotty the dairy cow, owned by local farmers Willie and Nellie Rasor, gave birth to a two-headed calf. Sadly, the little critter died almost immediately after being born. Seeing an opportunity, however, the Rasor family had the calf stuffed, erected billboards along Route 40 to advertise the display, and charged visitors ten cents to view the animal. They later donated the calf to the town's historical society. Still open for monthly tours, the house's basement features a cute (if not creepy) barn scene where the two-headed calf stands on a pile of hay. Andy D. Day—a stuffed and mounted bull's head with four eyes, two noses, and four horns—looks out from behind the stall door.

The Confederate Raider's Head: Dover

A wax replica of a man's head sits in the refrigerator at the Dover Historical Society. It's not a prop for a local horror movie. It's the likeness of Confederate Captain William Quantrill, who fought a guerrilla campaign against Union forces during the Civil War. Quantrill and his soldiers terrorized folks from Kansas to Kentucky, ambushing wagons, destroying telegraph lines, raiding farms, and killing many along the way. Union troops finally shot Quantrill in 1865, and for the next 130 years, his remains were mired in controversy. Initially, Quantrill was buried in an unmarked Kentucky grave, but in 1887, his childhood friend William Scott dug up the bones to reunite them with Quantrill's family in Dover. Quantrill's mother claimed to have buried her son at the Fourth Street Cemetery in 1889, but it's hard to say what actually ended up in the grave because Scott kept the skull and bones, hoping to sell them. No one was interested in buying, though. Scott's son eventually inherited the skull and gave it to a group of teenage boys who used it in initiation rites for their club.

In 1972, the fraternity donated the skull to the Dover Historical Society, and it was later buried in the Quantrill family plot, but not before Kent State University's anthropology department made two casts of the skull, complete with facial reconstructions. The university gave one of the casts to the Dover Historical Society's museum, and it remains there today in an antique refrigerator to prevent it from melting and warping. The peculiar history and curiosity that surrounds Quantrill's skull is a curse and a blessing for the museum: it attracts visitors, but museum officials wince at being associated with the dastardly rebel. The university kept the second cast.

For the last installment of "Offbeat Ohio," turn to page 235.

Did You Know?

After the floodwaters receded from Dayton in 1913, an employee with the city's Power and Light Company stumbled on a light bulb left in the debris. It didn't work, so there wasn't any real reason to keep it. But it was a relic from the disaster, so the employee saved it. In 2004, the Boonshoft Museum of Discovery put the light bulb on display during an exhibit titled "Curious Collections: An Exhibit Beyond Bizarre." The exhibit soon closed, and the light bulb is now stored in the museum's basement.

A Radio Adventure

Cincinnati businessman Powel Crosley Jr. made his mark on the airwaves but never found success selling the product he really loved: cars.

The First Step

In 1899, Cincinnati lawyer Powel Crosley bet his 12-year-old son, Powel Jr., $10 that he couldn't build a working automobile. Powel the younger took the bet. Short of funds, the boy borrowed $8 from his 10-year-old brother Lewis and went to work, buying parts and assembling the car. He used a buckboard wagon as the body, got an electric motor running, borrowed batteries from the local opera house, and hired a blacksmith to make a few miscellaneous parts.

Finally, the big day came. Lewis drove the car to the post office and back, and Powel Jr. collected his prize. He paid Lewis back the $8, and the boys split the profits, a dollar each.

Career Hopping

Crosley's interest in cars continued as he grew. As a student at the Ohio Military Institute, he dabbled in building cars in his free time. After graduation in 1905, he enrolled in the engineering program at the University of Cincinnati. School wasn't his strong suit, though. Crosley flunked out in less than a year and decided to study law instead. But he only lasted two years in that program before he dropped out of school entirely.

Crosley then went to work selling bonds to downtown businessmen, but he remained fixated on cars. In 1906, he undertook his first (professional) automobile-building venture: he built a car called the Marathon Six, which he hoped would compete with Ford's inexpensive Model N. He wanted to sell an affordable car so that every American could take to the road. But he was able to finish only one prototype before his financing dried up. The Marathon Six never got off the ground.

Crosley remained in the automobile industry. He worked in an automobile shop, advertised for a racing team, and built motorcycle sidecars before finally buying a mail-order auto parts business in 1916. That company was his first real success; in two years, Crosley sold more than $1 million in auto parts.

Pups and Harko

It was a completely new medium, though, that would make Crosley famous. In the 1920s, his son, Powel III, told his dad that he wanted a radio, so the pair went shopping. They discovered that the cheapest radio they could find cost an incredible $130! Horrified by the price, Crosley decided to build one himself. He ordered a pamphlet called "The ABCs of Radio" and built his son a radio for $35.

From there, he decided to manufacture affordable radios for the mass market. In 1921, he put out his first portable radio, called the Harko; it cost only $35. The Harko was a hit; in the first year, Crosley's company filled $5,000 worth of orders.

Next, Crosley bought a radio company and renamed it the Crosley Radio Corporation. He hired his brother Lewis to oversee manufacturing, and Lewis introduced the assembly line to the creation of Crosley radios. The company was soon the world's largest radio manufacturer, turning out 5,000 units a day.

The company's next product, the Crosley Pup, was even more successful than the Harko. The portable radio retailed for just $9.75, and advertisements used a terrier named Bonzo to hawk the product. Some customers who sent in positive reviews of the radio even got a free puppy. Crosley sold 14,000 Pups in just five weeks.

The Nation's Station

When the Harko hit the market, Crosley had seen another business opportunity: radio programming. Thanks to his affordable radios, more consumers had the hardware, but there wasn't much for them to listen to. Crosley first tried to remedy this with a 20-watt transmitter in his own home, where he played his own records on a wind-up Victrola. But by 1925, he'd increased the strength of the broadcast to 5,000 watts. At that level, his station—WLW—could be heard as far away as New York and Baltimore. Over the next decade, he continued to boost the signal, and finally, in 1934, Crosley built an 831-foot transmission tower in Mason, Ohio, and amped up the signal to 500,000 watts. According to some people, the signal was so strong that any metal object would play WLW programming: milking machines, barbed-wire fences, even rain gutters. Neighbors also complained that the strength of the radio signal made their lights flicker and created power surges in their homes. In 1939, Crosley lowered the wattage to 50,000, where it remains today.

WLW became a staple in American broadcasting, earning the nickname "the Nation's Station." People all over the country could tune in to hear big stars like Rosemary and Betty Clooney, Andy Williams, and Red Skelton. WLW also aired *Ma Perkins*, one of the first radio soap operas, and launched the career of Rod Serling of *Twilight Zone* fame. During World War II, the United States government aired the Voice of America on WLW. The ongoing program broadcast information about America's progress during the war to countries around the world. Adolf Hitler, angry that American propaganda was able to reach such a wide audience, called Voice of America the "Cincinnati Liars."

Back to the Car

In the late 1930s, Crosley had tried again to get back to his first love: manufacturing an affordable automobile. He launched the Crosley Car in 1939; it retailed at $325 (for the coupe) and $350 (for the sedan) and was the cheapest model on the market. But it was also tiny—just 10 feet long, with wheels 12 inches in diameter and a 4-gallon gas tank. It wasn't very powerful, either, and had trouble climbing hills with a full load of passengers.

Crosley's later models were bigger and more powerful; he even created the first sports car—the Hotshot, a convertible two-seater with a folding canvas top and headlights mounted in detachable pods. But after World War II, American consumers wanted bigger cars. Crosley's car company closed in 1952 after selling about 75,000 cars. Crosley retired soon after and died in 1961.

Did You Know?

Two musicians you probably didn't know were from Ohio:

• Dwight Yoakam. Not all country music stars are from the South or the Southwest. Yoakam was raised in Columbus and attended Ohio State.

• Al Jardine. One of the founding members of the Beach Boys, Jardine was born in Lima. He later learned about surfing and sunshine when he moved to California in high school.

Name That Town

From Bucyrus to Xenia to Defiance, many Ohio towns have been named for famous places and people. Here are some of the most notable place names in the Buckeye State.

Bellefontaine

According to rumor, Bellefontaine gets its name from nearby springs that made the area ideal for settlement. The word *belle-fontaine* is French for "beautiful fountain."

Bucyrus

This town takes its name from the Greeks' famous enemies, the Persians. Colonel James Kilbourne, who laid out the town, merged the words "beautiful" and "Cyrus." (Cyrus the Great was a famous king who created the Persian Empire and fought the Babylonians.) Why Kilbourne chose to the name the town after "beautiful Cyrus," though, no one knows.

Cairo

A reference to the famous city in Egypt, this name is popular enough that there are two Cairos in Ohio. They can be found in Allen and Stark counties.

Defiance

Defiance gets its name from Fort Defiance, the last American fort on the country's early western boundary. Built in 1794 by the order of General "Mad" Anthony Wayne, the fort was named as such because it was so well protected that Wayne challenged the "English, Indians, and all the devils of hell" to try and take the fort. (It never fell.)

Friendship

Located in southwestern Ohio, this name shows its founders' intentions.

Gallipolis

Another city with a French influence is Gallipolis. The name means "city of the Gauls" in Greek and was named by French immigrants who escaped revolutionary France and settled there.

Hicksville

A Midwestern town named Hicksville begets a chuckle from many, but this one gets its name, like many towns do, from its founder. When land in Ohio was opened up for sale in 1820, a pair of shipping merchants from New York, named Henry W. Hicks and Samuel Isaac Smith, purchased the area that became Hicksville. Why? They felt the region between Defiance and Fort Wayne, Indiana, needed a town.

Knockemstiff

The town has found fame (or infamy) in Ohio lore for having a haunted 18th-century cemetery and a haunted cliff where a person leaped to his death. But the town's name probably comes from one of two things: a massive brawl in a town tavern or the fighting ability of its young men.

Lima

Well known for being one of the first U.S. oil-boom towns, Lima was named after Lima, Peru, because the quinine bark used to treat malaria in and around the town came from that South American city. The flat terrain of northwest Ohio included many swampy areas prone to mosquitoes and malaria, something the new settlers struggled with during the 1800s and making quinine an invaluable resource.

Mecca

The people who founded this town in 1811 named it Mecca because they'd finally completed their search for a new home, the way Middle Eastern pilgrims completed their religious journeys to the more famous Mecca.

Medina

The pioneers who settled this area south of Cleveland originally wanted to call their town Mecca, but there was already an Ohio town with that name (see above). So instead, they chose Medina, the burial place of the Islamic prophet Muhammad and a town well known for being a biblical stop for righteous pilgrims. The town's founders chose the name because, during this period, biblical place names were popular.

For more towns, turn to page 242.

Did You Know?

Harry Andrews, who single-handedly constructed an elaborate "castle" he called Chateau La Roche in Loveland, was Ohio's oldest living notary. (He charged only 25 cents for his services.) He also built the road that leads up to the castle, and constructed a secret room in the castle's garden. The room was *so* secret that no one—not even the people who lived in the castle—knew it was there until it fell down from neglect years after Andrews' death. Its entrance was carefully hidden among the arches in the garden's wall.

The Secret Life of Carolyn Keene

The popular Nancy Drew book series was officially authored by "Carolyn Keene," a pseudonym for several writers who crafted the novels. The first—and, by many accounts, most famous—of those ghostwriters was Toledo newspaperwoman Mildred Wirt Benson.

Finding Nancy's Voice

In 1929, Edward Stratemeyer, head of a book production company called the Stratemeyer Syndicate, decided to create a series of detective-adventure stories to be published by Grosset & Dunlap. Stratemeyer had already successfully marketed the Hardy Boys series and now imagined a single spunky heroine who would appeal to girls. He suggested several names for the protagonist, including Stella Strong, Nan Nelson, and Diana Dare. The publishers, however, liked Nan Drew, which they lengthened to Nancy Drew.

All of Stratemeyer's books were written by ghostwriters, working writers who crafted the novels from outlines provided by the syndicate and authored under a pseudonym. The ghostwriters were paid a flat fee and owned neither the stories nor the character. For the Nancy Drew series, Stratemeyer chose the pseudonym Carolyn Keene.

All he needed was a writer, and Stratemeyer already had one in mind. She had been churning out young-adult books in some of his other series for a few years and was fast and efficient. Her name was Mildred Wirt.

From Hawkeye to Buckeye

Mildred Wirt (later Mildred Wirt Benson) was born Mildred Augustine in Iowa—the Hawkeye State—in 1905. She grew up in the small town of Ladora and received a bachelor's degree in journalism from the University of Iowa. In 1927, she got a master's degree from the same school, the first woman to do so. While working on her graduate studies, Mildred started writing for the Stratemeyer Syndicate; her first books were in the Ruth Fielding series, which revolved around a movie star and director who solved crimes.

During this time, she also married fellow journalism student Asa Wirt and moved with him to Cleveland, where he'd gotten a job with the Associated Press. It was there that she was assigned the task of crafting the first Nancy Drew mystery.

Anonymous (But Hard) Work

Stratemeyer gave Wirt her first Nancy Drew assignment in 1929. It was for a book titled *The Secret of the Old Clock*, about Nancy Drew's search for a missing will. Wirt wrote the book in only a few weeks and then sent it back to Stratemeyer for editing. (One of the Syndicate's most consistent complaints was that Mildred's Nancy was too sassy.) She was paid $125 for that first book. Over the years, the payments shrank (to $85 during the Great Depression) and grew, but she never received more than $250 for a Nancy Drew project—no matter how many books were sold or how many movies and TV shows were made.

The syndicate also required that its writers never disclose their role in crafting books in the series. This allowed Stratemeyer to easily use new writers on books for old series.

From Drews to News

Mildred and Asa Wirt moved to Toledo in 1938 when Asa was transferred there by the AP. Mildred continued writing for Nancy Drew and other series; she also took a newspaper job at the *Toledo Times*. In 1947, Asa Wirt died after a prolonged illness. A little later, Mildred fell in love with George Benson, one of the editors at the *Toledo Times*; she married him in 1950.

In the early 1950s, the Stratemeyer Syndicate, beset by financial problems, started doing almost all of its writing in-house. By that time, Mildred Wirt Benson had written 22 of the first 25 books in the Nancy Drew series. But Harriet Stratemeyer Adams, Edward's daughter, took over the writing for the series.

Into the Limelight, Finally

Mildred continued writing for the *Toledo Times*, and her connection to Nancy Drew remained a secret until 1980, when Grosset & Dunlap sued Harriet Adams for copyright infringement. She'd moved the Nancy Drew series to Simon & Schuster in 1979 because that publisher offered her a better financial deal. The case went to trial and forced the syndicate to acknowledge the real people behind Carolyn Keene. At least six writers had worked on Nancy Drew books over the years, with Mildred Wirt Benson being one of the most prolific. In the end, the court found for the Stratemeyer Syndicate.

Mildred Wirt Benson died in Toledo in 2002 at the age of 96. By then, she had written thousands of newspaper articles, hundreds of short stories, and 130 books. She worked right up until the end, handing in her final column the day she died.

Sing A Song

How well do you know the music of the Buckeye State?

1. "Ohio," performed by Crosby, Stills, Nash, and Young, is a protest song written in reaction to what?

A. The Vietnam War

B. President Richard Nixon's Watergate scandal

C. The Kent State shootings

2. The Pretenders released the song "My City Was Gone" in 1983. Which member of the band is actually from the Buckeye State?

A. Chrissie Hynde

B. Pete Farndon

C. Martin Chambers

3. The 1936 Blue Sky Boys' version of "Banks of the Ohio"—an 1800s murder ballad—appeared in the soundtrack of which 1973 film?

A. *Paper Moon*

B. *Live and Let Die*

C. *The Exorcist*

4. In 2003, Devo, which formed in Akron in 1972, produced a new version of their popular song "Whip It," to be used in television commercials for which product?

A. Cool Whip

B. Jell-O

C. Swiffer

5. In what year did Canton native Macy Gray win a Grammy Award for her song, "I Try"?

A. 2000

B. 2001

C. 2002

6. Industry rumors claim that the Cleveland-based band Nine Inch Nails got its name from a few inspirations. Which is *not* one of them?

A. The nails of the female record holder from *Guinness Book of World Records*

B. The fingernails on Freddy Kruger

C. The spikes from the story of Jesus' crucifixion

7. Which of the following Ohio musicians performed for Nelson Mandela at his 70th birthday tribute in 1988?

A. Marilyn Manson

B. Sawyer Brown

C. Tracy Chapman

For answers, turn to page 305.

Did You Know?

One of Toledo's best-known hangouts is Tony Pacos, a hot dog chain made famous by the character of Klinger (Jamie Farr), who talked up the dogs on the TV series *M*A*S*H.*

Just a Guy Who Makes Hamburgers

In 1969, when Dave Thomas opened the first Wendy's Old Fashioned Hamburgers in Columbus, he dreamed of one day having three or four restaurants in the city. Today there are 70 Wendy's restaurants in Columbus and more than 5,000 worldwide.

Dave Thomas was born in New Jersey in 1932, but much of his childhood was spent moving around the country with his adoptive father, Rex, who was always looking for work. (Dave's adoptive mother, Auleva, died when he was six.) Dinners out with his father were among Dave's fondest childhood memories, and when he was eight, he decided that he would one day open his own restaurant.

Learning the Biz

Dave got his first restaurant job—working the counter at the Regas Restaurant in Knoxville, Tennessee—when he was just 12, and he quickly immersed himself in the business. The young man was driven and quickly learned from his bosses and coworkers the essentials of the restaurant business: to accept nothing but the best standards in quality, customer service, and attention to detail.

In 1948, Dave's father decided to move again, but the now-16-year-old chose to stay behind in Fort Wayne, Indiana, where he'd taken a job at the Hobby House restaurant. He enjoyed the work and looked up to Phil Clauss, the restaurant's manager. At the Hobby House, Dave worked every job there was—from busboy to the front counter to the kitchen. Clauss taught Dave how to perform each position well so that he would know every aspect of running a restaurant.

It was also in Fort Wayne that Dave met Colonel Harland Sanders (of Kentucky Fried Chicken fame). In 1962, he went to work for Sanders, taking over four failing KFC restaurants in Columbus. Dave turned the restaurants around and eventually sold them back to Sanders at a profit. He used the money to open his own restaurant.

On His Own

The year was 1969, and Dave Thomas had spent more than 20 years working on the floor, behind the counter, in the kitchen, and behind the desk of various restaurants. He was more than qualified to start his own, and on November 15, Thomas opened the first Wendy's Old Fashioned Hamburgers on Broad Street in Columbus. He named the restaurant after his daughter Melinda Lou, whose nickname was "Wendy."

That first venture was so popular with Columbus residents that Thomas opened a second restaurant in November 1970; two more followed in 1971. By 1972, the first Wendy's outside Columbus opened, and then the franchise expanded beyond Ohio with the introduction of a Wendy's in Indianapolis. Thomas' success was the result of several things, the most prominent of which were creating a family-friendly atmosphere, ensuring that the food was made to order, and using fresh ingredients. He also spoke of five values to live by—in business and in life:

1. "Quality is our recipe." The burgers need to taste good, of course, but the rule also applies to way employees should live their lives—with quality in mind.
2. "Do the right thing." Integrity was paramount on the list of values one possessed.

3. “Treat people with respect.” Thomas simplified this golden rule as “Just be nice.”
4. “Profit is not a dirty word.” It resulted in growth, new opportunities, and putting oneself in a position for number five . . .
5. “Give something back.” Dave Thomas donated millions of dollars to various causes and established the Dave Thomas Foundation for Adoption, which gives assistance to adoptive parents and children across the country.

That Famous Commercial

By the early 1980s, Wendy’s franchises had spread across the country, but their profits were decreasing due to competition . So Thomas and the Wendy’s team decided to use television commercials to revive the business. Perhaps most memorable were the spots that featured 81-year-old Clara Peller shouting “Where’s the beef?” after examining the hamburger of a rival chain and finding its beef patty dwarfed by a large bun. Peller’s demand soon became a part of U.S. pop culture. A Nashville deejay named Coyote McCloud recorded a song called “Where’s the Beef,” and presidential candidate Walter Mondale even worked the phrase into his 1984 campaign, questioning the résumé of his rival, Gary Hart.

Thomas himself also starred in several Wendy’s commercials in the late 1980s. Wendy’s executives thought that Thomas (who had retired in 1982) could best convey what was great about his restaurant and its hamburgers. Thomas appeared in several commercials to pitch his product, and consumers were quick to catch on. Wendy’s profits started to rise again. Today, Wendy’s (based in Dublin, Ohio) is the number-three fast-food chain in the world (behind McDonald’s and Burger King).

Dave's Legacy

Dave Thomas died on January 8, 2002, at the age of 69 and is buried in Columbus' Union Cemetery, but he left behind more than the successful Wendy's chain. He had long worked to raise awareness of the needs of adoptive children and had established the Dave Thomas Foundation for Adoption in 1992. The foundation's aim was to increase the number of U.S. children who were moved out of foster care and into adoptive homes. Over the last 15 years, the foundation has found much success, serving more than 140,000 children and raising more than $23 million.

Did You Know?

The Wright brothers were from Ohio but made their first successful flight in North Carolina, so both states try to claim the duo as their own. Over the years, a détente has evolved with Ohio being recognized as the place where the brothers lived and developed their inventions and North Carolina being the site of the first flight. To document this, both states print an homage to the Wrights on their license plates: Ohio includes the slogan "Birthplace of Aviation Pioneers" or "Birthplace of Aviation," and North Carolina's is "First in Flight." Also, both Ohio and North Carolina use an image of the Wright brothers' glider *Flyer I* on their state quarters.

Weird Ohio

More strange tales from the Buckeye State.

Putting the "Fanatic" Back in Fan

Brent Huffines and his wife Kattie were preparing for the birth of their first child in 2007 when the subject of names came up. Brent knew what he wanted: Tressel Hayes Huffines. Kattie, however, wasn't so sure she wanted her firstborn to be named after the popular Ohio State coaches Jim Tressel and Woody Hayes. "I laughed. I thought he was joking. I was *shocked* to learn he was serious," said Kattie. But she relented.

Brent, ecstatic that he'd convinced his wife to go with his name choice, explained his reasoning to reporters: "If nothing else, it assures the Buckeye tradition stays in the family. Can you imagine someone named Tressel Hayes going to Michigan for college?" He then added, almost to himself: "Tressel Hayes Huffines—sounds as sweet as an OSU victory over Michigan!"

The Liberty Scream

The small town of Liberty is the quintessential quiet Midwestern town . . . except for the mysterious scream. Almost everyone in town has heard it—Jamie Young even recorded it. "It scared me," she told reporters. "I didn't want to finish my walk."

Experts have studied the recording, yet no one is quite sure what it is. It's definitely no known animal, and there's no evidence that it's a ghost. But at least the mysterious scream hasn't done anything more than scream. "I don't think it's going to wind up grabbing any of us and running off with us," says flea market dealer Walt Wilson.

The NASCAR Senior Circuit

On a cold winter night in January 2007, police embarked on a high-speed chase through Madison and Henry counties that could have come from a Hollywood movie. The car was driving erratically, swerving in and out of oncoming traffic, and reaching speeds of up to 110 mph. When the car finally pulled into a truck stop south of New Castle, officers surrounded the vehicle and ordered the driver to "come out with your hands up!" Expecting the worst, they drew their guns. But instead of a hardened criminal, they got Marcia Cashel, a 72-year-old retired schoolteacher. When asked why she fled, Cashel told them that she didn't believe they were really police officers.

If You Don't Like the Way I Drive, Stay Off the Sidewalk

Dondi Bowles of Vermillion was arrested for driving while intoxicated . . . on his lawnmower. Officers noticed the 20-horsepower riding mower cruising down the sidewalk on a Friday night in May 2006. Bowles, 50, admitted he'd had a few beers but said, "I didn't know you could get a DUI on a lawnmower. If I knew that, I would've walked." (That would have taken only slightly less time for Bowles to get home; the mower's top speed is barely 10 mph.) The police informed him that driving any vehicle while impaired—even in your own yard—is illegal.

For more weird Ohio stories, turn to page 297.

Endangered Ohio

There are 128 species of animals on the endangered species list in the state of Ohio . . . and nine on the extinct list.

Danger!

The state of Ohio contains the native habitats of about 56 species of mammals, 200 species of birds, 84 species and subspecies of amphibians and reptiles, 170 species of fish, more than 100 different mollusks, and 20 types of crustaceans. On top of that are thousands of species of insects and other invertebrates. Most are not in any foreseeable danger, but, as in so many places around the world today, some are in trouble.

The Ohio Department of Natural Resources divides those species into six different categories: endangered, threatened, concern, special interest, extirpated, and extinct.

What Do Those Terms Mean?

Endangered: A native species threatened with complete extermination from the state due to one or more causes, such as habitat loss, pollution, predation, interspecific competition, or disease.

Threatened: A species whose survival in Ohio is not in immediate danger, but to which a threat exists. (And it may soon be added to the endangered list if the threat persists.)

Species of Concern: A species that might become threatened in Ohio under continued or increased stress.

Special Interest: A species whose range is naturally outside Ohio but is capable of breeding in the state. These species are relatively few in number.

Extirpated: A species that was found in Ohio at the time of European settlement but which has since disappeared from the state.

Extinct: A species that was found in Ohio at the time of European settlement but has since disappeared from its entire range.

Endangered

The animals on Ohio's endangered list include 128 species divided into 14 different groups: birds, mammals, fish, beetles, moths, and so on. (Some, but not all, also appear on the list of federally protected animals.) Here are some of those animal groups:

Mammals

Indiana bat
Allegheny woodrat
Bobcat
Black bear
Snowshoe hare

Reptiles

Copperbelly water snake
Eastern plains garter snake
Timber rattlesnake
Eastern massasauga
Lake Erie water snake

Amphibians

Eastern hellbender
Blue spotted salamander
Green salamander
Cave salamander
Eastern spadefoot

Birds

American bittern
Bald eagle
Bewick's wren
Loggerhead shrike

Northern harrier
Peregrine falcon
King rail
Sandhill crane
Piping plover
Common tern
Black tern
Yellow-bellied sapsucker
Golden-winged warbler
Kirtland's warbler
Lark sparrow
Osprey
Trumpeter swan
Snowy egret
Cattle egret

The list continues with 24 species of fish, 24 mullosks, 13 types of dragonfly, 13 moth species, and many more.

Threatened

There are 47 different species on Ohio's threatened species list. They include the barn owl, the spotted turtle, the mud salamander, and the brook trout. There are 90 more on the species of concern list, including such animals as the pygmy shrew, the badger, the great egret, the lake whitefish, and the precious underwing moth. The special interest list (the mostly out-of-state species) is made up of 41 entries and includes several bird species and one each of moth and butterfly species.

The extirpated species list has 34 kinds of animals that still flourish in other parts of North America but are no longer found in Ohio. This list includes the bison, timber wolf, mountain lion, porcupine, common raven, greater prairie chicken, several fish and mollusk species, and the mustard white butterfly.

Extinct

There are nine animal species that existed in Ohio (and other places) when the European arrived but, to the best of anyone's knowledge, no longer exist anywhere in the world. The animals on this list are the passenger pigeon, Carolina parakeet, harelip sucker, blue pike, leafshell mollusk, forkshell mollusk, round snuffbox mollusk, and Cincinnati riffleshell Scioto pigtoe mollusk.

Some of those animals, like the passenger pigeon and the round snuffbox (a mollusk once found in Lake Erie), were wiped out a long time ago. But others, like the blue pike, are recent extinctions: the Lake Erie fish was declared extinct in 1983. Those nine forever-gone animals are a reminder of the dangers of ignoring the situation for the 128 species on Ohio's endangered list—and those on the threatened list, too.

Ohioans who want to learn more can go to the Web site for the Ohio Department of Natural Resources, Division of Wildlife. That agency offers volunteer programs to help clean up rivers, streams, woods, and whatever areas need maintaining for the wildlife that call them home. There are lots of plants in trouble, too—so if you're more of a plant person, you can check out the Web site to learn about ways to help them. Good luck, Ohio.

Did You Know?

More great inventions by Ohioans:

- Charles F. Brush invented the arc lamp, used for electric city lights in 1879.
- Harvey Firestone (founder of Firestone Tire) developed pneumatic, smooth-ride car tires.
- Claude H. Foster invented shock absorbers and the car horn.
- Photographer Andrew Iddings developed the 3-D stereoptic camera.
- John McTammany invented the player piano.

The Wright Brothers . . . and Sister

When we think of aviation pioneers, most of us think of Wilbur and Orville. But hey! What about Katharine?

One Big Family

Midwesterners Milton and Susan Wright had seven children: Reuchlin, Lorin, Wilbur, Orville, and Katharine (twins Otis and Ida died in infancy). The family moved several times during the late 1800s before finally settling in Dayton, Ohio.

Life in the Wright household was great for the kids. Orville Wright once wrote, "We were lucky enough to grow up in an environment where there was always much encouragement to children to pursue intellectual interests; to investigate whatever aroused curiosity." For Orville and his brother Wilbur, curiosity often turned to flight. When the boys were young, their father gave them a toy helicopter, a little wooden contraption with a rotor. They played with it until it broke and then built their own. It was their first flying machine.

From Bikes to Planes

The two youngest Wright brothers, of course, went on to be famous. They first owned and operated a successful bicycle shop in Dayton and then turned their attention to airplanes. The brothers didn't actually invent the airplane, though. Fixed-wing aircrafts had been around since the early 1800s, and Leonardo da Vinci had dreamed up plans for a flying machine a lot earlier than that. But those early aircrafts were missing an important component: a steering control. The Wright brothers solved that problem. At the turn of the 20th century, they headed to North Carolina to test their controlled glider. In 1903, Orville flew and managed to steer the first controlled aircraft. A year later, they added a motor and went into the airplane business.

And Then There Were Three

This is all common knowledge, of course. What most people don't realize is that the Wright duo was actually a trio. Katharine Wright was the youngest of the Wright children, and she grew up particularly close to Orville and Wilbur. She was also an invaluable participant in the brothers' flying success. It's likely that Katharine helped to calculate many of the flight formulas Orville and Wilbur used to get their planes off the ground. She sewed the fabric wing covers on the early gliders, worked in the bicycle shop while the brothers tinkered with their flying machines, and paid the bills, cooked, and cleaned so that Wilbur and Orville could concentrate on their inventions.

An Exceptional Spokeswoman

Katharine was also a spokesperson for her brothers' airplane business. Orville and Wilbur were shy and did their best to avoid the limelight. So Katharine traveled extensively on her brothers' behalf, promoting their successes and helping to make them famous. She raised funds for the brothers' ventures by giving speeches and soliciting donations. She was so well loved as the Wright brothers' ambassador that she became the first woman to attend a meeting of the Aero Club de France (a gentleman's club for aviation buffs) and received numerous accolades from the French government, including the Legion of Honor medal.

Katharine even started a fashion craze. When she flew with her brothers, she tied a rope around the hem of her skirt to keep it from blowing up. Soon, most other women who flew on airplanes tied down their skirts as well.

A Brother Scorned

So why is it that Katharine's contributions never made the history books? Many people believe it's because she and Orville had a falling-out later in life.

Katharine was one of her brothers' most vocal advocates, but she also had a life of her own. She was the only Wright child to graduate from college. In 1898, she received a teaching degree from Oberlin College and then got a job as a Latin teacher at a local high school. Katharine served as president of Dayton's Young Women's League and the Oberlin Alumni Group. She was a founding member of the Dayton Women's Club and helped organize a women's suffrage march in Dayton. In 1926, she got married.

It was this last event that led Orville to nearly disown his sister. According to legend, Wilbur, Orville, and Katharine were so close that they'd made a pact never to marry. After Wilbur's death in 1912, Katharine and Orville kept house together in Oakwood, Ohio, and maintained their pact. But in the mid-1920s, when she was in her 50s, Katharine got caught up in a romance with a former schoolmate. After a long courtship, the couple finally decided to marry—much to Orville's annoyance.

Orville was so angry with his sister that he refused to attend her wedding and didn't speak to her for more than two years afterward. It wasn't until she was on her deathbed in 1929 that they reconciled.

Jilted Orville Rewrites History

Many historians say these bitter feelings explain Orville's campaign to erase his sister from the history books. Just as she was starting to gain recognition for her work in early aviation—at about the same time she got married—Orville wrote letters to journalists claiming that Katharine's contributions to the invention of the airplane had been exaggerated.

Although it isn't clear how far Orville really went to discredit his sister (at his request, all his papers were burned when he died), it is clear that Katharine's role in the Wright brothers' legacy has been ignored through the years. It's only in the past decade that historians have finally begun to recognize the contributions of Katharine Wright.

Did You Know?

In 1919, Sherwood Anderson published *Winesburg, Ohio*, one of the most depressing novels about Ohio to date. A loosely tied collection of stories, *Winesburg* depicts the town's residents as they describe their lives and broken dreams to a newspaper reporter—one character has deformed hands, while another was banished from a nearby town after a fatal accident. Fortunately for Winesburg residents, Anderson based the book on his hometown of Clyde, not the real Winesburg, Ohio.

Ohio Wisdom

"Many of life's failures are people who did not realize how close they were to success when they gave up."

—Thomas A. Edison

"Destiny is no matter of chance. It is a matter of choice. It is not a thing to be waited for, it is a thing to be achieved."

—William Jennings Bryan

"I'm a firm believer that in the theory that people only do their best at things they truly enjoy. It is difficult to excel at something you don't enjoy."

—Jack Nicklaus

"If wrinkles must be written on our brows, let them not be written upon the heart. The spirit should never grow old."

—James Garfield

"Chase after the truth like all hell and you'll free yourself, even though you never touch its coat tails."

—Clarence Darrow

"If birds can glide for long periods of time, then why can't I?"

—Orville Wright

"There never was a time when, in my opinion, some way could not be found to prevent the drawing of the sword."

—Ulysses S. Grant

Ohio Comes First

Ohio is home to the first ambulance service (1865), the first city to use police cars (Akron), and the first hot dog (1900). Embedded in this puzzle are four more firsts claimed by the Buckeye State. *(For answers, turn to page 306.)*

Across

1 Blues singer Bessie
6 Duds
10 French cleric
14 Davis of *Evening Shade*
15 Not worth ___
16 Auteur's work
17 Uneven, as a road
18 Mickey ___ (loaded drink)
19 Scandal
20 Ohio first
23 Orally
25 Rejection of church dogma
26 Ohio had the first professional, salaried one
30 It's up your sleeve
31 Prince of the desert
32 Philosopher of dialectics
36 Online acronym for laughing
38 Flower leaf
40 Dems, dose, and ___
41 Conductor Dorati
43 Surrenders
45 Mail carrier's rd.
46 Another Ohio first
49 Michener book
52 Feed as cows and horses do
53 Ohio's Armstrong was the first
57 Ciera or Bravada maker
58 Actress Skye
59 Staff mark for violas
63 Adversaries
64 Guns the engine
65 Actress-dancer Rivera
66 Golfer's cry
67 Ben & Jerry's alternative
68 Seeps

Down

1 Blubber
2 School at E. Lansing
3 Suffix with hero
4 Move through the tulips, in song
5 Carnie cry
6 Hook for landing large fish
7 "Yeah, that's gonna happen!"
8 Rice-A-___
9 Former UN under-secretary-general Ralph
10 1978 Triple Crown winner
11 "Rubbish!"

12 Doldrums
13 Like some calories
21 *Hitchhiker* writer Douglas
22 Remini of *The King of Queens*
23 Homer king Hank
24 Old TV commercial letters
26 Theda of silent films
27 Parasite
28 Pariah
29 Swap
33 Jami of *Still Standing*
34 Lauder of lotions
35 Wolfish look
37 Game invented by American Indians
39 "___ my Eggo!"
42 Rested
44 Hot desert wind
47 Literary ridicule
48 Quixote squire Panza
49 "Ciao!"
50 Kipling bear
51 Rear for rear
54 Worked on a bed
55 The sixth deadly sin
56 Army chow
60 Claiborne or Smith
61 Sorbonne summer
62 They're between mi's and so's

Meet Me in Cincy

From abolition to art, modern Cincinnati reflects the city's varied and colorful history.

Town: Cincinnati

Location: Hamilton County

Founding: 1788

Current population: 317,361

Size: 78 square miles

County seat: Yes

What's in a Name?

A surveying party founded Cincinnati in 1788. The members named it Losantiville, a name that took words from French, Latin, and German and meant "the city opposite the mouth of the Licking River." Two years later, Scotsman and Continental Congress president Arthur St. Clair renamed the town "Cincinnati" after an exclusive and historic social society to which he belonged: the Society of the Cincinnati. That name stuck.

Claims to Fame:

- Cincinnati boasts the largest U.S. collection of Italianate architecture. Most of it is located in the city's Over-the-Rhine neighborhood, the largest national historical district in the United States.
- The city has several nicknames: Cincy, the 'Nati, the Queen City, Queen of the West, the Blue Chip City, the City of

Seven Hills, and Porkopolis (because Cincinnati was a main U.S. meatpacking center during the mid-19th century).

- Procter & Gamble, the Kroger Company, and the United States Playing Card Company all call Cincinnati home.
- The city hosts the second-largest Oktoberfest in the world.
- Cincinnati offers several nationally acclaimed museums: the Cincinnati Art Museum, one of the first public art museums in the Midwest; the National Underground Railroad Freedom Center (Cincinnati was a major Underground Railroad destination in the 1800s); the Contemporary Arts Center, one of the first American museums built specifically to display modern art; and the Taft Museum, one of the most heralded small art museums in the country.
- Cincinnati firsts:

  First bag of mail carried by a hot-air balloon (1835)

  First Jewish hospital in the United States (1850)

  First municipal fire department and first city to use a fireman's pole (1853)

  First professional baseball team (the Red Stockings, later just the Reds, in 1869)

  First concrete skyscraper (the Ingalls Building in 1902)

  First public television station (WCET-TV in 1954)

Did You Know?

Wendy's fast-food chain (founded in Columbus and now based in Dublin) was the first restaurant to use a drive-through window with a speaker box.

Got Glass?

Rich in resources like sand, water, coal, and natural gas, Ohio is a glassmaker's paradise.

Beginning in the late 1800s through the mid-1900s, glassworks blossomed throughout Ohio. The companies produced stained glass, window glass, colored glass, cut glass, blown glass, and much more. They manufactured everything from dinnerware to ashtrays to mirrors. So who were all these glassmakers, and what were their stories? Here are some highlights.

The Tiffin Glass Company

Founder: A. J. Beatty from Steubenville

Where: Tiffin

Famous For: Stemware called "Tiffin Modern," parrot lamps (just what it sounds like), and pieces made of black satin (very smooth) glass

The Scoop: Beatty's glassworks came to Tiffin in 1888 because the city enticed him with an offer he couldn't refuse—free natural gas for five years, a wad of cash, and a first-rate parcel of land. The company opened on August 15, 1889, on Fourth Avenue and Vine Street. Three years later, Beatty merged with the much larger United States Glass Company.

The Ohio glassworks kept the name Tiffin, however, and continued turning out products for almost 100 years. They worked through the Great Depression and spent the 1930s picking up the customers of their failed competitors. In 1955, the Tiffin Glass Company bought several popular molds from the now-defunct Pennsylvania-based Duncan and Miller Glass Company. Throughout the next two decades, the factory changed owners several times but still managed to supply stemware to high-end stores like Tiffany and Macy's. Finally, in 1979, Tiffin Glass was sold, though its factories continued to operate until 1984.

Heisey Glass Company

Founder: Augustus H. Heisey from Hannover, Germany
Where: Newark
Famous For: Fine crystal, delicate glassware, and their simple logo: a diamond with an H etched inside (designed by the owner's son)
The Scoop: Heisey began his glassmaking career in Pennsylvania when he worked for the George Duncan Company. He also married Duncan's daughter, Susan, and when George Duncan died, the Heiseys and Susan's brother, James, inherited the company.

But Heisey knew that Ohio, with all of its natural resources, was a perfect place to build a glass company. He traveled to Newark and convinced the city to give him land and to subsidize his new factory in exchange for bringing jobs to their town. In 1896, Heisey and his wife moved to Ohio and opened the Heisey Glass Company. (James stayed in Pennsylvania and became the head of his father's company.) By 1900, Heisey had become one of the most popular glassmakers in the United States and had gotten a reputation for elegance.

After Augustus Heisey died in 1922, his son E. Wilson (Wils) Heisey took over. It was under Wils' guidance that Heisey glass became more colorful. His pieces had names like

Moongleam, Flamingo, and Tangerine. When Wils died in 1942, the next Heisey brother, T. Clarence, took the top job. His shop specialized in animals—everything from horses to donkeys to pairs of angelfish bookends . . . all made of colorful glass.

Heisey's specialized, high-end products eventually made it impossible for the company to turn a profit and stay in business. Heisey closed its doors in 1957. The Imperial Glass Company of Bellaire, Ohio, bought many of the Heisey molds, and in 1985, the Heisey Collectors of America Club bought them and returned them to Newark. Today, the molds reside at the National Heisey Glass Museum on West Church Street.

Libbey Glass Company

Founder: William L. Libbey

Where: Toledo

Famous For: High-end specialty products like a reddish Victorian-era glass made from real gold and a spun-glass dress for Spain's Princess Eulalia

The Scoop: William L. Libbey bought the New England Glass Company in 1877. When he died, his son Edward took over and moved the business from Cambridge, Massachusetts, to Toledo, Ohio. It was set up on four acres on Buckeye Street, and there were 50 additional lots for glassworkers' homes. Edward Libbey hired British designer Joseph Locke in 1882, and together the men developed Amberina, a reddish Victorian-era glass made from real gold. They also showed off Libbey glass at the World's Columbian Exhibition in 1892 and the St. Louis World's Fair in 1904. And in 1893, they made the spun-glass dress for Princess Eulalia.

Over the next 20 years, Edward Libbey continued to

expand and improve his business. He merged with other glass-makers to form larger companies. He established the Toledo Museum of Art. And, on his death in 1925, his estate donated $2 million to build a design school and concert hall at the museum. Thanks to the efforts of Edward Libbey, Toledo earned the nickname "Glass City." The Libbey Glass Company continues to operate there and remains one of the world's largest glassware manufacturers.

Did You Know?

Want to pay your respects to some famous departed sons and daughters of Ohio? Here's where to go.

- Erma Bombeck (humorist): Woodland Cemetery, Dayton
- Sammy Kaye (bandleader): Lakewood Park Cemetery, Rocky River
- Paul Lynde (Uncle Arthur on *Bewitched*): Amity Cemetery, Knox County
- Agnes Moorehead (Endora on *Bewitched*): Dayton Memorial Park, Dayton
- Thurman Munson (baseball player): Sunset Hills Burial Park, Canton
- Eliot Ness (brought down Al Capone): Lake View Cemetery, Cleveland
- James Thurber (cartoonist): Green Lawn Cemetery, Columbus
- Cy Young (baseball player): Peoli Cemetery, Peoli

Seven Things You Don't Know About the Golden Bear

He was born in Columbus and is one of the world's most celebrated golfers. But how well do you know Jack Nicklaus?

1. He overcame polio.

In 1953, when he was just 13, Nicklaus was stricken with polio. Fortunately, his was a mild case, and he recovered. But at the time, he endured a two-week illness, lost stability and hand/eye coordination, and shed 20 pounds. He still suffers from post-polio syndrome and has been plagued by sore joints ever since.

2. He's the most decorated, most prolific, and most consistent golfer in history.

From the time he turned pro in 1961 until his retirement from the PGA Tour in 2005, Nicklaus won an unmatched 73 PGA Tour events, including six Masters (1963, 1965, 1966, 1972, 1975, 1986), four U.S. Opens (1962, 1967, 1972, 1980), three British Opens (1966, 1970, 1978), and five PGA Championships (1963, 1971, 1973, 1975, 1980). He's also the only golfer to win all four majors at least three times and the only player to win the U.S. Open in three different decades.

3. He held down multiple jobs.

Even as he was becoming a promising golfer, Nicklaus still worked multiple jobs. As a young man, he split his time between selling insurance, working for a company that made pants, and playing golf with the pants company's top customers. The money was good but the work made Nicklaus miserable, so he turned pro in 1961.

4. His professional career got off to an inauspicious start.

Few golfers storm out of the gates at their first professional tournament, and Nicklaus was no exception. Battling both his own nerves and seasoned veterans, the Golden Bear finished his first tournament—the 1962 L.A. Open—with a check for a paltry $33.33. (The winner won thousands of dollars.) Nicklaus came in 50th place in the event, 21 strokes behind the winner. He improved, though, and won the U.S. Open later that year by defeating Arnold Palmer in an 18-hole playoff.

5. He's legal tender.

As popular as Nicklaus is in America, he's equally beloved in Scotland, where he won the British Open at St. Andrews Links in 1970 and 1978. On July 12, 2005, the Royal Bank of Scotland Group honored him with the release of a commemorative five-pound note featuring Nicklaus cradling a championship trophy. Apart from Queen Elizabeth II and the late Queen Mother, Elizabeth I, Nicklaus is the only living person to have appeared on a Scottish note.

6. He put the "i" in "Ohio."

On October 28, 2006, he returned to his alma mater—Ohio State University—to become the dot above the "i" of the marching band's signature formation. This Ohio State tradition is considered to be the greatest honor the band can give a non-band member, and it's been shared by only 12 other "civilians," including Hall of Fame football coach Woody Hayes, comedian Bob Hope, and heavyweight champion Buster Douglas.

7. He got his nickname in high school.

Nicklaus' famous "Golden Bear" nickname has nothing to do with his blonde hair or his large physique. The moniker is derived from his alma mater—Ohio's Upper Arlington High School—where the teams have long been known as the Golden Bears.

Career Stats:

- He was named the PGA Tour money winner—meaning he won more money at PGA Tour events that year than any other golfer—eight times (1964, 1965, 1967, 1971, 1972, 1973, 1975, 1976).
- He was named the PGA Player of the Year five times (1967, 1972, 1973, 1975, 1976).
- He was inducted into the World Golf Hall of Fame in 1974.

Did You Know?

Numerous sites around Ohio bear the Wright brothers' name. There's the Wright-Patterson Air Force Base in Greene and Montgomery counties, Wilbur Wright Middle School in Dayton, and Wright State University in Dayton. The Dayton Aviation Heritage National Historic Park commemorates their contribution to air travel.

Here's Johnny!

"As I hurtled through space, one thought kept crossing my mind: Every part of this capsule was supplied by the lowest bidder." —John Glenn

A Supersonic Flight

John Herschel Glenn was born in Cambridge, Ohio, on July 18, 1921. Two years later, he moved with his family to New Concord, Ohio. His father owned a plumbing business, and his mother took in Muskingum College students as boarders. Growing up, young John struck up friendships with many of the students who passed through his home. He loved to read and learn, and the college students—and his parents—were happy to teach him. He was especially interested in science and flying.

In the late 1930s, Glenn graduated from New Concord High School and headed to nearby Muskingum for college. There he studied engineering and graduated with a BA. He then enlisted in a flying school called the Naval Aviation Cadet Program. And in 1943, he married Anna Castor, his childhood sweetheart.

Later that year, Glenn headed for the South Pacific, where, during World War II, he flew 59 combat missions. When the Korean War broke out in 1950, Glenn again volunteered for combat duty and flew 63 missions—accompanied by his wingman, the famous Boston Red Sox slugger Ted Williams.

In 1953, he was appointed to a Navy and Marine program for which he flew cutting-edge aircraft. On one of those missions, in July 1957, Glenn flew the first supersonic transcontinental flight—from Los Alamitos, California, to Floyd Bennett Field in New York. The flight took 3 hours, 23 minutes, and 8 seconds—a record-breaking time. When he flew over his hometown of New Concord, his family and friends were waiting to cheer him on.

Not Your Average Space Cadet

Glenn's stellar reputation as a military pilot made him a natural choice for NASA. He joined the organization in 1958 and the next year was assigned as one of the original astronauts in the Mercury program, the first manned space program in the United States; its goal was to put a human being into orbit.

John Glenn piloted Mercury's first manned space orbiter, *Friendship* 7, on February 20, 1962, but it wasn't all smooth sailing. Shortly after blastoff, NASA officials feared that the heat shield on Glenn's craft had malfunctioned. They—and the Americans who watched the mission updates on television—worried that the orbiter would overheat on reentry. A piece of the orbiter's heat shield was malfunctioning, causing concern that the entire spacecraft might catch fire when it reentered the Earth's atmosphere. Luckily, the equipment did its job, and Glenn returned safely. He was the first person to travel into outer space, and he became an American hero.

So Glenn seemed destined for the Apollo moon mission several years later, but NASA disagreed. The agency considered Glenn too valuable for another dangerous trip to space. Officials in NASA (and some say President Kennedy himself) thought that if something went wrong on the mission to the moon and Glenn lost his life, the public outcry would end the manned space program. So NASA grounded John Glenn. He retired from in the agency in 1964.

A Whole New Career

Glenn was looking for a new job, and he chose public service, but his first political campaign was a bust. In 1964, Glenn challenged incumbent Ohio senator Stephen Young, hoping to win the primary and become the Democrats' choice for the November election. Just before the primary, though, Glenn slipped and hit his head in a bathtub. The injury forced him to withdraw from the race.

He ran again—unsuccessfully—in 1970 but then in 1974 was finally victorious; he defeated former Cleveland mayor and Republican Ralph J. Perk to become an Ohio senator. He ultimately spent 25 years in the Senate, where he served as chairman of the Government Affairs Committee and was chief author of the Nuclear Nonproliferation Act of 1978. He retired in 1999.

His political career was distinguished but it wasn't untainted. In the late 1980s and early 1990s, he was part of the Keating Five scandal. This escapade centered on Charles H. Keating Jr., president of a failed savings and loan. Five senators—including Glenn—were accused of having improperly accepted large campaign funds from Keating's investment group. Investigations into the scandal lasted for several years. In the end, Glenn was found to have demonstrated "poor judgment" but was otherwise exonerated, as was fellow accusee John McCain, the Arizona senator who went on to champion campaign finance reform.

Oldest Man in Space and Beyond

At the age of 77, John Glenn was living quite a life. He was a decorated war hero, had gone into space, and was serving his final year as his home state's representative in Congress. But he wasn't ready to relax and retire quite yet. Instead, he returned to his roots. More than 35 years after his first space flight, Glenn served onboard the Space Shuttle *Discovery's* October 29, 1998, flight. His mission: to study on the effects of space travel on elderly astronauts. The space flight lasted nine days.

Today, John Glenn continues to work and do his home state proud. He teaches at Ohio State University's John Glenn School of Public Affairs, an institution that encourages students and other young people to get involved in public service. He's also a professor in the Political Science Department at OSU.

Did You Know?

In the 1950s and 1960s, Ohio housewife Evelyn Ryan had to find a way to feed her 10 children because her husband spent most of his salary on alcohol. So she started entering commercial jingle writing contests, which she won with astounding frequency. Her jingles for Lipton soup, Burma-Shave, Dr. Pepper, and other products won the Ryans new appliances, bicycles, grocery shopping sprees—and once, enough money for a down payment on a new house, right when the family faced eviction. Amazingly, it's a true story . . . told in the book *The Prize Winner of Defiance, Ohio*, by Evelyn Ryan's daughter, Terry.

The Real Fugitive?

Former Ohio doctor Sam Sheppard has his name linked with both movies and murder. In the case of the former, though, Hollywood bigwigs deny the connection.

How the Story Got Started

On September 17, 1963, Roy Huggins, creator of the popular Western TV series *Maverick*, launched a new series, *The Fugitive*. Dr. Richard Kimble (played by David Janssen) comes home one night to find his wife murdered. He had seen a one-armed man fleeing as he arrived, but no one believes his story that this one-armed intruder killed his wife. Kimble is wrongly convicted for his wife's murder and sentenced to die. However, the train carrying him to his execution derails, and Kimble escapes, becoming . . . the fugitive (and spending four seasons being pursued by the indefatigable Lieutenant Gerard).

The Reel Story

In 1993, the story of the doc-on-the-run was re-created for a new generation of viewers in a film starring Harrison Ford as Richard Kimble and Tommy Lee Jones as Lieutenant Gerard. The movie was a huge success and was nominated for six Academy Awards, including Best Picture. Tommy Lee Jones walked away with an Oscar for Best Supporting Actor.

The Real Story

Huggins denied that he based *The Fugitive* on a true story, but the events in the series are suspiciously close to a true-life murder trial that fascinated the American public for years.

Richard Kimble's life on the run is reminiscent of the events surrounding the 1954 murder trial of Cleveland doctor Sam Sheppard. One July morning, Dr. Sheppard called police to tell them he'd been attacked by a bushy-haired man who'd broken into his suburban Cleveland home. The intruder had knocked the doctor unconscious, and when Sheppard came to, he discovered that his wife Marilyn—who was four months pregnant—had been murdered.

The shocked public was sympathetic, but the cops were suspicious. They wondered why Sheppard couldn't find the T-shirt he'd worn that night. They said the crime scene didn't look like a typical burglary—it was too tidy and looked staged. Plus, nobody found the murder weapon or the bushy-haired intruder. Public feeling turned against Sheppard after he admitted to an adulterous affair that he'd previously denied.

The nation's press corps declared Sheppard guilty, and the jury agreed, sentencing him to life in prison. For a time, the case seemed solved. Or was it?

Along Comes A Suspect

While Sheppard was serving time, police arrested a thief who had possession of Marilyn's wedding ring. The suspect, Richard Eberling, admitted that he'd burgled the home of Marilyn's sister-in-law, who inherited the ring after Marilyn's death. Eberling, a window washer, also said he'd worked at Marilyn's home days before her murder and that he'd cut his finger while he was there. Still, the police let Eberling go after he passed a lie detector test.

Meanwhile, the U.S. Supreme Court was going over the prejudicial press coverage against the doctor—a "carnival" that the judge never tried to control or keep from the jury. In 1966, the high court granted Sheppard a new trial. At that second trial, the doctor was acquitted.

The Epilogue

Unable to establish a successful medical practice, Sheppard performed as a professional wrestler under the name Killer Sheppard. He also drank heavily and died of liver failure at age 46, just four years after his release.

In 1996, Sam and Marilyn's son, Sam Reese Sheppard, who had slept through the murder all those years ago, tried to clear his father's name by using DNA evidence to prove Richard Eberling was the bushy-haired intruder. Unfortunately, the effort was futile: the DNA evidence showed that a third person could have been in the room on the night of the murder, but it had been too contaminated for a clear identification. Eberling had been convicted of murdering an elderly woman and was suspected of killing three other women as well. Eberling died in prison without ever publicly confessing to Marilyn Sheppard's murder, though his cellmate claimed that Eberling confessed just before his death.

Did You Know?

The juniper sedge is a species of sedge—a grasslike plant—that grows only under juniper trees on limestone outcroppings called *alvars*. The plant wasn't even known to science until 1986 when it was discovered at Lynx Prairie in Adams County (more recently it's been found in Kentucky).

Modern Ohio Stars

On page 99, we asked about Ohio's shining stars from old Hollywood. Now see if you can match these modern Ohio celebrities to their descriptions.

1. Drew Carey
2. Arsenio Hall
3. Maggie Grace
4. Halle Berry
5. Sarah Jessica Parker
6. Luke Perry
7. Molly Shannon
8. Dave Grohl
9. Gloria Steinem
10. Jack Hanna

A. This "superstar" drew much of her acting inspiration from her schoolgirl days at St. Dominic's Catholic elementary school in Shaker Heights.

B. This Cleveland-born actress won an Academy Award in 2002.

C. For 15 years, he was the chief overseer of some of Columbus' most beloved animal inhabitants.

D. This actor began his career as a stand-up comedian before going on to star in TV show that bore his name. He's known for his crew cut and Buddy Holly glasses—though the glasses are only a prop; he had surgery to correct his vision years ago.

E. This "sexy" actress began her career as a Broadway child star. She was cast in productions of *The Sound of Music* and

The Innocents and played the lead in *Annie.*

F. He became famous as a TV heartthrob, but this native Ohioan also acted in movies like *The Fifth Element* and *Buffy the Vampire Slayer.*

G. This blond actress really got *Lost* during her TV show's second season. Although a main character, she wasn't safe from a fellow castaway's bullet.

H. This one-time stand-up comic was friends with Eddie Murphy and was the star of his own talk show in the mid-1990s.

I. A renowned journalist and lecturer, this Ohioan was a cofounder and the original publisher of *Ms.* magazine.

J. A quintuple threat—on drums, guitar, bass, piano, and vocals—this frontman is sometimes called the "nicest man in rock."

For answers, turn to page 306.

Did You Know?

Charles Goodyear, for whom the famous Akron tire company is named, spent time in a Pennsylvania debtors' prison in the early 1800s. While there, he worked on his first rubber experiments, trying to decrease the stickiness of natural rubber by adding a magnesia powder. He went on to invent the nonsticky, durable vulcanized rubber that made the modern tire and rubber industry possible.

Go Jump in a Lake

Ohio may be thousands of miles from either coast, but it boasts access to one of the largest freshwater lakes in the world. As a result, the typically tropical sports of surfing, windsurfing, and scuba diving are all possible in the Buckeye State.

Get Stoked!

Catching a tubular wave is hardly the first thing most people think of when talking about Lake Erie. And there are definitely a few elements missing from the typical endless summer—primarily no clear blue water and no ocean. But since the mid-1950s, the lake has attracted a dedicated group of surfers who paddle out from Ohio's coastlines to meet the waves.

The same forces of nature that are responsible for battering and sinking numerous ships through Great Lakes history also give rise to rideable waves in the right conditions. When the seasons change and the wind whipping across Lake Erie picks up, waves as high as a surfer's chest (sometimes even higher) start to break off Ohio's shores. Those freshwater waves are lighter—saltwater is dense—so lake surfers have to use wider, more buoyant boards than their coastal counterparts. But otherwise the sport is pretty much the same.

Do the Wave

Ohio gets its best waves in the winter, of course, when storms batter the lake. But that can be a downside. Erie's winter water temperature sometimes dips to freezing, and surfers have to dodge floating chunks of ice. So to protect themselves, Ohio's lake surfers must wear protective wetsuits and monitor each other for signs of hypothermia.

The surf spots on Lake Erie are closely guarded secrets because the surfers want to make sure their waves stay uncrowded. One popular and well-known surfing spot is in Cleveland's Edgewater State Park, which features a small beach that surfers can paddle out from. Just be careful if you're surfing Edgewater after a storm; heavy rains create runoff that leeches into the water there. If you're interested in Edgewater or other spots, there are many Web sites dedicated to surfing in Ohio where riders trade tips, discuss upcoming weather reports, and share pictures of their most recent rides.

Surf's Up (Windsurfing, That Is)

Board surfing may be the domain of a hardy few, but windsurfers are a common sight on Ohio's more than 2,500 lakes and rivers. Grand Lake St. Marys in the central part of the state and Toledo's Maumee River are two of Ohio's popular windsurfing destinations. The Maumee River even boasts a windsurfing club (the Toledo Area Boardsailing Association) and a local windsurfing shop.

If you can't get to a lake, Ohio's large reservoirs, such as the 600-acre Breslin Reservoir near Lima or Alum Lake in Columbus, will do in a pinch. Many reservoirs are elevated, with the surface of the water being as high as many of the trees around them. As a result, the reservoirs often get high, uninterrupted winds—a boon for windsurfers.

Under the Lake

Scuba divers typically seek out coral reefs and bright tropical fish, but in Ohio, divers specialize in wrecks. Lake Erie offers more than 100 shipwrecks—anything from sunken warships to merchant vessels that fell prey to the lake's raging storms. Six of the wrecks have been marked with mooring buoys thanks to the Ohio Maritime and Archaeological Survey Team, Inc. (MAST). These include the side-wheel steamer *Morning Star*, located off of Cleveland's shore in 65-foot-deep water.

Because scuba diving is so popular, Ohio has a large number of inland dive shops near many of the state's quarries. These shops offer training and certification, and instructors often create artificial reefs in the quarries by sinking small boats, buses, and cars. Portage Quarry, near Bowling Green, has a jet resting on its bottom. The jet provides an practice platform for search-and-rescue divers to hone their skills on a real plane lying 35 feet underwater. Of course, curious recreational divers can explore the plane, too.

Did You Know?

In 1919, when Ohio Stadium was being built at OSU, the school held a contest to find fight songs for its football team. Frank Crumit—an Ohio University alumnus but also a rabid Buckeye fan—composed and submitted the "Buckeye Battle Cry" and won one of the coveted spots. More than 80 years later, his song remains an integral part of OSU football: The marching band's Ramp Entrance is performed to the song, it ends Script Ohio, and it's played every time the Buckeyes score.

Six Things You Don't Know About Paul O'Neill

Any discussion of Major League Baseball's greatest competitors is sure to include Paul O'Neill. After all, the Columbus native won five World Series championships, including one with the Cincinnati Reds. Here are six things you might not know about one of Ohio's most famous hometown heroes.

1. He has a literary family connection.

O'Neill's great-grandmother was Mary Clemens, a first cousin of Samuel Clemens—better known as Mark Twain.

2. Baseball is in his genes.

For the O'Neills, baseball is more than just a sport; it's also the family business. Paul's father, Chick O'Neill, pitched in the California League (a single-A minor league) after World War II, and his grandfather, Art O'Neill, played for the Mustangs—a Billings, Montana, minor league team—in 1909.

3. He was inspired early.

A lifelong fan of the Reds, O'Neill used to accompany his family to Cincinnati's Crosley Field, where they'd root for the Reds. When he was six years old, O'Neill's parents took a photo of him posing in the right field stadium bleachers . . . in front of Pittsburgh Pirates Hall of Famer Roberto Clemente. Not only did O'Neill grow up to play right field, but he wore number 21, the number Clemente wore.

4. He knows about perfection.

O'Neill is the only player in major league history to have played on the winning side in three perfect games. The games in question were pitched by the Reds' Tom Browning on September 16, 1988, at Riverfront Stadium; by Yankee David Wells on May 17, 1998, at Yankee Stadium; and by Yankee David Cone on July 18, 1999, also at Yankee Stadium.

5. He sometimes grooves to a different beat.

In addition to being a standout athlete, O'Neill is also an enthusiastic amateur drummer who has performed onstage with Grammy Award–winning rocker John Mellencamp.

6. He's done a lot of sweeping.

O'Neill is one of only 11 players in major league history to have participated in three successful World Series sweeps. He accomplished the feat in 1990 with the Reds and in 1998 and 1999 with the Yankees. In fact, O'Neill and former Yankees legend Joe DiMaggio are the only two players to have done this since 1939.

Career Stats:

- O'Neill played for 17 seasons with two major league teams: the Cincinnati Reds (1985–1992) and the New York Yankees (1993–2001).
- He batted .288, hit 281 home runs, and accumulated 2,105 hits over the course of his career.
- He was a five-time all-star (1991, 1994, 1995, 1997, 1998).
- He was the American League batting champ in 1994, posting a batting average of .359.

The Friendly Ghosts

People who visit Granville's Buxton Inn have discovered that not all haunts are fire and brimstone; some are sweet as . . . well . . . pie.

The Spooks

Orrin Granger, Bonnie Bounell, and others.

The Inn

In 1812, Orrin Granger built Granville's two-story, brick Buxton Inn. (As one of the town's founders, he also built a post office and stagecoach stop.) The inn was first known as the Tavern, a name given to it by travelers on the stagecoach route from Zanesville to Columbus; they could get a drink and lodging while they passed through town. In the basement, the drivers and stable workers who accompanied those travelers could cook their own meals and enjoy a warm place to sleep while on the road.

In 1865, Granger sold the Tavern to Major Horton Buxton, who renamed it the Buxton Inn. Buxton ran the inn until he died in 1902 and the business then passed on to a series of owners, including a singer and actress named Ethel "Bonnie" Bounell, Nell Schoeller and her cat Major Buxton (named for the deceased innkeeper), and later Orville and Audrey Orr, who bought the inn in the 1980s and continue to run it today. The Buxton Inn also holds the distinction of being the oldest inn in Ohio still operating out of its original building.

Supernatural Cravings

Paying guests aren't the only ones who visit the Buxton, however. The ghosts of Orrin Granger and Bonnie Bounell have been known to show up unannounced, and although they don't try to frighten or harass visitors, they do give many people pause.

The first documented sighting took place in the late 1920s when Fred Sweet, son of one of the inn's later owners, ventured downstairs for a midnight snack. He arrived in the dining room and saw the transparent figure of a man sitting at the table eating the last slice of pie. According to Fred, the pie eater introduced himself as Orrin Granger and proceeded to narrate the inn's history. The ghost also praised the way the owners were running the inn; then he smiled and disappeared. Over the years, Granger has showed himself to many other guests. He doesn't seem shy, they say, and appears to particularly enjoy floating by the dining room's fireplace.

The Lady in Blue

More recently, the Orrs and other guests have reported seeing a female apparition on the property. Orville Orr was the first to experience the entity. One night, while locking up for the evening, he heard someone walk up the stairs, across the balcony, and then out of the house. But when he investigated, he found no one and discovered that none of the upstairs doors had been unlocked. Later, workers doing renovations on the inn started seeing a lady in a blue dress roaming the property. Locals identified the spirit as former owner Bonnie Bounell. Bounell had been well known and well liked in town during her tenure as Buxton's owner and often wore her favorite color . . . blue.

Over the years, Bounell has become Buxton's most-sighted spook. During her life, she lived in the inn's room #7 and died in room #9, so she's commonly seen patrolling those areas. In fact, she once startled a guest who entered room #7 one night.

According to the guest, Bounell was sitting at the edge of the bed, and she asked whether he'd been getting enough sleep during his stay. Then she disappeared, leaving a sweet perfume smell in her wake.

The Rest

Granger and Bounell are the most often seen and most easily identified ghosts to haunt the Buxton Inn, but many guests have reported other sightings over the years. Some have seen Major Buxton sitting on a rocking chair in the dining room. The spirits of drivers and stable workers roam the basement. Disembodied hands sometimes appear near guests standing by the fireplaces. Doors open and close on their own, mysterious footsteps climb up and down stairs, and Nell Schoeler's cat Major Buxton has been seen wandering the inn's hallways. He occasionally even rubs gently against a patron's leg. (Some people speculate the gray cat painted on the Buxton Inn's sign was created in the likeness of this feline ghost.)

Overall, the apparitions are said to be friendly. Most people who visit the Buxton Inn report enjoying their stay, even with all the unexplained activities. So if you're ever in Granville and looking for a place to stay, drop in at the Buxton. But if you get a craving for a midnight snack, don't be surprised if old man Granger himself beats you to that last piece of pie.

Did You Know?

One player—Bill Bond—suited up for three of Columbus' hockey teams: the Checkers, the Seals, and the Owls.

...n Fests, Part 2

On page 111, we introduced you to some of Ohio's wackiest festivals. Here are a few more to teach you how to have a good time.

Banana Split Festival

Where: Wilmington

When: Early June

What: Ask people in Wilmington, and they'll tell you that Ohio is the birthplace of the banana split (first served in 1907 to students at Wilmington College). Who cares that Latrobe, Pennsylvania, also makes the claim? This is Ohio! To celebrate their historic contribution to dessert, Wilmingtonians honor the split every summer at a 1950s-themed festival filled with crafts, classic cars, and a build-your-own-banana-split booth.

Oktoberfest Zinzinnati

Where: Cincinnati

When: Late October

What: With more than 500,000 attendees, Cincinnati's Oktoberfest claims to be the largest in the country. The party began back in 1976 as a way to honor the German heritage of the people of southwestern Ohio. Today, the festival is known for its grand amounts of food (more than 80,000 bratwurst one year) and its famously large Chicken Dance (a record 48,000 people participated in 1994). Guest leaders of the Chicken Dance (you know the one . . . it's a staple at weddings) have included Weird Al Yankovic, the Monkees' Davy Jones, and Mötley Crüe's Vince

Neil. The chicken dance record is not the only one the Zinzinnati folks have set. In 1998, Oktoberfesters set another world record when bandleader Al Hirt led the world's largest kazoo band, a group made up of 25,000 kazooists.

Sauerkraut Festival

Where: Waynesville

When: Mid-October

What: Thousands of visitors have descended on Waynesville every year since 1970 for the Sauerkraut Festival. They participate in a cabbage-growing contest (with prizes for the largest, greenest, most magnificent, and most pathetic cabbages), a spelling bee, and a contest for the best dish made with sauerkraut—past winners include "Sauerkraut Quesadillas" and "Sauerkraut Pockets." Food booths also serve sauerkraut pizza and sauerkraut doughnuts. Yum.

Avon Heritage Duct Tape Festival

Where: Avon

When: Mid-June

What: Avon is the self-proclaimed "Duct Tape Capital of the World" (it's also home to Duck brand duct tape), so it's no wonder that the townspeople came up with a festival to showcase the wondrous versatility of duct tape. There's an exhibit of duct tape sculptures—crafted by experts like Canadian duct tape sculptor Todd Scott—and an exhibit of duct tape fashion.

Tiro Testicle Festival

Where: Tiro

When: Late April

What: This annual event takes place at a biker bar called the Tiro Tavern, which serves the bovine delicacy known as mountain oysters. It all began about 30 years ago when "some guy just brung 'em in and cooked 'em up," says a spokesman from the tavern. And that's about all there is to it. No games or contests or a parade or anything like that—just the mountain oysters and the many visitors who come from all over the state to participate. Oh, they do sell T-shirts—they say "Tiro Testicle Festival: You'll have a ball!"

Did You Know

These Ohio town names have some fascinating origins:

- **College Corner** was part of the township selected by the government to be the site of Miami University.
- **Coolville**: a far out, groovy beatnik enslave? Nope. It was named by a settler named Simeon Cooley.
- **Put In Bay** may have originally been named Pudding Bay, but the official story is that a Revolutionary War general had his ships "put in" the bay here for security.
- **Mount Healthy** was Mount Pleasant until townspeople discovered that another village already had the name. So they picked Mount Healthy to commemorate the town's avoidance of an 1850s cholera epidemic that ravaged parts of Ohio.

Cleveland Indians By the Numbers

Whether you know them as the Indians or the Tribe, there's no debating the fact that Cleveland's major league team is a hit with the city it calls home. Since the Indians' inception in 1901, the ball club has won five American League pennants and two World Series titles. No wonder Chief Wahoo is always smiling.

1

Number of Ten Cent Beer Night promotions run by the team. The event took place during a game on June 4, 1974. The Indians had to forfeit due to the crowd's unruly conduct and displays of drunken behavior, including a naked man sprinting to second base and a father and son running into the outfield and mooning the crowd.

2

Number of Major League films to feature the Cleveland Indians (*Major League* in 1989 and *Major League II* in 1994). (The third film in the trilogy—*Major League: Back to the Minors*—focused on the Buzz of Salt Lake City, a minor league affiliate of the Minnesota Twins.) The first film grossed $80,419,236 and was nominated for an award of the Japanese Academy for Best Foreign Language Film.

3

Indians who have won the American League's Most Valuable Player award (George Burns, 1926; Lou Boudreau, 1948; Al Rosen, 1953).

4

Number of stadiums the Indians have called home: League Park, 1901–1909; League Park II, 1910–1946; Municipal Stadium, 1932–1993; and Jacobs Field, 1994–present. The team has also had four names since its inception: the Blues, the Bronchos, the Naps, and the Indians.

5

Number of seasons Indians Hall of Fame pitcher Bob Feller led the league in innings pitched (1939, 1940, 1941, 1946, and 1947).

11

Number of seasons Gilmore, Ohio, native Cy Young played for the Indians (1890–1898 and 1909–1910). Young retired as the winningest pitcher in major league history with a record of 511 wins and 316 losses (more than any other pitcher in history). His record with the Indians was 267 wins and 160 losses.

22

Runs scored by the Indians in a 22–0 victory over the New York Yankees on August 31, 2004. It was the worst defeat in Yankees history.

26

Number of triples hit by infamous outfielder "Shoeless" Joe Jackson during the 1912 season, the most in Indians history. Jackson, while with the Chicago White Sox, was later banned from baseball after allegedly participating in the "Black Sox" scandal, in which he and some of his teammates were accused of conspiring to throw the 1919 World Series.

98

Number of times Indians Hall of Fame shortstop Joe Sewell struck out during his 11 years and 5,621 at-bats with the team. Sewell still owns the American League record for the fewest career strikeouts.

111

Number of wins during the 1954 season, the most in franchise history.

455

Number of consecutive home sellouts from 1995 until 2002. The streak was so impressive that the Indians retired the number 455 in order to honor their fans.

43,345

Seating capacity of Jacobs Field, the Indians home stadium. The team attracted an average of 24,667 fans per game during the 2006 season.

Did You Know?

While researching *Uncle Tom's Cabin*, Harriet Beecher Stowe discovered that Zillah, her housekeeper in Cincinnati, was actually a runaway slave. Determined to help the woman, Stowe and her husband drove Zillah to the next stop on the Underground Railroad, the home of an abolitionist farmer. Zillah later escaped to Canada.

They Grow 'Em Smart in Ohio!

When it comes to education, the Buckeye State doesn't fool around: It has 13 state universities, 46 liberal arts colleges and universities, 2 medical schools, 15 community colleges, 8 technical colleges, and more than 24 independent nonprofit colleges. We had room for only 35 schools in this pennant-shaped word search, but hats off to Ohio's half a million students!

ANTIOCH
BLUFFTON
BOWLING GREEN
CASE WESTERN
CEDARVILLE
CLARK
CUYAHOGA
DENISON
DEVRY
EDISON STATE
FRANCISCAN
HEIDELBERG
HIRAM
HOCKING
KENT STATE
KENYON
MARIETTA
MIAMI UNIV
MOUNT UNION
MUSKINGUM
NORTHWESTERN
OBERLIN
OHIO STATE
OHIO WESLEYAN
OLD DOMINICAN
U OF AKRON
U OF CINCINNATI
U OF DAYTON
URSULINE
WILBERFORCE
WILMINGTON
WITTENBERG
WOOSTER
XAVIER
YOUNGSTOWN

N I
B G
Y X
Z F S M
Y R V E D C
Z A N O Y N E K
D N F O B E R L I N
H C D M I A M I U N I V
G I T A N N I C N I C F O U
R S U B I E U N O M J O O O D F
E C O K H C E T A M I L H F Y R O F
B A A Z R R W R N S B D I D R Y H G F P
N N C S Z A I R G U T D O A E N I L U S R U
E O K E E H L T Q G O O W Y U N O T F F U L B E
T T R V D W B C L H N M E T A T S T N E K X A V I E R M X
T G W K W A E Q X E D I S O N S T A T E N Z Q B Z L R O E
I N O V A F R S W I D N L N P E A G O H A Y U C
W I O L G F F V T D R I E W A T T E I R A M
Y M S S N E O B I E M C Y R O Z E C P R
O L T M I E R U T L R A A V O B X S
U I E O K N C S M B L N N J N E
N W R I C Z E U Z E L E K P
G B H F O W G D U R K S
S X C M H N T A K G
T A N T I O C H
O Y R K R
W O S P
N U
M E
E T

For answers, turn to page 307.

Invented in Ohio

Thanks to these three Ohioans and their inventions, our lives are a little bit easier.

An Incorruptible Cashier

Invention: The cash register

Inventor: James J. Ritty

The scoop: In the 1870s, saloon owner and Dayton native James J. Ritty was fed up with his employees stealing from him. He'd found that his cashiers often "miscounted" the day's receipts, skimming a little off the top for themselves. Ritty wanted to invent a machine that would count his money accurately at the end of each business day.

An idea came to him while he was traveling aboard a ship crossing the Atlantic. During the voyage, Ritty took a tour of the engine room, where he saw a device that counted the revolutions of the ship's propeller. He theorized that if a machine could record the propeller turns, it could certainly register the money customers paid to a cashier. So he returned home to Dayton and built that machine. It consisted of two rows of keys to punch out dollars and cents and a dial that showed and recorded the sums deposited. He called his machine the "Incorruptible Cashier."

Ritty began using the machine right away, and he patented it in 1879. Four years later, he sold the patent to a group of local investors who went on to improve the design (they added the drawer that holds the money and divides it by denomination) and create the National Cash Register Company. (*To read more about the National Cash Register Company, turn to page 148.*)

(Non) Stick-it!

Invention: Teflon

Inventor: Roy J. Plunkett

The scoop: In April 1938, Plunkett, a New Carlisle native, was working in New Jersey as a research chemist for DuPont. While investigating refrigerants, Plunkett accidentally discovered a powder called polytetrafluoroethylene, a substance that we know today as Teflon.

It was a revolutionary find, though at first no one was sure what it could be best used for. During World War II, scientists used Teflon to coat gaskets on the atomic bombs because Teflon could withstand the intense heat and corrosion the bomb gave off. Finally, in 1954, a pair of French scientists discovered that pans coated with Teflon prevented food from sticking during cooking, and the modern kitchen marvel was born.

Plunkett received many accolades for his discovery. He was awarded Philadelphia's John Scott Trust Medal, an honor bestowed on men and women who come up with ingenious inventions. In 1973, he was inducted into Massachusetts' Plastics Hall of Fame and, in 1985, into Ohio's National Inventor's Hall of Fame.

Pop!

Invention: The pop-top can

Inventor: Ermal Fraze

The scoop: Before the 1960s, opening a tin can wasn't as easy as it is today. You needed a can opener—called a can key—to pop a drinking hole in the top of the can. One day in 1959, Ermal Fraze, a tool manufacturer and inventor living in Dayton, forgot to bring his can key to a family picnic. Rather than go thirsty, he used a car bumper to open it. The problem continued to plague him, though, so he decided to invent a can that didn't require a key to open it.

After a lot of experimenting, Fraze came up with a can that included a lever that acted as the opener. But the hole the lever made was sharp and jagged and could injure people who drank from it. Scrapping that idea, Fraze refined his design until it included a safe, precut hole covered by a disposable pull tab. The new can was an instant hit, and by 1965, more than 75 percent of U.S. beer manufacturers were using Fraze's design.

In the 1970s, in response to environmentalists who worried that the pull tabs were contributing to America's litter problem, Fraze further modified his can so that the tab didn't come off the top of the can. In 1977, he patented the "push-in and fold-back tab design" used on most canned drinks today.

Did You Know?

What good is it drinking a warm bottle of pure spring water when the only ice cubes you have to cool it down with are full of nasty tap water? That's the question that inspired a Dublin, Ohio, company to create "Aquaice." Instead of buying bottles of water and then pouring them out into ice cube trays, consumers can buy the unfrozen ice cubes in Aquaice's specially designed, individually filled trays. Just put the the trays in the freezer, wait one hour, remove, peel off the plastic top, and *voilá!* Purified ice cubes! (Price: $8.99 for 100 cubes.)

Frog Town

One of Ohio's most populous cities, Toledo has been making its mark on Ohio history since the early 19th century.

Town: Toledo
Location: Lucas County
Founding: 1836
Current population: 308,973
Size: 81 square miles
County seat: Yes

What's in a Name?

No one is sure how Toledo got its name, but the most repeated legend is that a merchant suggested the word "Toledo" because it was "easy to pronounce, is pleasant in sound, and there is no other city by that name on the American continent." The legend doesn't mention if that merchant had visited Spain or heard of the town of Toledo, Spain, though he may have. Interesting, too, is the fact that Ohio's Toledo is pronounced differently than the Spanish version. In Spain, the city's name is "Toe-leh-dough"; in Ohio, it's "Tuh-lee-dough."

Claims to Fame:

- Toledo got one of its nicknames, "Frog Town," for the numerous amphibians that once populated the Great Black Swamp, a former wetland in northwestern Ohio that was drained during the 1800s and is now farmland. Toledo is situated just north of the former swampland.

- The city's newspaper, the *Blade*, has been around since 1835, but it became famous during the Civil War when journalist David Ross Locke wrote a series of satiric commentaries under the pseudonym "Rev. Petroleum V. Nasby." The commentaries, called the Nasby Letters, were intended to rally support for the Union, even though Nasby himself was pro-Confederacy. Locke created such a hateful character in Nasby—a bigoted, lazy, uneducated slavery advocate—that he condemned the slave-loving South by making fun of it. President Abraham Lincoln was among the many fans of the Nasby Letters.
- The Toledo Art Museum, one of Ohio's most well known museums, was founded in 1901 by local glassmaker Edward Drummond Libbey. The museum includes everything from 19th-century European paintings to Greek and Roman works. But recently, the museum gained fame for its Glass Pavilion, which opened in 2006. In fitting tribute to the museum's founder and to Toledo's nickname "Glass City," the pavilion houses both an impressive glass art collection and a glassmaking studio space. As always, admission to the museum and the Glass Pavilion is free.

To read more about Edward Libbey and Ohio's glassmaking history, turn to page 198.

Did You Know?

In 2007, the Rock and Roll Hall of Fame in Cleveland inducted its first hip-hop group: the New York–based Grandmaster Flash and the Furious Five.

Offbeat Ohio (Again)

Our discussion of Ohio's roadside attractions concludes with a stamp, a deity, and a field of corn.

World's Biggest Rubber Stamp: Cleveland

In 1992, the City of Cleveland accepted a unique art donation: a 28-foot-tall, 48-foot-wide replica of a rubber stamp. The aluminum-and-steel structure featured the word "FREE" on its stamp pad.

The stamp's story, though, actually begins ten years earlier. In 1982, Standard Oil of Ohio commissioned two Dutch artists, Claes Oldenburg and Coosje van Bruggen, to build a statue for its lobby. Oldenburg and van Bruggen, famous for creating gigantic replicas of everyday objects, built the world's biggest rubber stamp. Unfortunately, Standard Oil soon changed management, and the new folks didn't like the gigantic piece of pop art. They placed it in storage for seven years until the cost of storing it got so high that they decided to donate it to the city.

Cleveland initially declined the gift—the city didn't want to pay for the installation or maintenance. When the oil company agreed to cover all costs, the city accepted. Today, the statue is on display in Willard Park and continues to provoke debate. Some locals feel the word "FREE" represents the city's proud heritage, but others feel it only represents the piece's price tag.

Field of Corn: Dublin

Although some of Ohio's public art provokes awe or debate, Dublin's contribution is downright corny. A half-mile down Frantz Road, 109 human-sized ears of corn stand in homage to Sam Frantz, who developed several hybrid forms of the husky grain. In the early 1990s, the Dublin Arts Council hired artist Malcolm Cochran to create something that would remind the community of its agricultural roots. Cochran learned that Frantz had used an acre and a half of farmland in Dublin to plant his hybrid corn seeds. So the artist decided to make that the focus of his piece. The giant concrete-and-metal corncobs are all about six feet high and are "planted" in rows at even intervals.

King of Kings: Monroe

Baptisms at the Solid Rock Church can be quite inspirational. They're held behind the church in a body of water that features a 62-foot, 16,000-pound statue of Jesus. The statue depicts Jesus from the waist up, arms outstretched above him, rising out of the water. Lawrence and Darlene Bishop, who started the evangelical Christian church in 1978, commissioned artist James Lynch to create the statue. Lynch used wood, Styrofoam, and concrete for the structure and a fiberglass mat and resin exterior to keep it weatherproof. The statue was erected in 2003 and is visible from I-75.

For the first two installments, turn to pages 91 and 164.

Did You Know?

Ohio was a non-slave state in the years leading up to the Civil War. The town of Getaway was the first stop in free territory for slaves escaping Kentucky and West Virginia.

The Book That Changed the World

"I wrote what I did because as a woman, as a mother, I was oppressed and brokenhearted with the sorrows and injustice I saw, because as a Christian, I felt the dishonor to Christianity, because as a lover of my country, I trembled at the coming day of wrath."
—Harriet Beecher Stowe

When Harriet Beecher Stowe published *Uncle Tom's Cabin* in 1852, the novel helped invigorate the abolitionist cause in America. It made the depravity of slavery tangible to millions, inspired the public, and contributed to the outbreak of the Civil War. But where did Stowe get her ideas for the story? Many of them came from her experiences during the early 1800s, when she and her family lived in Cincinnati.

Birth of an Abolitionist

Harriet Elizabeth Beecher was born June 14, 1811, in Litchfield, Connecticut. Her father, Reverend Lyman Beecher, was a prominent and influential abolitionist minister. Her mother Roxanna died when Harriet was only five. Young Harriet was one of 11 children born to the Beechers, and many of her siblings also became famous reformers: Her brother, minister Henry Ward, was an abolitionist; her sister Catharine founded schools for female students across the United States; and her youngest sister, Isabella, became a key player in the early women's suffrage movement.

It was Lyman Beecher, though, who first taught his brood about the evils of slavery. In the 1820s, he was renowned throughout New England for his antislavery sermons, and he adamantly believed slavery was a sin.

Cincinnati Calling

In 1832, Harriet and her family moved to Cincinnati, where her father became the first president of the Lane Theological Seminary, a school for Presbyterian ministers, which was known for its fierce antislavery teachings. It was in Cincinnati that Harriet met and married Calvin E. Stowe, a professor at the seminary. The couple had seven children, six of whom were born in the city.

Also in Cincinnati, Harriet sharpened her writing skills. She was a member of the Semi-Colon Club, a literary society in which members wrote articles and then read and discussed them. In 1833, she coauthored a book, *Primary Geography for Children*, with her sister Catharine. The book offered a positive depiction of Catholicism and showed the sisters' feelings of religious tolerance, something that was unusual for Protestants at the time.

Cincinnati also introduced Harriet to the tangible barbarity of slavery. The city was situated across the Ohio River from a slave-holding community in Kentucky and was populated by both escaped slaves and slave owners. Harriet had a chance to talk with many of them. She heard and was horrified by the firsthand accounts of conditions among enslaved people. Her family's own cook, Eiza Buck, had been a slave in Louisiana and Virginia and told Stowe gruesome stories of the abuse endured by slave women.

The Catalyst

It was the introduction of the Fugitive Slave Law of 1850, though, that stirred Stowe to action. This law, based on the

Fugitive Slave Law of 1793, allowed slave owners to hunt runaway slaves in free territories and make legal claims to recapture them. It also established a fine of $500 for anyone who impeded an owner's efforts to retake a slave or who rescued, harbored, or abetted fugitive slaves. The Fugitive Slave Law of 1850 also required that officials in free states return runaway slaves to their Southern masters.

After the law passed, Stowe's sister-in-law wrote to her, saying, "Harriet, if I could use a pen as you can, I would write something that would make this whole nation feel what an accursed thing slavery is." Stowe agreed, famously announcing, "I will write something."

Getting to Work

Within weeks of the passing of the Fugitive Slave Law, Stowe began researching slavery and its ramifications. She interviewed slaves and slave owners in Ohio and read extensively on the subject. Also in 1850, her husband Calvin accepted a position at Bowdoin College and moved the family to Brunswick, Maine. Stowe continued writing, using her experiences in Cincinnati to guide her novel.

She began to craft a tale of Tom—a loyal and heroic slave who is sold to a local slave trader—and of Eliza—a slave who lives on the plantation with Tom and whose son is sold to the same trader. Stowe based the character of Tom in large part on Josiah Henson, a slave from Maryland who escaped to Canada in 1830 and later wrote a book about his life. Eliza's story, however, came from Stowe's own experience and from a true story told to her by an Ohioan named John Rankin, who, as an Underground Railroad conductor in Ripley, helped thousands of slaves escape to freedom.

Imagining Eliza

In 1849, Stowe's son Charley died—he was only 18 months old. The boy contracted cholera when an epidemic swept through Cincinnati, and while mourning his death, Stowe imagined what it must be like for enslaved mothers to lose their children for a different reason: because the children were sold.

In the novel, rather than give up her son Harry to slave traders, Eliza flees with him and her husband to Ohio, Canada, France, and finally Liberia. In one of the story's most harrowing moments, Eliza crosses the icy Ohio River from Kentucky with bounty hunters on her tail and her baby in her arms. This was the story Rankin told Stowe in 1850; it was the real-life experience of a woman he had sheltered.

Changing Hearts and Minds

Stowe finished her story in 1851 and published it first as a serial in the *National Era*, an abolitionist newspaper. In 1852, the story was published as a novel in two volumes under its full title, *Uncle Tom's Cabin: Life Among the Lowly*. In its first week, the book sold an amazing 10,000 copies. (*The Scarlet Letter*, a popular novel also published in the early 1850s, sold only 2,500 copies in its first 10 days.) Within a year, Stowe's novel had sold 300,000 copies and was a best seller throughout the United States, England, Europe, and Asia.

The novel was both praised for its humanity and attacked as biased and inaccurate. In the North, readers were horrified by the brutal descriptions of slavery and flocked to the abolitionist side. *Uncle Tom's Cabin* is often credited with stirring so much antislavery furor among Northern whites that it contributed to the outbreak of the Civil War. In the South, though, many people criticized Stowe as an outsider who couldn't possibly depict Southern life accurately. These critics pointed out that she had never visited or lived in the South and had never even seen a plantation. They took *Uncle Tom's Cabin* as an affront, banned the book, and threatened to arrest anyone who possessed it.

Harriet Beecher Stowe died in 1896 and was buried in Andover, Massachusetts. But Ohio continues to claim and honor her with the Harriet Beecher Stowe House in Cincinnati. The museum is the former home of Stowe's father and is located on what was the campus of the Lane Seminary. Harriet lived in the house until she married Calvin Stowe in 1836.

To read more about Ohio's role in the Underground Railroad, turn to page 79.

Did You Know?

Ohio is home to some huge, well-known corporations. Here are just a few:

- Abercrombie & Fitch
- Proctor & Gamble
- White Castle Restaurants
- Victoria's Secret
- Goodyear
- Big Lots
- CompuServe
- Red Roof Inn
- Huffy Corporation
- King Soopers
- Roto-Rooter
- Revco Drugs
- Owens Corning
- Chiquita Brands International

Name That Town, Part 2

On page 171, we told you about the origins of the names of some Ohio towns. Here are four more.

River Styx

This town takes its name, in a roundabout way, from the River Styx of Greek mythology. Ohio's Styx River runs near the town and is a tributary of Chippewa Creek in Medina and Wayne counties. The settlers who named the Styx River couldn't resist paying homage to the Greeks' most famous waterway. As a result, the town and some of the roads nearby all bear the name of River Styx.

Russia

The flat plains and immense snowfall common to the area around this Shelby County town reminded its Russian settlers of their homeland and its French settlers of the region in which they'd fought in during the reign of Napoléon. So they named it as such.

Versailles

Folks in this town can thank the French . . . again. Versailles was originally named Jacksonville after American president Andrew Jackson. But the French immigrants who settled the area in the early 1800s changed the name in 1837 when one of them, horribly homesick, talked the townsfolk into a name that reminded him of home.

Xenia

Located in the southwestern corner of the state, Xenia was founded in 1803 and got its name from the Greek word for "hospitality." Xenia, Ohio, is one of only a few midsized towns in the United States that begins with the letter X.

Did You Know?

Roger Quinn—director of Case Western University's Robotics Lab—is leading a team of professors and scientists who are working on building mini robots modeled after insects. Why insects? Six-legged creepy crawlies walk with what's known as a "tripod gait," meaning that two legs on one side of the body and one on the other are touching the ground at all times. This makes it possible for the insects to travel over rough terrain without missing a step; their movement remains as stable as a three-legged stool. So far, Quinn's team has come up with three types of bug robots:

- Cockroaches that scramble along on six mechanical legs powered by mechanical muscles.
- Crickets that use their oversized back legs to jump.
- Ants that mimic the strength of the bug: they can lift the equivalent of their weight (about six pounds) and still walk.

Someday, the Case Western robots might function as lifesavers or explorers. The creators imagine them climbing through rubble to find earthquake survivors or exploring the forbidding Martian terrain for NASA. For now, though, the wired bugs remain in Ohio while their creators try to perfect this newest technological species.

Cincinnati Bengals By the Numbers

Welcome to the Bengals' lair, where Who Dey the tiger dines on fried Ravens, burned Brownies, and salted Steelers; opponents are "welcomed to the jungle"; and the orange-and-black machine is rough-errr, tough-errr—the finest ever seen!

0

Number of teams the Bengals' chant claims will beat Cincy: "Who dey, who dey, who dey think gonna beat them Bengals? Nobody!"

1

Number of long-time Bengals players inducted into the Pro Football Hall of Fame. Tackle Anthony Muñoz earned the honor in 1998; he was named to 11 straight Pro Bowls from 1982 to 1992. (Charlie Joiner was inducted as well, but he spent only three years in Cincy.)

2

Number of Super Bowls in which the Bengals played and the number of Super Bowls lost to Joe Montana and the San Francisco 49ers. In 1982, they lost 26–21, spoiling Bengals quarterback Ken Anderson's record-making afternoon, and in 1989, they lost 20–16 when Montana tossed the winning touchdown pass with just 34 seconds left. Grrrrrrrrrr.

3

Stadiums the Bengals have called home over the years: Nippert

Stadium (1968–1969), Riverfront Stadium (1970–1999; also known as Cinergy Field from 1996 to 1999), and Paul Brown Stadium (2000–present).

5

The Bengals lowest combined game score, a 5–0 loss to Buffalo in 1978.

9

Number of head coaches in the team's history; only three have winning records: Bill Johnson (1976–1978), Forrest Gregg (1980–1983), and Marvin Lewis (2003–present).

11

Total yards rushing allowed by the defense in the team's 44–28 victory over the Browns on December 12, 1999, the final game played at Riverfront Stadium.

26

Number of years with no Bengals team. The original team formed in 1937 and folded in 1941. The new Bengals reemerged as an expansion team in 1967 thanks in large part to the efforts of Hall of Fame coach Paul Brown, who also founded and coached the Browns.

29

The number of Ben-Gals (cheerleaders) on the squad.

54

The only retired Bengals jersey number. It belonged to offensive lineman Bob Johnson, the team's first-ever draft pick.

85

Receiver Chad Johnson's jersey number. In 2006, Johnson used the number as inspiration for his new nickname—"Ocho-Cinco"—in honor of Hispanic Heritage Month. Ocho was fined $5,000 for putting his new moniker on his jersey.

278

Yards rushed in one game in 2000 by Corey Dillon. This broke Walter Payton's 1977 NFL record of 275 yards (Corey's record was broken in 2003 by Jamal Lewis, who rushed for 295).

1988

Rookie year of running back Elbert "Ickey" Woods. His "Ickey Shuffle" led to the No Fun League . . . ahem . . . the NFL penalizing players for "excessive celebration" during the game.

$110 million

Contract extension that quarterback Carson Palmer—the "Big Kahuna"—negotiated in 2005, right before he suffered (and overcame) a potentially career-ending knee injury in a wild card playoff game against the Pittsburgh Steelers.

Did You Know?

Local legend says that early settlers in the town of Torch carried pine torches when they walked to church services in the evening. Hence, the name.

JER-RY! JER-RY!

TV Guide once named The Jerry Springer Show the "Worst TV Show Ever." But before Springer became the king of trash TV, he was an immigrant, lawyer, news anchorman, and one of the most popular mayors in Cincinnati's history.

In the Beginning

Gerald Norman Springer was born on February 13, 1944, in a tube station in London. He was a baby of the Blitz—when German fighter planes bombed England's capital nightly during World War II—and his parents, both Jews, had fled Nazi Germany. In 1949, the family moved to the United States, and Springer has said that his earliest memories are of seeing the Statue of Liberty from the boat sailing into New York Harbor.

The Springers settled in the New York City borough of Queens, and Jerry attended high school there. He then went on to Tulane University and law school at Northwestern University in Illinois. His first job out of college was as a campaign aide for Robert F. Kennedy's 1968 bid for president. After Kennedy was assassinated, Springer got a job at a Cincinnati law firm and began to consider his own career in politics.

If At First You Don't Succeed . . .

The year was 1969, and Jerry Springer was 25 years old. He decided to run for Congress, even though he'd been in Cincinnati for only six months. He was also a liberal, running in the city's most conservative district, so it was no surprise that he lost. What was surprising was that he didn't lose by much: 55 percent to 45 percent. That bolstered his confidence, and he ran for the Cincinnati City Council the next year. That time, he won.

Springer was a fresh voice in the city's political machine. He opposed the Vietnam War and advocated public works. He managed to convince the council to build Riverfront Stadium, home of the Cincinnati Reds for 20 years, with private dollars instead of public, even though he was the only advocate of the idea and most stadiums were publicly funded at the time. Fellow Cincinnati politicians remember him as one of the most gifted natural politicians they'd ever seen.

From Scandalized Politician to Mayor

Springer served on the council until 1974 when a scandal stalled his career. A police investigation into a Kentucky massage parlor revealed a prostitution ring, and Springer's name showed up in the business records. He'd been a patron—and had paid by personal check.

Springer resigned his council seat and apologized to his constituency—and to his wife. It looked like his career might be over, but he stood up to public ridicule and jokes and earned the respect of the city. Springer won back his city council seat in 1975.

Three years later, Springer ran for mayor in Cincinnati and won. During his single term, Springer managed to get health clinics and recreation centers built in many of Cincinnati's poorest neighborhoods, and he negotiated the end of a transit strike. He also wrestled a circus bear for charity. (The bear won.)

In 1980, he ran for governor of Ohio. But although his charisma had won him many supporters in Cincinnati, most of Ohio had never heard of him. He lost.

"Take Care of Yourselves"

Springer's next job was as a political reporter for Cincinnati's NBC affiliate, WLWT. At the time, the network had the lowest ratings of any news show in the city. With little to lose, the network gave Springer free reign to turn that around. Within two years, he was the city's most popular anchor. His signature commentaries—like the ones he still uses to end his shows—were probably the reason Springer also ended each program with the catch phrase "Take care of yourself, and each other." He still uses it today.

For the next decade, Jerry Springer was the voice of the news in Cincinnati. WLWT News became the top-rated local news program, and Springer won 10 local Emmys. He was so popular that, in 1991, the network gave him his own show: *The Jerry Springer Show*. Jerry initially split his time between the daytime talk show and his news anchor job until the network decided that his liberal Cincinnati news persona clashed with his role as national charismatic talk show host. So he left the news, and Cincinnati, for Chicago and the big time.

He's Interviewing Who?

Springer's exploits as a trash TV talk show host are legendary, but his program actually started out as a clone of *The Phil Donahue Show*. Springer was intelligent, conducted highbrow interviews, and delivered commentaries—similar to what he'd been doing on the news. He interviewed Jesse Jackson and Oliver North and tackled topics like gun control and homelessness. But after three years, the show's ratings were in the toilet and he was in danger of being canceled.

That same year, Springer's show got a new executive producer: Richard Dominick, who believed that if a program wasn't entertaining with the sound off, it wasn't good television. Under Dominick's guidance, the guests on Springer's show morphed from serious to farcical, and the more outrageous the subject matter got, the higher the ratings climbed. Soon, Springer was hosting shows with titles other talk shows wouldn't touch, like "Christmas with the Klan," "I Married a Horse," and "Granny Works in a Brothel."

In 2000, Jerry Springer's contract was renewed for $6 million a year. But despite his show's success, he has kept his eye on politics and serious journalism. In 1997, he was hired as a commentator on a Chicago TV station (although protests from the station's anchors forced him to resign just four days later). He remains active in and works as a fundraiser for Ohio's Democratic Party. And there were even rumors that he was thinking about running for a seat in the Ohio State Senate in 2004. (Springer ultimately decided his TV obligations would make a campaign impossible.) Given the number of transformations he's undergone already, though, few people are willing to count him out just yet.

Did You Know?

More Ohioans with a sense of humor:

"I don't like spinach, and I'm glad I don't, because if I liked it I'd eat it, and I just hate it." —**Clarence Darrow**

"I'm so old, they've canceled my blood type."
—**Bob Hope**, on his 100th birthday

The Great Chase

In 1862, a group of Ohioans sneaked into the Confederate South in one of the most daring raids in Civil War history.

The Makings of a Raid

In 1862, James J. Andrews—a Virginian by birth but a Union scout and sometimes-spy by choice—came up with a plan to hijack one of the Confederacy's trains. Andrews believed that if he could take control of the train and make it back into Union territory (destroying Confederate bridges, tracks, and telegraphs along the way), he could do serious damage to the Confederates' supply lines along the Western and Atlantic Railroad. The railroad was vital to the Confederate army because it connected Georgia, Tennessee, and Kentucky and provided branches to other southeastern areas of the Confederacy. Destroying the railroad would frustrate the Confederates and, if timed properly, could slow troop reinforcements to the Confederate line.

Andrews presented his idea to the Union's Major General Ormsby Mitchel, who gave him the go-ahead. Andrews then recruited 22 soldiers and one civilian from Ohio to join him on the secret mission.

Taking the Train

Andrews informed his men of their goal: they would hijack a train called the *General* in Georgia and would then drive it north through Tennessee and Kentucky and over Union lines. Dressed as civilians, then Ohioans left for Georgia in early April 1862. They faced torrential rains and had to travel separately in small groups so as not to arouse suspicion. In the early morning of April 12, they reconnected near a town called Big Shanty outside Atlanta. (They were two soldiers short, however; two men overslept and missed the rendezvous.) The *General* was scheduled to stop at Big Shanty so the crew and passengers could have breakfast, and indeed, it rolled into town as scheduled. After the people on board departed the train and settled in for their morning meal, Andrews and his men (who came to be called "Andrews' Raiders") sneaked on board. They fired up the engine and pulled away from the stop.

The Chase

Things seemed to go well at first. The soldiers had commandeered the train and were moving slowly but steadily north. The problem, though, was that they needed to get more fuel and wait for the tracks to clear of other trains. These obstacles ate up precious time and gave the train's Confederate conductor, William Fuller, a chance to follow them. He set out on foot for the next station on the line. From there, he got on board another train, began to chase the raiders, and called for help from local posses.

With Fuller in hot pursuit, the raiders didn't have much time to burn bridges, destroy the track, and cut telegraph wires in their wake. The closer Fuller got, the more frantic Andrews' Raiders became, and their mission started to fall apart. They were able to cut a few telegraph wires, but they never managed to burn any bridges or pull up any track. Finally, after 87 miles, the *General* ran out of fuel. Still in Georgia and with no hope of rescue, the Raiders abandoned their mission. They scattered into the surrounding woods, but all were eventually caught.

The Confederates had no sympathy for the pro-Union Yankees from Ohio. The men were interrogated, beaten, and seven of them, including Andrews, were hanged. The remaining

14 were jailed. Over the course of the next year, eight of those escaped from prison, and finally, in March 1863, the last six were returned to the Union in a prisoner swap.

Medals of Honor

On their return to Ohio, the men were hailed as heroes. Over the next few years, 20 of the Raiders received the Medal of Honor. (As civilians, Andrews and another layman were ineligible, and two of the soldiers were overlooked, as their records were lost to bureaucracy.) The medal had been created in 1862 to honor soldiers who "distinguish themselves by their gallantry in action."

The youngest Raider, a Kenton man named Jacob Parrott, was the first person ever to receive the new Medal of Honor. Secretary of War Edwin Stanton, himself from Steubenville, Ohio, interviewed Parrott and was especially impressed with the young man's calm recollection of the raid and the treatment the prisoners had received while in Southern hands.

Did You Know?

The 1862 James J. Andrews raid on Confederate train lines became part of popular legend, and was later chronicled in two films: the 1927 silent comedy *The General*, and 1956's *The Great Locomotive Chase*. It was also the subject of 20th-century composer Robert W. Smith's *The Great Locomotive Chase*, a musical score that includes railroad engine sound effects.

Weigh to Go, Toledo

Ever wonder who came up with the idea for the no-springs scale . . . and why? We did.

You're Fired!

At the turn of the 20th century, business at the Dayton-based National Cash Register Company was booming. (*To read more about NCR, turn to page 148.*) Henry Theobald had risen through the company's ranks quickly. He began his NCR career as a stenographer and by the age of 34 was a general manager. But in 1901, he found himself out of a job. Having failed to get NCR founder John Patterson's approval before making a change to one of the company's manufacturing processes, Theobald was fired.

Weighing Options

Unemployed but equipped with business skills and confidence, Theobald thought about going into business for himself. He just needed a product to sell, and soon he decided to market a new type of scale.

In 1898, inventor Allen DeVilbiss Jr. had come up with a scale that used a gravity-and-pendulum system to provide accurate, automatic weight and cost measurements of goods. Until that time, most scales used springs to measure weight, but they could be inaccurate. Even slight changes in temperature could affect the scales' results. The DeVilbiss scale didn't have that problem, but it was much more expensive to manufacture, so it sold for a higher price.

Still, Theobald saw a lot of business possibilities in the new scale. After all, butchers, grocers, and general store merchants needed scales. So Theobald bought the DeVilbiss Scale Company, including the patent for the no-springs scale. He opened his own business—the Toledo Computing Scale Company (later just Toledo Scale)—and hired DeVilbiss on as his first factory manager.

Look Out for Thieves

The new scales may have been more accurate than their springy counterparts, but by the company's fourth year in business, it was losing money. The product was expensive, and merchants weren't flocking to Theobald's showrooms. So he decided to take the no-springs design to the people. All he needed was a catchy slogan.

In 1904, Theobald created the "No Springs, Honest Weight" campaign to make his scales stand out. He discredited his competitors by implying that any shop owner who didn't use a no-springs scale was stealing from his customers. Theobald also encouraged lawmakers to regulate commercial scales. And what was the best way to do that? By buying a Toledo Scale, of course.

Scaling Up

By 1906, consumer demand for honest weight had increased and merchants began to advertise their use of Toledo Scales to attract customers. Theobald included with each Toledo Scale a sign that said "We Protect our Customers by Using Toledo Scales—No Springs—Honest Weight Guaranteed" for merchants to display as an assurance for their customers. Some merchants even purchased electric signs that flashed "Toledo Scale—No Springs—Honest Weight" every time an item was weighed. Theobald also encouraged merchants to hold "Honest Weight" events to announce the purchase of a new Toledo

Scale. Company salespeople would attend and explain the advantages of the new scale.

By 1914, Toledo Scales dominated the market. In 10 years, Theobald had sold more than 75,000 scales. Henry Theobald died in 1924, but a series of presidents and managers continued to build the business in Ohio until 1975, when the company's corporate headquarters moved out of Toledo. Today, the company is part of a corporation called Mettler Toledo, headquartered in Columbus. The little scale company started in 1901 by an unemployed cash register company manager is now an international, publicly traded corporation.

Did You Know?

In the late 1800s, following an expedition to Greenland, explorer Robert E. Peary brought a meteorite back to the United States. The meteorite—called Ahnighito, which means "the tent" in the Inuit language—was so large that it wasn't officially weighed until 1956, when Toledo Scale created a special device to calculate its weight: a whopping 34 tons. Today the meteorite is on display at New York City's Museum of Natural History.

Goodyear . . . Then and Now

Goodyear's come a long way, baby!

Then: Charles Goodyear, for whom the company was named, was a 19th-century inventor and the first American to vulcanize rubber (a process that makes rubber more durable and less sticky). He died in 1860 with $200,000 of debt.
Now: His name is associated with the third-largest tire company in the world.

Then: The first Goodyear factory opened in Akron in 1898. Founder Frank Seiberling borrowed $3,500 from his brother-in-law to start the company. Sales in the first month of business totaled $8,246.
Now: In 2006, Goodyear's net sales totaled $20.3 billion.

Then: In 1898, Goodyear employed 13 people.
Now: More than 80,000 work at Goodyear plants and offices around the world.

Then: Frank Seiberling needed a logo for his growing company. In 1900, he came up with the idea of using a winged foot of the Roman god Mercury set in the middle of the word "Goodyear." Seiberling felt that Mercury—the god of trade and a swift messenger—embodied Goodyear's products and business style. The new logo first appeared publicly in a 1901 edition of the *Saturday Evening Post*.
Now: The modern logo includes a smaller, more stylized

winged foot than the original, but it remains the company's symbol and is one of the most recognizable trademarks in the world.

Then: In 1917, Goodyear set up the first interstate trucking route, called the Wingfoot Express. Seiberling initially wanted the trucks to deliver goods nonstop between Akron and Boston. (The routes were later expanded to include cross-country treks.) That initial trip was more than 700 miles each way and required a two-man crew: one drove while the other rested. The Goodyear trucks weighed three to five tons and had interiors that were modified to include a sleeping cab (the first in the trucking industry) and space for a variety of goods and supplies—everything from spare tires to shoe soles to grain, lumber, and eggs. In 1918, the trucks even made a special trip, carrying a group of Boy Scouts 3,000 miles along the East Coast during a Scout excursion.

Now: Interstate trucking is one of the easiest and most efficient ways to move goods overland.

Then: The first helium-filled Goodyear blimp took to the skies in 1925. Named the *Pilgrim*, it was an enormous advertisement that barnstormed the United States and introduced Goodyear to a mass audience. Over the next 80 years, Goodyear built and flew more than 300 different blimps, with Akron being the hub of blimp manufacturing.

Now: The Goodyear blimp is one of the most recognizable airships in the world. The company now maintains a fleet of three blimps: *Spirit of Innovation*, based in Florida; *Spirit of America*, based in California; and *Spirit of Goodyear*, based in Akron.

The Pride of the Buckeyes

The OSU marching band has been thrilling fans since 1878. But if you think you know everything about the "best damn band in the land," think again.

1. It had a modest beginning.

Today, the OSU marching band is a 192-piece extravaganza, but back in 1878, it was just a 12-piece flute-and-drum corps. When professional musician Gustav Bruder became the first band director in 1896, he increased the size of the band to 64. In 1920, he combined his band with the Varsity Band, bringing the number to 100. (That year, he also introduced OSU's first showy, strutting drum major: Edwin "Tubby" Essington.) Over the next half century, the band size continued to increase until 1976, when it reached the current 192 marching members (225 total members, including alternates).

2. You don't have to be a music major to play in the band.

Only about 20 percent of the students in the OSU marching band are music majors. Members come from a variety of disciplines, and the most common is engineering. The band does, however, have strict standards and auditions. Every member has to audition, and the tryout process is arduous: it consists primarily of several days of playing and marching alone and in groups. Whether male or female, trumpeter or sousaphone player, new or veteran member, everyone is held to the same standards and participates in the same audition process. And once students make the band, they are continuously challenged to keep their spots. Bandleaders conduct weekly music and uniform checks, and before every performance, alternates are expected to challenge band members with a mini-audition. If a band member falters during the challenge, the alternate takes his or her place in the formation.

3. Skull Session started out as a pregame rehearsal.

Back in 1932, the band's leader, Eugene Weigel, decided that he wanted the band members to memorize their musical numbers, rather than read them as they played. Before each game, to make sure the band was ready, he held a last rehearsal (called a "skull session") in the school's old stock-judging pavilion. Students, family, and friends could come watch the rehearsal, and over the years, it became a popular tradition to attend Skull Session before a game. By 1940, it was so popular that the band had to issue tickets (free ones). In 1957, Skull Session moved to St. John Arena. Today, Skull Session is a pep rally/rehearsal. Two hours before each home game, the band plays through all of its numbers. Tickets are still free, and on average, 10,000 fans show up. The football team and coach come, too, and usually say a few words before game time.

4. Dotting the "i" happened by chance.

Eugene Weigel also introduced "Script Ohio"—as just one of several new formations in 1936. The band performed it twice that year, and Weigel choose trumpet player John Brungart to dot the "i" just because he happened to be "in the right place at the right time." Brungart's dot wasn't the elaborate kick, turn, and bow that it is today, however. He just hopped into place and played along with "Buckeye Battle Cry." Two years later, sousaphone player Glenn Johnson replaced Brungart—again by chance: Weigel gestured to him and said "switch places with the trumpet player in the dot." Johnson did, and during one game in the 1938, he came up with the dot dance when the drum major showed up out of time. There were a couple of beats left in the song, so Johnson did a kick, turn, and bow to use up the time. The crowd loved it, and the move became the formation's signature.

5. The "i-dotter" changes with each game.

Each year, the band's fourth-year sousaphone players get to choose the game in which they'd like to perform the role of "i-dotter." The fourth-year sousaphone player who's marched in the most pregame formations gets to choose first. From there, the rest of the fourth-year sousaphone players pick a date (other band members pick up any leftover dates). Postseason games require a "dot-off": eligible players perform their kick, turn, and bow, and then the sousaphone players vote for a winner.

The "i-dotter" in Script Ohio is always either a sousaphone player or the rare honorary guest. To read about one such guest (golfer Jack Nicklaus), turn to page 202.

Did You Know?

Ohio takes its name from the Iroquois. In their language, *ohio* means "great river."

It's Just Business

How much do you know about Ohio-born businesses?
Take this quiz and find out.

1. In 1897, Jerome M. Smucker opened his business in Orrville, Ohio. What was his company's first product?

A. Jam
B. Jelly
C. Cider

2. Jeeps, which have been manufactured in Toledo since 1941, get their name from two meanings. Which of the following is *not* one of them?

A. The doglike character Eugene the Jeep from the *Popeye* cartoon, who had the ability to fly, jump, and seem ingly defy physics.
B. A slang term for "truck."
C. A World War I reference for new recruits and unproven vehicles.

3. Hartzell Propeller, Inc. (based in Piqua, Ohio) has been making propellers since 1917, three years after Orville Wright struck up a friendship with his neighbor, George Hartzell, and inspired the man to get involved with aviation. Before Wright arrived, though, Hartzell manufactured an entirely different product. What was it?

A. Lumber
B. Flour
C. Cornmeal

4. The American Whistle Corporation—based in Columbus—is the only U.S. company that manufactures the (ubiquitous) safety whistles used at sporting events, in school PE classes, and by police. What are those whistles made of?

A. Aluminum

B. Brass

C. Tin

5. How did William Procter (from Ireland) and James Gamble (from England) meet? (They later became the founders of the conglomerate Procter and Gamble.)

A. They married sisters.

B. The both studied soap making with the same chemist.

C. They met on a ship bound for America.

For answers, turn to page 308.

Did You Know?

In 1883, a man named John Grimm was killed by a falling tree in Marion, Ohio. His gravesite (also the site of the accident) is on Cardington Road, just southeast of town. It's marked by a white marble slab surrounded by four upright limestone slabs. A worn metal sign gives sparse details of the man's confrontation with the tree, but that might not be the whole story: There are rumors that Grimm might actually have been done in by his own brother, possibly because the two were rivals for the same job.

The Man Behind the Underpants

One of our favorite authors here at the BRI is Dav Pilkey, who wrote such best sellers as Captain Underpants and the Wrath of the Wicked Wedgie Woman *and* Captain Underpants and the Attack of the Talking Toilets. *He was also born and raised in Ohio.*

An Inspired Childhood

Dav Pilkey spent his youth in Cleveland and went to college at Kent State. As an adult, he's authored more than 43 books and created six series. Perhaps the best known is his Captain Underpants series, which is based on a character he created in second grade. Pilkey credits his childhood and elementary school with being the source of much of the content of the series—the practical jokes, the Flip-O-Rama flip books, and George and Harold's comics. Although he now lives in Oregon, Pilkey's Ohio upbringing provided a lot of inspiration for his best-selling books for kids (and hip adults).

- George Beard and Harold Hutchins, the main characters of the Captain Underpants series, live in Piqua, Ohio. The author selected this town because it once held the annual Great Outdoor Underwear Festival.
- In many books, villains attack the gym teachers, and no one cares. This is the author's revenge for the many mean gym teachers he came across in elementary school.
- In *Captain Underpants and the Attack of the Talking Toilets,* Pilkey uses the term "invention convention," which was inspired by an annual event of the same name that his uncle (a teacher) hosted at his Berea, Ohio, school.

- The title for *Moonglow Roll-O-Rama* was inspired by the Moon-glo Roller Rink in Kent.
- *The Dumb Bunnies Go to the Zoo* was inspired by a trip Pilkey's sister took with her family to the Cleveland Zoo.
- *The Paperboy* was inspired by Pilkey's experiences delivering the Ohio newspaper the *Lorain Journal*. The paper that the book's character delivers was named after the author's father's sailboat, the *Morning Star*.
- Oscar, the star of *The Hallo-weiner*, is based on a dog that belongs to some of Pilkey's Ohio friends.

Challenged!

In 2002, the American Library Association reported that the Captain Underpants series was the sixth most challenged in the United States. In 2003, *The Adventures of Super Diaper Baby* was challenged specifically and came close to being banned from a school library in Texas. Of all the conflict, Pilkey says:

> It was never my intention to offend anybody. My intention . . . was to make kids laugh. If a kid is reading my books and laughing, I've done my job. Of course, I knew all along that some people would be offended by the book, but that didn't really bother me. Humor is a very subjective thing.

Spelling Isn't Everything

One of the reasons some people find Pilkey's books objectionable (besides the obvious bathroom humor) is the ubiquity of spelling and grammatical errors in the stories. But the author maintains that the errors serve a purpose. He says:

> I've heard from some grown-ups who were not happy about the misspelled words and bad grammar in this book, but I think they're missing the point . . . The

point of all the mistakes in George and Harold's comics is: it doesn't matter . . . It's my hope that these kids will read George and Harold's comics, notice the mistakes, and realize that creativity doesn't depend on proper spelling, flawless grammar, or even perfect artwork [Harold's drawings aren't much more than stick figures]. I'm hoping these "less than perfect" comics will encourage kids to try being creative on their own, without the often paralyzing fear of messing up.

Underpants Facts

- Pilkey's second book, *Dog Breath*, was rejected by more than 30 publishers until Scholastic agreed to publish it. *Dog Breath* has become Pilkey's best-selling picture book to date.
- Unique artwork is as important an element to Pilkey's books as the story. In fact, some of the stories have been written in just 15 minutes, but Pilkey has spent months or up to a year illustrating. He's explored many media and art techniques, and it comes as no surprise that his favorite painters are ones who did not follow the rules—van Gogh, Rousseau, and Chagall.
- The first draft for Pilkey's *'Twas the Night Before Thanksgiving* was eaten by a herd of cows.
- The cover of the first edition of *The Dumb Bunnies* had a can of Spam on the cover, but the makers of Spam were not pleased and threatened a lawsuit. The can was stickered over, and the word was removed in the next printing.
- Science genius and Captain Underpants character Professor Pippy P. Poopypants is modeled after Albert Einstein.
- The Jerome Horwitz Elementary School that George and Harold attend was named after the given name of Curly of *The Three Stooges*.

The Number One Fun Car

In the mid-1940s, two Athens-based inventors came up with the idea of selling a microcar that consumers could construct themselves. They called it the King Midget.

All the King's Men

After World War II, America's economy was booming and American pocketbooks were full. Never in the country's history had so many people had so much discretionary income . . . and what better way to spend their money than on fun items? Elaborate children's toys, washing machines, and televisions became the norm. And in neighborhoods all over the country, King Midget minicars took to the open road.

Claud Dry and Dale Orcutt came up with the King Midget car while working as pilots during World War II. In 1946, they opened an auto parts company in Athens, Ohio, and started working on their concept. They wanted to build and sell a small, affordable car, and they used their knowledge of aeronautics (learned during their military days) to make it light, sleek, and easy to maneuver. To set themselves apart—and to offset costs—they also decided to let people put the cars together themselves. They named the car after their auto parts company: Midget Motors Corporation.

King One and King Two

The first King Midget was a single-passenger car called the Model 1. It was sold two ways: as a kit that contained an assembly book, the frame, axles, springs, steering wheel, and diagrams for the sheet metal plates (builders had to buy the single-cylinder engine separately); and in the slightly more expensive assembled form. It looked like a soapbox derby car and had no roof, but it ran on its own power. The second model (appropriately called Model 2) was a swankier ride. It was still a bare-bones vehicle—the Model 2 had no speedometer or reverse gear—but it could seat two passengers, offered an optional automatic transmission, and had a top. It was also durable: the Model 2 could carry more than its own weight. It sold for just $500.

Both the Model 1 and 2 were about the size of a golf cart. (In fact, Dry and Orcutt offered a golf cart model that included two golf bag racks and a quiet muffler system, so as not to disturb other players.) These models included footrests on the front fenders, wide traction on the rear tires, and special low gearings, and they could be driven on an actual road. But with an engine equivalent to many of today's riding lawnmowers, they maxed out at around 15 miles per hour.

King of the Road

Dry and Orcutt sold Midget Motors Corporation and the rights to the King Midget cars in 1966. Emissions and safety regulations ultimately made the small cars too expensive to produce. But between 1946 and 1969, the company racked up some impressive stats, leading to the little cars earning the title of "the number one fun car." King Midgets were . . .

- The only small car continuously manufactured for nearly a quarter of a century.
- The sixth largest automobile manufacturer in the United States.

- Incredibly fuel efficient—their small engines yielded more than 50 miles per gallon.

The rights to King Midgets, their parts, and their design changed hands several times over the last three decades. In 2001, a Norwalk, Ohio, automobile collector named Mike Beebe became the latest buyer. He still calls the company Midget Motors and hopes to build a Model 4 King Midget one day soon.

The King's Jamboree

A former owner of the company and avid collector, Dave Stults started a registry of King Midgets and an annual gathering of Midget owners: In 1991, 18 Midget owners congregated in Westport, Indiana (Stults' hometown), for the first King Midget Jamboree. The next year, he helped form the King Midget Car Club at the Jamboree in Athens, Ohio. To date, the club has more than 200 active members.

Did You Know?

"Buckeye Battle Cry" holds a special place in the hearts of Buckeye fans, but the school's oldest fight song is "Across the Field," written in 1915 by OSU student William A. Dougherty.

The Dreamer

You've heard his name, and some know his story. But there's more to Ohio congressman and fringe presidential candidate Dennis Kucinich than meets the eye. He was one of the youngest people to hold a major political office, and he endured a public financial crisis that should have buried him. But Kucinich rebounded, was eventually vindicated, and went on to continue his political career.

The Boy Mayor vs. the Banks

Dennis Kucinich was born in Cleveland in 1946 and attended Case Western University. He got his first political job in 1969 as a member of the Cleveland City Council, and became the city's mayor in 1977. He was called the "Boy Mayor," not only because he was young (just 31) but also because he was small in stature (he stands only 5 feet 7 inches tall).

In the late 1970s, the city of Cleveland was in a tight spot. Local banks were calling in loans they had provided the city, and Cleveland didn't have any money. So the banks offered a deal: they would renew the city's credit line if Cleveland would sell its public electricity company—Municipal "Muny" Light—to a private competitor, CEI.

The Boy Mayor said "no dice." Some of the directors of CEI were also directors of the banks, and Kucinich saw the sale as a boondoggle to enrich the businessmen. So he held firm and refused to sell.

The banks followed through with their threat and pressed Cleveland into default. It was an embarrassment for the city and near-instantaneous political exile for Kucinich. He lost his reelection bid in 1979.

Spiritual Lessons

After all that, Kucinich found it difficult to get a job in Cleveland, so he went out west to do some soul-searching. He stayed at the home of his friend Shirley MacLaine and became a vegan. Kucinich earned money by lecturing and consulting, but every time he dipped a toe back into politics, he failed. Then, in 1993 while he was sitting on a beach in Malibu, his phone rang.

Vindication

It was a reporter from the *Cleveland Plain Dealer*. The newspaper had been investigating his decision not to sell Muny Light and had found that Clevelanders benefited greatly in the long run by keeping the company city-owned. The reporter wanted Kucinich's comment. He said, "I was certain that in time, I would be vindicated in the position I took."

The *Plain Dealer* ran an editorial supporting Kucinich's decision: "The truth is out: Saving Muny Light was good for Cleveland," the paper wrote. Clevelanders became Kucinich supporters once again.

Rerun

Kucinich took the opportunity and got back into politics. He ran for the Ohio State Senate in 1994 with the slogan "Because he was right." He won that election and then ran for the U.S. House of Representatives two years later. He won that, too.

As of 2007, Kucinich was serving his sixth term in the House, where he is known as one of the chamber's most progressive members. He's also known as a bit of an oddball. In 2001, he introduced a bill opposing the development of space-based weapons—specifically, any "radiation, electromagnetic, psychotronic, sonic, laser, or other energies . . . for the purpose of information war, mood management, or mind control."

In 2004, Kucinich ran for president, but his campaign never really got much steam behind it. Even in Ohio, he received only 9 percent of the vote in the Democratic primary. But he did receive the support of many celebrities, including Ani DiFranco, Willie Nelson, and Elliott Gould, in addition to his friend MacLaine.

The Dating Game

He also got a date out of it. Of his ideal first lady, Kucinich, a two-time divorcé at the time, said, "I certainly want a dynamic, outspoken woman who was fearless in her desire for peace in the world and for universal single-payer health care and a full-employment economy. If you are out there, call me." A Web site called PoliticsNH.com took the challenge and chose a winner through Internet voting. Gina Marie Santore, a 34-year-old assistant to a New Jersey sheriff, had an oatmeal-and-bananas breakfast with Kucinich in New Hampshire during the primary season. They talked about health care and pharmaceutical advertising, and he gave her a peck on the cheek when they parted. But alas . . . the match wasn't to be. It turned out that Santore already had a boyfriend.

Did You Know?

In 1899, postmaster Henry Hill was responsible for naming the town of Novelty, so named because he felt like he had to come up with something "novel."

From Door Knocking to Lip Smacking

Here's how a cosmetics company named for a little girl became one of the most successful businesses in Ohio.

Bonne Bell Is Born

It all started in 1916 when Kansan and cosmetics salesman Jesse Grove "J. G." Bell and his wife read a serialized version of Emerson Hough's novel *The Man Next Door* in the *Saturday Evening Post.* There was a character in the story named Bonne, and the more the Bells read, the more they liked her. In 1923, when their second daughter was born, they named her after that character; she became Bonne Bell.

When Bonne was four years old, J. G. Bell moved his family to Lakewood, a suburb of Cleveland. Bell had heard that business there was booming (not so in Kansas). At the time, half of America's population lived within 500 miles of Cleveland, offering a huge market for any company. Bell decided on cosmetics—it was what he knew best, after all. In 1927, he opened his own business and named it after his youngest daughter.

Cooking up Cosmetics

J.G. produced his first cosmetics on a hot plate in the basement of his rented Lakewood house. He saved money by going door-to-door himself and selling the products in plain brown packaging. At first, the sparse packaging put off his customers, but he was a skilled salesman and convinced them that the product was much more important (and more impressive) than its wrapper.

New Sales Strategy

Next, J.G. set his sights on young people. He considered them an untapped market, and he thought that he could do better business if he created products especially for them. In 1936, he bought the formula for a skin lotion from a local chemist, who had created it for dermatologists. Bell put his skills as a salesman to work again and marketed the lotion as the best skin product available for teenage skin. It was a hit.

J.G. ran the company himself until he retired in 1959, and throughout his tenure, he insisted on well-developed, high-quality products. Bonne Bell continues that tradition today. The company does numerous safety tests on its ingredients but forbids animal testing. J.G. Bell died in 1970 at the age of 80.

Lip-Smacking Good

In 1959, Jess Bell—J.G.'s son and Bonne's brother—took over, and he was the one who dreamed up the company's most popular (and enduring) product. In the early 1970s, Jess came of with the idea of scented and flavored lip balms. He originally envisioned the lip balms as something that would appeal to outdoorsy types; he added the flavors to differentiate them from similar products on the market. He launched the first (strawberry-flavored) Lip Smacker in 1973, and, in the years since, created dozens of additional flavors. The company even partnered with recognizable giants like Starburst, Skittles, and Dr. Pepper to create commercially recognizable Smackers.

Jess Bell retired in 2000 and died in 2005; his son, Jess A. "Buddy" Bell, took over as chairman and CEO. Today, Buddy runs the family-owned company from its headquarters in Lakewood, Ohio.

What About Bonne?

Bonne Bell, the business' namesake, died in 2005. But during her lifetime, she served on the company's board, allowed her signature to be used on early company logos, and appeared in several advertising campaigns.

Did You Know?

The Roseville Pottery Company, which was founded in Roseville in 1890 but headquartered in Zanesville from 1892 to 1954, is one of the most recognizable and collectable brands of pottery in the world. Roseville's first high-quality art pottery line was called Rozane (the name a combination of the company's two hometowns), and its pieces were bright red, green, or tinted to look like fine Italian glass. The company was most famous, though, for its "middle-period" (1920s and 1930s) works. These resembled art deco pieces and had floral designs and matte finishes. Today, Roseville pottery is popular among collectors, and rare pieces like umbrella stands and floor vases can go for thousands of dollars.

Ohio's Presidents

This Midwestern state is the birthplace of seven presidents. Take a look at the native sons that Ohio sent to Pennsylvania Avenue.

Between 1868 and 1900, all elected presidents were born in Ohio—or, in the case of Grover Cleveland, shared a name with an Ohio city. Even into the 20th century, the Buckeye State remained a political powerhouse. Between 1964 and 2004, every presidential candidate who won the White House also won Ohio. And because both Democrats and Republicans became president during that time, Ohio has proven itself to be a bipartisan electorate. Here are the histories of six of the seven Ohio-born men to move into the White House. (*Read about William Howard Taft on page 76.*)

President: Ulysses S. Grant
Years in office: 1869–1877

The first Ohio-born president was Ulysses S. Grant. He was actually born Hiram Ulysses Grant in Point Pleasant, Ohio, in 1822. When he enrolled at West Point, the school listed his middle name as his first and recorded his middle initial as "S." Grant never corrected the error, and the name stuck.

During the Civil War, U. S. Grant became "Unconditional Surrender" Grant when, as a Union colonel, he demanded and received unconditional surrender from the Confederate forces at Fort Donelson, Tennessee. In 1863, Grant led the Union's western army to a spectacular victory at Vicksburg, Mississippi, capturing 20,000 troops and control of the Mississippi River. In 1864 President Abraham Lincoln promoted him to commanding general of the entire Union army, and for the next year, Grant used the superior numbers of Union troops to defeat the South. Confederate General Robert E. Lee surrendered to Grant at Appomattox Courthouse, Virginia, in April 1865, ending the war.

It was natural that the victorious Union general would be considered a prime presidential candidate, and Grant won easy victories as the Republican nominee from Illinois in 1868 and 1872. His main focus was the Reconstruction of the South and enforcement of the 15th Amendment, which gave African Americans the right to vote. In his second term, however, the Crédit Mobilier and Whiskey Ring scandals shook his administration. In his last address to Congress, Grant acknowledged errors of judgment but "not of intent." A well-received world tour helped restore his reputation at home, and he finished his best-selling memoirs, which would help pay off his substantial family debts, four days before he died. He is buried in New York City.

President: Rutherford B. Hayes
Years in office: 1877–1881
Born in Delaware, Ohio, in 1822, Hayes served as brigadier general during the Civil War, a member of the House of Representatives, and governor of Ohio. In 1876, he won the Republican nomination for president. On Election Day, Hayes was behind by 260,000 votes to Democrat Samuel J. Tilden in the popular election. However, the results were too close to call. Republicans supporting Hayes charged three Southern states with voter fraud: they believed that newly enfranchised African American voters had been intimidated from going to the polls. To win the election, Hayes needed to take all three states.

A 15-person electoral commission, composed of eight

Republicans and seven Democrats, examined the charges. By one vote, the commission gave all three states and the election to Hayes just two days before he took the oath of office. To prevent Democrats from protesting the decision, Hayes agreed to withdraw federal troops from the South, ending the Reconstruction. Hayes did not seek reelection, died in 1893, and is buried in Fremont, Ohio.

President: James A. Garfield

Time in office: March 4, 1881 to September 19, 1881

Born on a farm in Orange, Ohio, in 1831, and a major general during the Civil War, James A. Garfield was a well-liked Republican senator when he won the White House in 1880. But a disgruntled man passed over for a federal job shot Garfield in July 1881. For two months the president lay at the White House while surgeons tried to remove the bullet near his spine. He finally died just six months into his presidency. Some modern researchers believe that if the doctors had left the bullet alone, Garfield might have survived.

President: Benjamin Harrison

Years in office: 1889–1893

Benjamin Harrison (born in North Bend, Ohio, in 1833) was part of the only grandfather-grandson pair to be elected president. When he was seven, his grandfather William Henry Harrison became president. The elder Harrison had been born in Virginia but was living in Ohio when he was elected. He served just one month in office (a cold he caught while delivering the longest-ever inaugural address, which clocked at a bit under two hours, did him in). His grandson Benjamin had better luck. Benjamin Harrison, who also served as a Republican senator from

Indianapolis and a brigadier general in the Civil War, defeated incumbent president Grover Cleveland in 1888 in a very close vote. In fact, Harrison lost the popular vote but won the electoral count 233 to 168. On Inauguration Day, Cleveland accompanied Harrison to his inauguration. Four years later, Harrison returned the favor when Cleveland won the presidency back.

President: William McKinley
Years in office: 1897–1901
The election of 1896 was perhaps the first modern election. It was the first year that candidates really campaigned. Before then, candidates gave speeches here and there but actually did very little before an election. However, popular Ohio governor and Niles native William McKinley gave dynamic speeches from his own front porch to crowds of thousands who came by train to see him. (His opponent, William Jennings Bryan, also used the railroad; he traveled all over the country to speak.) The Republican McKinley also outspent the Democrat Bryan by 10 to 1 in the first widespread national media campaign and won easily.

McKinley was reelected in 1900, but on a trip to Buffalo six months later, he was shot by an anarchist. Like James Garfield 20 years before him, McKinley's recovery was affected by poor medical procedures, and he died a week later. Vice President Theodore Roosevelt became president. McKinley is buried in Canton, Ohio.

President: Warren G. Harding
Years in office: 1921–1923
The last person elected president from Ohio was newspaperman Warren G. Harding, who was born in Corsica, Ohio, in

1864. Harding owned a successful and politically powerful Ohio newspaper, the *Marion Star*. During his first term as an Ohio senator, Harding was a long-shot candidate for the Republican presidential nomination in 1920 because he had won only his home state in the primaries. Because the convention that year was deadlocked among three other candidates, party leaders chose Harding as a compromise. In the first general election after the end of World War I, Harding campaigned to return the country to what he called pre-war "normalcy." He won by a landslide.

But as president, Harding got into trouble. The Teapot Dome scandal, which concerned the misuse of the government's oil reserves, plagued him, and he underwent a national tour to revive political support. In 1923, during the trip, he died suddenly of a heart attack while in San Francisco. (Vice President Calvin Coolidge took over.) Harding is buried in Marion, Ohio.

Did You Know?

These Ohioans have a Buckeye state of mind:

"I'm just a lucky slob from Ohio who happened to be in the right place at the right time." —**Clark Gable**

"I love the normalcy of Cleveland. There's regular people there." —**Drew Carey**

Lovely Loveland

This Cincinnati bedroom community has a lot to love.

Town: Loveland
Location: Hamilton, Clermont, and Warren counties
Founding: 1878
Current population: 11,677
Size: 4.7 square miles
County seat: No

What's in a Name?

The town is named for James Loveland, who operated a general store and post office in the area in the 1800s. Locals used to say, "Leave the mailbag off at Loveland's," meaning the store. But over time, the name came to represent a growing town. The area that became Loveland was first settled in 1795 but wasn't incorporated as a village until 1878. (In 1961, it was incorporated as a city.)

Claims to Fame:

- Loveland is known as the "Sweetheart of Ohio," and for good reason: it's held a Valentine program every year since 1972. The city's chamber of commerce sponsors the event, which has a different theme each year, poetry and Valentine card–design competitions, and the election of a "Valentine Lady" who acts as the program's ambassador. (She visits businesses, schools, and nursing homes during her one-year reign.) The town's post office hand stamps Valentine's Day cards with a cachet that reads "There is nothing in this world so sweet as Love," and the U.S. Postal Service even chose Loveland as the spot at which to unveil its 1994 Love stamp.

- The 5,000-square-foot, medieval-inspired Chateau La Roche (Rock Castle), located one the banks of the Little Miami River, was built (dungeon and all) by hand by one man. Harry Andrews, a World War I medic born in 1890, wanted to bring back valor and knighthood to the modern world. He began the castle in 1929 and worked on it until he died in 1981. He got all the supplies himself, hauling 50,000 stones from the nearby riverbed to form the walls; when he ran out of stones, he made bricks by pouring cement into milk cartons and then removing the cartons when the cement dried. Andrews also formed an organization called the Knights of the Golden Trail, whose members were charged with the task of "helping save civilization." When Andrews died, he left the castle to the Knights who live there to this day and maintain it as a tourist attraction. Every year on Halloween, they decorate the castle to resemble a haunted house.
- Loveland is one of 35 towns in Ohio to have land in more than one county.

Did You Know?

Jamie Farr, an Ohioan and the star of the TV series *M*A*S*H*, says, "I wanted to be an actor, a famous actor, and I wanted my hometown of Toledo to be proud of me."

It Happened in 1803

Ohio became the 17th state, but that's not all that happened in that busy year.

January

Scottish inventor William Symington successfully sailed the *Charlotte Dundas*, the first towing steamboat, the first practical steamboat, and the first boat to show that steam power was practical for shipping.

February

The U.S. Supreme Court decided the case of *Marbury vs. Madison*, which established the principle of judicial review.

April

The United States bought the 530,000-acre Louisiana Territory from France. The total Louisiana Purchase price was more than $20 million, and the sale opened up much of the land west of the Mississippi River for settlement. The U.S. Senate ratified the purchase on October 20.

May

American essayist and poet Ralph Waldo Emerson was born in Boston, Massachusetts.

August

Meriwether Lewis left Pennsylvania to begin the historic exploration of the land west of the Mississippi. William Clark joined him in Indiana on October 14, and the two spent the next three years exploring the American West.

September

English scientist John Dalton published his atomic theory for the first time.

October

Samuel Adams, one of America's founding fathers, died in Massachusetts. Adams signed the Declaration of Independence, was a delegate at the First Continental Congress, and helped to organize the Boston Tea Party. (The Boston Beer Company's Sam Adams beer is named for him.)

November

British captain Henry Shrapnel was promoted to major. Earlier that year, the British army had started using the bullets ("shrapnel shells") that he invented in the late 1700s.

Also that year

- New York's city hall was built.
- John James Audubon conducted the first banding studies on American birds.
- Britain resumed war with France over Malta.
- Two new elements were discovered—cerium and palladium.

Did You Know?

Bo Schembechler, best known for his tenure as head football coach at the University of Michigan, earned a master's degree from Ohio State in 1952. (Traitor!)

A Game of Horse

How did a horse belonging to France's Napoleon III (nephew of the famous French emperor) end up in Marion, Ohio?

It's all thanks to Ohioan Jacob Howser, a partner in a Marion company that imported stock animals. Howser wanted to diversify Ohio's equine population and introduce new breeds. Napoleon III and his son had a prized Percheron draft horse—named Prince Imperial for Napoleon's son—to sell. So in 1868, Howser traveled to France, bought the animal for $3,000, and brought him back to Ohio.

A Horse's Life

Prince Imperial was one of the first Percheron (now called Norman) horses to be imported to North America. The breed is named after the French region of Perche, where it was first bred and whose citizens were renowned for their champion stock. Percherons are hardy, powerful, and rugged; they often pulled French stagecoaches and were used as workhorses on farms, traits that made Prince Imperial right at home in 19th-century Ohio's agricultural economy.

Because he was so unique, Prince Imperial was incredibly marketable. In addition to breeding programs, Howser decided to make some extra money by putting the animal on display. He traveled the country with Prince Imperial, showing him off at shows and fairs around the country and calling him "the greatest curiosity of this or any age."

Stuffed!

When Prince Imperial died in 1888, Howser decided to keep

the stallion working. He put the horse on ice and sent him via railroad to Rochester, New York, to the Ward Scientific Company. There—at the company named for Henry Augustus Ward, a scientist and the man who stuffed P. T. Barnum's circus elephant, Jumbo—taxidermists preserved and stuffed Prince Imperial and then sent him home. The cost: an incredible $8,000. Afterward, Howser continued to exhibit the stallion, and when they weren't traveling, he kept Prince Imperial in the living room of his house.

When Howser died, his sons showed the horse, and when they passed away, their sons followed suit. Finally, in the early 1900s, one of Howser's grandsons had enough. He sold Prince Imperial to a local family who restored him, mounted the body on wheels, and tugged him through local parades. In the early 1930s, the family donated Prince Imperial to the Marion County Historical Society.

Forever in Heritage Hall

Today, Prince Imperial is on display at Heritage Hall on East Church Street in Marion. He's easy to spot—nestled between an antique popcorn wagon and an exhibit devoted to President Warren G. Harding. In addition to his many accomplishments, Prince Imperial is credited with once having the world's longest mane (9 feet 9 inches) and longest bangs (7 feet).

Did You Know?

In bowling lingo, "Cincinnati" means an 8-10 split.

The Ohio State Fair By the Numbers

From a three-day expo in 1850, the Ohio State Fair has evolved into a 12-day August extravaganza that brings in more than $200 million each year and is one of the largest fairs in the United States.

4

Number of big rigs needed to haul Country Candy Warehouse's stash of more than 500 different candy items to the fair each year. The company's candy display at the fair is the largest in the United States.

20 cents

Cost of admission to the first Ohio State Fair. Today, tickets are $8 for adults and $7 for children.

28

Number of categories in the annual home-brewed beer competition. The brews are judged before the fair and winning beers are selected for aroma, flavor, appearance, "mouth feel," and overall impression.

45°F

Temperature at which the fair's Dairy Products Building is kept. Inside this building are the famous heifer and calf sculptures—all made out of butter. The first sculptures appeared in 1903, and in the years since, they've become a fair tradition. In the 1960s, sculptors added new subjects, and they change each year. Some notable butter sculptures of the past include

Neil Armstrong, Darth Vader, Jack Nicklaus, a Tonka Truck, and Dave Thomas of Wendy's. Ohio has also expressed its patriotism through dairy depictions of the Liberty Bell and a bald eagle.

70

Number of permanent employees of the Ohio Expo Center (where the fair is held). About 1,000 seasonal workers are also hired every year.

144 feet

Length of the yellow Giant Slide, which stands 45 feet tall and has 105 steps. More than 1,000 fairgoers enjoy the slide every hour and careen down it at an average speed of 15 mph.

175

Average number of food vendors dishing their fare each year. Fairgoers can eat everything from hot dogs to deep-fried Twinkies to hot apple dumplings à la mode and orange Creamsicle floats.

1850

The first year the fair was held in Cincinnati. It was the brainchild of the Ohio Board of Agriculture, which initially planned to hold the first statewide celebration in 1849. A cholera epidemic that year forced the organizers to wait until 1850. Over the next 22 years, the fair moved to various other cities, but finally, the Board of Agriculture decided that Columbus, being the state capital and easily accessible by train, should be the event's permanent home. Since 1886, the fair has been held at the Ohio Expo Center on Woodard Avenue.

1928

Year the John Philip Sousa Band performed twice at the fair.

7,500

Approximate number of lights illuminating the Ferris wheel.

12,707

Entries in 2005's Open Livestock Competition. The animals up for review included dairy goats, llamas, sheep, Boer goats, beef and dairy cattle, pigs, horses, poultry, and rabbits.

13,400

Hot dog samples smeared with Ben's Sweet and Hot Mustard—a condiment made in Kingston, Ohio, from a secret family recipe—that were passed out in 2006.

25,000+

Sandwiches the Ohio Pork Producers Council sold at the 2005 Ohio State Fair. They also sold more than 1,000 pounds of pork ribs.

$64,000

Cost of 1996's Grand Champion Barrow—for those unfamiliar with farm lingo, a barrow is a young, neutered male pig.

1,011,331

The record-breaking number of annual visitors who attended the fair in 2003. The single-day attendance record was 103,497, set on August 8, 2004. The first fair in 1850 brought in only about 25,000 to 30,000 people.

Welcome to the Cavs Nation

From less-than-memorable beginnings, the Cleveland Cavaliers have become one of the top franchises in the NBA.

Let's Go Ice Capades!

The 1960s and 1970s were decades of expansion for the National Basketball Association. The league had eight teams in 1954 and that number had grown to 14 by the 1969–1970 season. Three more were added for the next year, including the Cleveland Cavaliers. The original Cavs were a ragtag bunch, assembled from other teams' castoffs and several rookies. Bill Fitch was hired as the head coach; he made no false promises about their chances to contend: "Just remember, the name is Fitch, not Houdini."

The season got off to an inauspicious start when the Cavs were forced to play their first seven games on the road because the Cleveland Arena had been booked for the Ice Capades. Not surprisingly, the Cavs lost their first 15 games and finished 15-67, the worst record in the NBA.

A Sign of Things to Come?

A few years of gradual improvement saw the Cavs (now playing in their new digs, the Richfield Coliseum) not only make the playoffs but also win their division for the first time in 1976. After squeaking past the Washington Bullets in the first round, the Cavs were ousted by the Boston Celtics in the second round, four games to two. (As a small consolation, Bill Fitch won the NBA's Coach of the Year Award.)

The Cavs went on to make the playoffs the next two seasons, losing in the first round each time. Injuries to key players, Bill Fitch's resignation following the 1978–1979 season, and a new owner all contributed to many lean years. The Cavs didn't make the playoffs again until 1985.

Close, but No Cigar

The 1986 NBA Draft was a productive one for the Cavs, they selected center Brad Daughtery with the first overall pick, guard Ron Harper with the eighth pick, and also acquired guard Mark Price. Harper was traded before the 1989–1990 season, but Daughtery and Price became the faces of the franchise for much of the next decade, along with head coach Lenny Wilkens, who had the longest tenure (seven years) of any Cavs head coach since Bill Fitch. The Cavs made the playoffs eight times in ten seasons from 1987 to 1996 but never advanced to the NBA Finals. During that time, they lost five playoff series to the Chicago Bulls, who were led by the Cavs' nemesis, number 23: Michael Jordan.

Introducing the New 23

Following the 2002–2003 season, in which the Cavs posted their fifth consecutive losing record, Cleveland fans could finally chant "We're number one!"—though not for the reasons they'd like. The Cavaliers got the first pick in the 2003 NBA Draft, and they selected teen phenom and Akron native LeBron James.

For years, James had been the talk of the basketball world: while still in high school, he was featured on the covers of *SLAM*, *Sports Illustrated*, and *ESPN Magazine*. His high school games were attended by NBA players, coaches, and scouts; some were even televised nationally on ESPN. The kid was accustomed to fame and had little trouble adjusting to life in the NBA when he started playing for the Cavs at the age of 18. James scored 20.9 points his first season and was the youngest ever to win the NBA Rookie of the Year Award. He also chose to wear the number of his favorite player on his uniform: Michael Jordan's 23.

With LeBron James on their side, the Cavs went from winning 17 games in 2002–2003 to winning 35 games in 2003–2004 and then 42 in 2004–2005, missing the playoffs by one game. The 2005–2006 season proved to be a breakthrough campaign: the Cavs won 50 games and finished second in the Central Division. By then, James had a supporting cast in place, and the team continues to mature, giving the people of Cavs Nation hope that the future will bring their team a championship trophy. Let's go, Cavs!

Did You Know?

Here are some wise words from Ohio's native sons and daughters:

"We have an infinite amount to learn both from nature and from each other." **—John Glenn**

"A smile is a curve that sets everything straight." **—Phyllis Diller**

"A single twig breaks, but the bundle of twigs is strong." **—Tecumseh**

"Love is or it ain't. Thin love ain't love at all." **—Toni Morrison**

(No) Thanks, Ohio

Our deepest and shallowest gratitude for a few great—and not-so-great—people that Ohio has given us.

No Thanks for . . . William Quantrill, born in Dover in 1837. Quantrill was known for his violent tendencies even as a child; he tortured animals and was involved with petty crimes from his early years. He continued his ways when he left Ohio for Kansas in 1860—there he was charged with robbery and murder. Quantrill then fled to Missouri, where, at the start of the Civil War, he joined a Confederate regiment. But the discipline of army life wasn't for him, and by the end of 1861, he had broken away and formed Quantrill's Raiders, an infamously brutal Confederate guerrilla group. These bushwhackers raided Union towns, ambushed Union patrols, and robbed mail coaches. In the most well known of their dozens of violent acts, Quantrill and a gang of several hundred attacked Lawrence, Kansas, in 1863, killing more than 200 men and boys. He was finally killed by Union forces in 1865. (Among his followers: Frank and Jesse James.)

Thanks for . . . Mary Ann Bickerdyke, born in Knox County, Ohio, in 1817. "Mother Bickerdyke" volunteered as a nurse in Galesburg, Illinois, during the Civil War and ended up traveling with Union armies. Eventually, she set up more than 300 field hospitals for wounded soldiers. She became known as one of the most popular and outspoken female figures of the war and was so beloved by the troops that, at General William Tecumseh Sherman's request, she rode down Pennsylvania Avenue when the war ended.

After the war, Bickerdyke nursed people in slums from New York to San Francisco and worked ceaselessly to help veterans and nurses receive pensions for their war service. Mother Bickerdyke died in 1901 at the age of 84. In 1903, a monument depicting Mother Bickerdyke kneeling beside a wounded soldier and holding a cup to his lips was erected in Galesburg. (It's still there.)

No Thanks for . . . Lou Rothkopf, born in Cleveland in 1902. Rothkopf was a Prohibition-era gangster and leader of the brutal Cleveland Syndicate, a criminal organization that prospered by smuggling booze from Canada across Lake Erie and into the United States. After Prohibition, the syndicate turned to gambling. As an associate of the likes of Meyer Lansky, Bugsy Siegel, and Al Capone, Rothkopf represented Cleveland at the 1929 Atlantic City conference, considered the first major national "Mafia summit" and the beginning of the mob's national organization. Rothkopf committed suicide in 1956, a year after the suicide of his wife.

Thanks for . . . Harlan Ellison, born in Cleveland in 1934. Ellison is considered one of the greatest science fiction and surrealist writers of the 20th century. He started his career in the 1950s and is still at it. Ellison also wrote many memorable episodes of TV shows like *Outer Limits*, *Route 66*, and *The Alfred Hitchcock Hour*. He has received numerous awards, including ten Hugo and four Nebula awards for his writing. And he wrote what many critics call the best *Star Trek* episode ever: "The City on the Edge of Forever," from the show's first season.

Ohio's Own

Ohio is the home—in some cases the only home—of a handful of fascinating plants and animals. Here are just a few.

Lakeside Daisy

On the shores of Lake Erie on Ohio's Marblehead Peninsula is the 19-acre Lakeside Daisy State Nature Preserve. It was established in the old limestone quarry there in order to save the endangered flower of that name, a bright yellow wildflower found only in that tiny area of Ohio and two similarly small sites across the lake in Ontario. It is the rarest of all of Ohio's endangered plants. Want to see the them? Every May, when the flowers are in bloom, the village of Marblehead celebrates the flower by hosting a festival known as Lakeside Daisy Day.

Ohio Brook Trout

Woodiebrook Creek and Spring Brook in the Chagrin River Basin in northeast Ohio are two of the only known continuous habitats of this native and threatened species. Evidence suggests that Ohio brook trout have lived in that area since the last Ice Age—about 12,000 years ago. They are an extremely sensitive species, with very specific ecological needs: cool temperatures and high oxygen levels, which can be found in the region's sandstone-based, cool, spring-fed creeks. The area is currently designated a state scenic area and numerous projects are underway to make sure the Ohio brook trout sticks around.

Heterotrissocladius Boltoni

This is a species of tiny aquatic-born bugs that become the tiny flying bugs you may have seen swarming above creeks and ponds in the wild. This particular type was discovered in 1992 in vernal pools (temporary pools of water that usually last from spring to summer) and in Ohio's creeks. The bugs were named after Michael Bolton. (Not the singer; this Michael Bolton is a biologist from the University of Akron.)

The Lake Erie Water Snake

These aquatic snakes are found on rocky cliffs and shorelines on a group of limestone islands in western Lake Erie. Their range extends a bit into waters owned by Ontario, but they are found primarily in Ohio. Lake Erie water snakes are gray when they reach adulthood—and can be up to 42 inches long. They're also excellent swimmers and feed primarily on fish. Because the islands are partially inhabited and very popular with boaters and campers, the snake's numbers have been dwindling for years. They were put on the endangered species list in 1991.

Bartley's Reed Grass

This is a rare grass species that was first discovered in south-central Ohio and is now known to exist in just a handful of states to Ohio's west. Bartley's reed grass grows around the edges of upland woods and on cool, north-facing sandstone bluffs. It also has the curious characteristic of almost never flowering or producing seeds—which is one of the reasons it's rare. Instead, it spreads vegetatively, like many grasses, by sending out runners that send up new leaves. The plant was named after Ohio farmer and amateur botanist Floyd Bartley.

Weird Ohio, Part 2

Here are more strange tales from the Buckeye State.
(Part 1 is on page 183.)

The Blame Game

Two men broke into the home of a Westerville woman in February 2006. According to the police report filed by the woman, the two crooks did nothing but argue about how to rob the house and what to steal. Finally, one of them said, "This is all George W. Bush's fault. He screwed up the economy." The crooks left without stealing anything.

Paper Moon

From 1997 until 2001, Newark police couldn't figure out why huge mounds of paper trash were accumulating overnight in an alley near Third Street. Finally, after a late-night stakeout, police apprehended and arrested 65-year-old Jerold West. West confessed to the crime—taking pieces of magazines, newspapers, and junk mail, crumpling them up, and depositing them into the alley. His reason? West said, "I get bored."

Something Smells

In December 1994, administrators at the Chrysler Jeep plant in Toledo told workers to stop wearing deodorant because it w flaking off and spoiling the paint on the new cars. After su visors did an "armpit check," two female employees file ances. Many other employees didn't appreciate the sm people who weren't wearing deodorant. Fortunately manufacturers heard about the problem and sent several shipments of "no-flake" deodorant.

Washington's Last Soldier

Today, John Gray rests in a family plot in Noble County, Ohio, his life marked by a plain, three-foot-high gray headstone. The memorial, though, boasts a grand declaration—"The Last of Washington's Companions"—because when he died at the age of 104, Gray was the last surviving veteran of the American Revolution.

The Revolutionary

John Gray was born on January 6, 1764, at Mount Vernon, Virginia—George Washington's sprawling estate. When he was still just a child, his father went to fight in the Revolution under the command of Washington, and John became the primary means of support for his family of nine. He and his brother hunted rabbits for food, and John worked the fields of neighborhood farms to earn money. In 1776, when John was 12 years old, his father was killed during the Battle of White Plains. He continued to support his family until he turned 18; then the young man signed up for the Revolution and proudly carried the musket of his fallen father onto the battlefield.

Gray spent less than a year in the Revolutionary army. nd like his father, he served under the command of General shington. When the war ended, Gray returned to Mount on and worked the estate's fields under the employ of ngton. Gray moved to Ohio in 1795, bought his own m in Noble County. and spent the rest of his life

Living Long

And what a long life he lived. Gray survived two wives in Virginia, one in Ohio, and all four of his children. He was alive when Ohio became a state in 1803. And he was witness to the War of 1812 and the Civil War.

Because Gray's term of military service had been less than a year, he wasn't entitled to a standard military pension. In the mid-19th century, however, Congress made an exception. Led by Ohio representative John A. Bingham, Congress granted Gray and other veterans honorary pensions of $500 per year. It wasn't a lot, but it was enough for the oldest surviving Revolutionary soldier to get by on.

Up to the Challenge

Gray didn't earn his title without a fight. Fellow veterans Daniel Bakeman (who died in 1869) and George Fruits (who died in 1876) challenged Gray's claim. But they lost out due to technicalities. Bakeman did get a military pension by the same act of Congress that afforded Gray his, but he couldn't prove that he'd actually served in the Revolution. Fruits never received a pension at all, and there were no records proving that he'd fought in the war.

Thus, Gray officially became the last surviving Revolutionary War veteran. He is buried in the McElroy Family Cemetery—about 250 yards from his former Ohio log cabin home—at Roadside Park off State Route 821 South.

Honoring Gray in Verse

In 1888, James McCormick Dalzell, who served in the 116th Ohio Infantry during the Civil War, wrote a poem about John Gray. It reads:

Time hath brought us to behold the last;
Last of all who won our early glory,
Lonely traveler of the weary way,
Poor, unknown, unnamed in song or story,
In his western cabin lives John Gray.

Dalzell, who wrote under the pen name Private Dalzell, also organized the first veterans' reunion in 1873 and served in the Ohio State Legislature from 1876 to 1879.

Did You Know?

Because of his fame, everyone wants a piece of astronaut (and Wapakoneta native) Neil Armstrong. After he learned that his autographs were being sold on eBay for $1,000 and up—and that many were forgeries—he stopped signing his name for fans. But souvenir hunters apparently will take anything they can get. In 2005, Armstrong's long-time barber, Marx Sizemore of Lebanon, Ohio, allegedly sold locks of his hair for $3,000. When Armstrong learned of the transaction, he threatened to sue unless Sizemore forked over the money. Sizemore quickly agreed to donate the proceeds to a charity of Armstrong's choice.

Answers

Literary Lions, page 16

Let's Get Down to Business, page 25

1. **A.** Ladybug beetles are often called "ladybirds," because when it comes to scientific classification, bugs and beetles are in different categories.
2. **C.** Buckeye tea? Come on!
3. **B.** Modern people might use flint to make a ring, but the stone had more practical purposes in history. Native Americans and early settlers used flint to make tools and weapons because the stone is so strong and durable.
4. **B.** When the first European explorers arrived in Ohio in the 1600s, cardinals were rare. Cardinals usually live in bushes and shrubs along the edges of forests, but the area was so

heavily wooded that it couldn't support the birds. By the late 19th century, though, so much of Ohio had been cleared for settlement that cardinals began making nests along the newly created forest edges. Today, the birds thrive in urban and rural areas throughout the state.

5. **A.** Red carnations were the favorite flower of President William McKinley, a native Ohioan. In 1904, three years after McKinley was assassinated at the Pan-American Exposition in Buffalo, New York, the Ohio State Legislature voted to make the carnation the state's official flower in order to honor the late president.
6. **B.** Between 430 and 480 million years ago, Ohio was covered by an ocean. *Isotelus* and other marine animals trolled the sea floor. In 1985, *Isotelus* became the state's official fossil.
7. **C.** In 1959, the state legislature held a contest to find a state motto. Twelve-year-old James Mastronardo suggested the winning entry: "With God, all things are possible," a passage from the Bible. Although the ACLU sued Ohio in the 1990s, claiming that the motto violated the U.S. Constitution's rule separating church and state, federal judges ruled that Ohio could keep its motto because it didn't endorse a specific religion or god.
8. **A.** The Dayton-raised McCoys released "Hang on Sloopy" in 1965. The song is about the Steubenville native and performer Dorothy Sloop, who sometimes went by the stage name "Sloopy."
9. **C.** The white trillium actually has four other names: the wake robin, snow trillium, great white trillium, and large white trillium.

Ohio Stars: The Classics, page 99

1. **G.** Born and raised in Cleveland, Jim Backus—best known as the voice of Mr. Magoo and as Thurston Howell III on *Gilligan's Island*—moved to New York as a teenager to study acting.
2. **C.** Dorothy Dandridge was nominated for a Best Actress Oscar in 1954 for her work in the film *Carmen Jones*. In 1999, Halle Berry—also from Cleveland—played Dandridge in a made-for-TV movie.
3. **E.** Tim Conway is most famous for his work on the *Carol Burnett Show*, but he also starred in *McHale's Navy* and the 1975 film *The Apple Dumpling Gang*.
4. **A.** Born and raised in Cincinnati, Doris Day received an Oscar nomination for her work in 1959's *Pillow Talk*.
5. **D.** Because he was so successful and such a huge movie star, Clark Gable was often called the "King of Hollywood."
6. **B.** Margaret Hamilton became famous for portraying the Wicked Witch in the *Wizard of Oz*, but before she moved to Hollywood, she was a Cleveland schoolteacher whose students included *Twilight Zone* actor William Windom and Jim Backus (see #1).
7. **J.** On their 1908 journey from England to Ohio, Bob Hope and his family were processed at New York's Ellis Island.
8. **I.** Jack Paar was born in Canton but moved to Michigan as a child.
9. **H.** Before becoming a movie star, Roy Rogers worked with his father at a Cincinnati shoe factory. But Rogers was so miserable at the job that he quit after only a year and moved to California soon after.
10. **F.** In her first two years as a film actress, Lillian Gish made 25 films and earned the title "First Lady of the Silent Screen."

From Ada to Youngstown, page 124

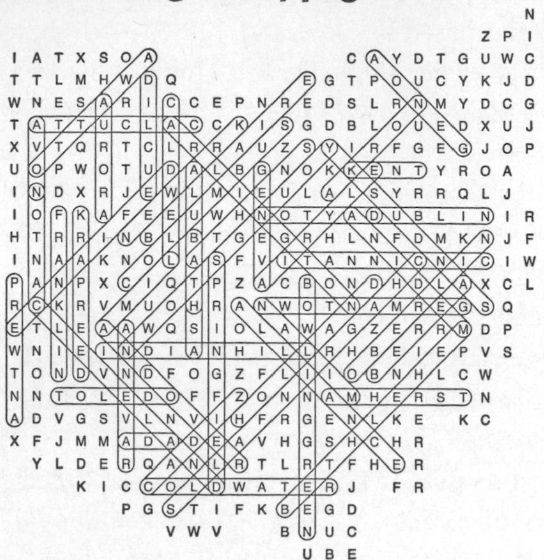

Ohio Literati, page 155

1. **C.** Toni Morrison's first novel, *The Bluest Eye*, is set in Lorain, Ohio, where she grew up.
2. **G.** The Walt Disney Company turned Bickham's *The Apple Dumpling Gang* into a hit 1975 movie.
3. **I.** Erma Bombeck died in 1996; she's buried at Woodland Cemetery in Dayton.
4. **E.** Adrienne Miller worked for *GQ* and *Esquire* magazines before publishing her first novel, *The Coast of Akron*, in 2005.
5. **A.** Hart Crane's father was successful Ohio candy maker Clarence Crane, who invented Lifesavers in 1912.
6. **H.** James Thurber was born in Columbus and graduated from the Ohio State University in 1917.
7. **D.** "Bitter Bierce," as Ambrose Bierce became known, was born in Meigs County but actually grew up in Indiana.
8. **B.** Sherwood Anderson wrote the short story "A Meeting South," about friend and contemporary William Faulkner,

whom he also influenced and encouraged to try his hand at writing his own fiction.

9. J. Zane Grey grew up in Zanesville, a town named for one of his ancestors: Ebenezer Zane, who built Ohio's first major road in 1796.

10. F. Rita Dove was the youngest person and the first African American to serve as the U.S. Poet Laureate.

Sing A Song, page 177

1. C. Photojournalist John Paul Filo's famous newspaper photo of teenager Mary Ann Vecchio kneeling and screaming over the body of one of the dead Kent State students inspired Neil Young to write "Ohio" and earned Filo a 1971 Pulitzer Prize.

2. A. Akron-born Christine "Chrissie" Ellen Hynde attended Kent State University's art school in the 1970s and was on campus during the infamous shootings.

3. A. In addition to the Blue Sky Boys, "Banks of the Ohio" has been recorded by many musicians, including Johnny Cash, the Carter Family, Joan Baez, Olivia Newton-John, and Doc Watson.

4. C. As followers of the Church of the SubGenius—a parody religion—Devo sometimes opened its own shows, performing as a Christian soft-rock group called "Dove (the Band of Love)."

5. A. The next year, in 2001, Macy Gray was booed after forgetting the words to "The Star Spangled Banner" before a Pro Football Hall of Fame exhibition game in Canton. For the performance, she donned a Cleveland Browns jersey and cap.

6. A. Trent Reznor, Nine Inch Nails' founder, claims that he chose the name because it could be abbreviated easily. (NIN is included in the band's logo.)

7. C. In 2004, Massachusetts' Tufts University awarded alumna and Cleveland native Tracy Chapman an honorary Doctor of fine arts degree for her social and artistic accomplishments.

Ohio Comes First, page 194

S	M	I	T	H	■	G	A	R	B	■	A	B	B	E
O	S	S	I	E	■	A	S	O	U	■	F	I	L	M
B	U	M	P	Y	■	F	I	N	N	■	F	L	A	P
■	■	■	T	R	A	F	F	I	C	L	I	G	H	T
■	A	L	O	U	D	■	■	■	H	E	R	E	S	Y
B	A	S	E	B	A	L	L	T	E	A	M	■	■	■
A	R	M	■	E	M	E	E	R	■	H	E	G	E	L
R	O	F	L	■	S	E	P	A	L	■	D	E	S	E
A	N	T	A	L	■	C	E	D	E	S	■	R	T	E
■	■	■	C	A	S	H	R	E	G	I	S	T	E	R
I	B	E	R	I	A	■	■	■	G	R	A	Z	E	■
M	A	N	O	N	T	H	E	M	O	O	N	■	■	■
O	L	D	S	■	I	O	N	E	■	C	C	L	E	F
F	O	E	S	■	R	E	V	S	■	C	H	I	T	A
F	O	R	E	■	E	D	Y	S	■	O	O	Z	E	S

Modern Ohio Stars, page 212

1. **D.** Drew Carey has stayed true to his Ohio roots. He was born in Cleveland, attended Kent State University, and set *The Drew Carey Show* in his hometown.
2. **H.** Arsenio Hall moved to Cleveland when he was two years old. He attended Ohio University and Ohio State, and his trademark "Whoop! Whoop! Whoop!" was inspired by the chants of members of the Cleveland Browns' Dawg Pound.
3. **G.** Born in Columbus, Maggie Grace grew up in Worthington, Ohio.
4. **B.** Halle Berry was named for Halle's Department Store, which opened in Cleveland in 1891 and closed in 1982.
5. **E.** Best known for her starring role in the television program *Sex and the City*, Sarah Jessica Parker was born in Nelsonville, Ohio, but her family moved to New Jersey when her Broadway career began to take off.

6. F. Born in Mansfield and raised in Fredericktown, Luke Perry actually auditioned for the role of Steve in *Beverly Hills 90210* before landing the part of Dylan.
7. A. Molly Shannon has quite the Ohio educational pedigree: for elementary school, she attended St. Dominic's in Shaker Heights, and she spent her high school years at the Hawken School in Gates Mills.
8. J. Dave Grohl was born in Warren, Ohio, in 1969 but moved to Virginia as a child.
9. I. Gloria Steinem was born and lived in Toledo until she left for Smith College in Massachusetts in 1952.
10. C. Jack Hanna was born in Tennessee, but he attended New Concord's Muskingum College and acted as the director of the Columbus Zoo from 1978 to 1993.

They Grow 'Em Smart in Ohio, page 228

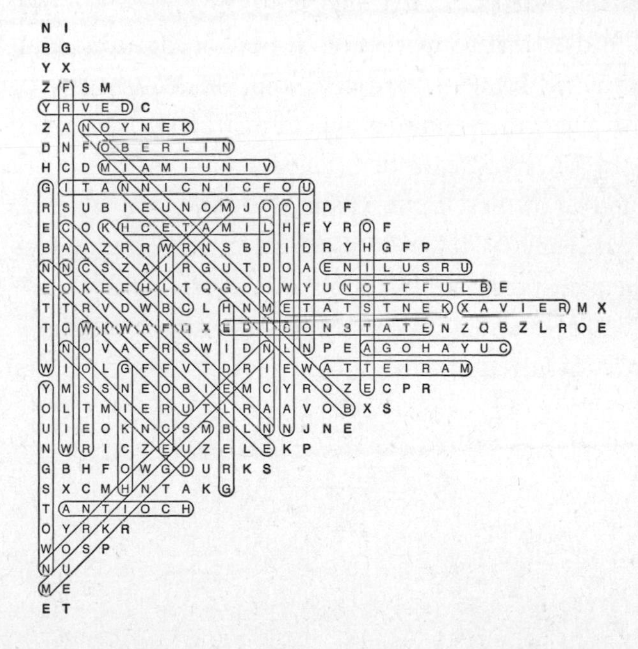

It's Just Business, page 262

1. **C.** Although the J.M. Smucker Company is now best known for its jams, jellies, and preserves, the first product Smucker made was apple cider from the trees Johnny Appleseed planted throughout Ohio.
2. **B.** The most common story about the origin of the name "Jeep" claims that it's the slurred abbreviation "GP," which stands for "general purpose." Recently, though, that story has been disputed and researchers offer the cartoon and World War I references instead. (DaimlerChrysler, which owns Jeep, doesn't offer an official explanation.)
3. **A.** Hartzell Propeller has played a role in many significant historical achievements over the years. But one of the most remarkable was the 1986 trip of the aircraft *Voyager*. Pilot Dick Rutan circumnavigated the globe in 9 days, 3 minutes, and 44 seconds, and set many speed records. His plane was powered, in part, by a Hartzell propeller.
4. **B.** Most of the American Whistle Corporation's whistles are plated with brass and nickel, but, on request, the company will make a customer a whistle plated with bronze, silver, or gold. They come nestled inside a solid walnut display case and sell for between $20 and $59.95.
5. **A.** In 1837, William Proctor and James Gamble formalized their business relationship in Cincinnati: each pledged $3,596.47 to get their company up and running. By 1859, sales of Proctor and Gamble products reached $1 million.

Be sure to check out more hot titles from

Available at bookstores, warehouse clubs, and in great bathrooms everywhere. Or visit www.bathroomreader.com.

Bathroom Readers' Press • 5880 Oberlin Drive • San Diego, CA 92121

The Last Page

Sit down and be counted!

Become a member of the Bathroom Readers' Institute! No join-up fees, monthly minimums or maximums, organized dance parties, quilting bees, solicitors, annoying phone calls (we only have one phone line), spam—or any other canned meat product—to worry about . . . just the chance to get our fabulous monthly newsletter (and if you want) some extremely cool Uncle John's stuff.

So send us a letter:

Uncle John's Bathroom Reader
Portable Press
5880 Oberlin Drive, Suite 101
San Diego, CA 92121

Or email us at unclejohn@btol.com.

Hope you enjoyed the book—and if you're skipping to the end, what are you doing reading this page? Go back and finish!